SEX
CRIMES

SEX CRIMES

*Ten Years on the Front Lines
Prosecuting Rapists and
Confronting Their Collaborators*

ALICE VACHSS

An Owl Book
Henry Holt and Company
New York

Henry Holt and Company, Inc.
Publishers since 1866
115 West 18th Street
New York, New York 10011

Henry Holt® is a registered
trademark of Henry Holt and Company, Inc.

Published in Canada by Fitzhenry & Whiteside Ltd.,
195 Allstate Parkway, Markham, Ontario L3R 4T8.

Library of Congress Cataloging-in-Publication Data
Vachss, Alice S.
Sex crimes : ten years on the front lines prosecuting rapists
and confronting their collaborators / Alice Vachss.—
1st Owl book ed.
p.   cm.
"An Owl book."
1. Vachss, Alice S.   2. Public prosecutors—New York
(State)—Queens County—Biography.   3. Sex
crimes—New York (N.Y.)
4. Queens (New York, N.Y.)   I. Title.
KF373.V3A3   1994   94-17954
345.747′101—dc20   CIP
[B]
[347.471051]
[B]

ISBN 0-8050-3502-8 (An Owl Book: pbk.)

Henry Holt books are available for special promotions
and premiums. For details contact: Director, Special
Markets.

First published in hardcover in 1993
by Random House, Inc.

First Owl Book Edition—1994

Printed in the United States of America
All first editions are printed on acid-free paper. ∞

1   3   5   7   9   10   8   6   4   2

For the ghost's true love, and mine,
and for the wolf

Most of the names in this book are fictitious. For victims, witnesses, and their families, this was done out of respect for their privacy. For judges, lawyers, and police officers, it was done because this book is about *what* they are, not *who* they are. I have used the true names of defendants and public figures throughout—these individuals have waived anonymity by their voluntarily acquired status. All other names, other than cited sources, have been changed or omitted. Some of the enemies I made during the course of my career in sex-crimes prosecution will take comfort from this decision. Like much of their lives, that comfort is illusory.

CONTENTS

FOREWORD TO THE OWL BOOKS EDITION

SEX CRIMES was first published in hardcover in July of 1993. Weeks earlier the United States Senate Judiciary Committee released "Violence Against Women: The Response to Rape: Detours on the Road to Equal Justice." Senator Joseph Biden's introduction summarized the report's research and conclusions, based upon a statistical analysis of 1990 crime data from each of the fifty states: "These findings reveal a justice system that fails by any standard to meet its goals—apprehending, convicting, and incarcerating violent criminals: *98 percent of the victims of rape never see their attacker caught, tried and imprisoned.*"

In September of 1993 I had the privilege of speaking at a rally for one of those 98 percent who found a way to fight back. Two years earlier a young woman from upstate New York had made the mistake of getting drunk in a local bar (called the Casablanca) in Gouverneur, New York, among people she thought were lifelong friends. Afterward five of these "friends" bragged about having sex with her while she was passed out. An investigation followed, and confessions. Eventually the "Casablanca Five" were indicted for rape. On the eve of trial (in June of 1993) the recently elected St. Lawrence County District Attorney allowed the five defendants to plead guilty to the misdemeanor of "sexual misconduct." The sentence imposed: a seven-hundred-and-fifty-dollar fine.

Perhaps the District Attorney thought there would be no protest. The victim was a small-town girl from a place so remote that the *New York*

Post later referred to it as "a rural county where deer outnumber Democrats 10-to-1." But Krista Absalom, thrust involuntarily into a limelight she never wanted, decided to use her own name and her own experiences against the laws and people who had betrayed her. With the extraordinary help and support of her sister, Clover Forsythe, they organized a group of angered, disenfranchised women into the St. Lawrence County Citizens for Women's Justice. The gloomy cold rain of autumn in upstate New York did not deter the hundreds of citizens who came to support their cause.

Because Krista represents so many of the issues that are closest to my heart, I would like to include for you some of what I told them. I gave my speech in the form of the prosecutor's summation that Krista, and St. Lawrence County, should have been entitled to hear. Five empty chairs were placed in front of the podium, to represent the five defendants who should have been on trial:

Ladies and gentlemen, women and men of this jury, it is an honor and a privilege to speak to you here today. It is up to you to decide the truth of this case. Not these five defendants. Not the judge. Not the District Attorney certainly. But not even me or Krista. You decide it based on the one thing that we use to determine truth in this country, to reach justice in this country, and that is the evidence that you have heard before you.

You have, or you would have if there were a trial in this case, heard many witnesses. You would have heard testimony from Krista herself that she went there that night, that it had been a bad day, a frustrating day, and that she wanted to forget her troubles by getting drunk. You may find that you don't like that behavior in a woman. But I ask you when you listen to the judge's instructions on the law, to see if you think you hear anything about that being a defense to rape.

Out of the words of Krista Absalom, we can find a truth. Because of all the people there, of all the people here, Krista was and is the one who least wanted to believe that she had been raped, who least wanted to believe that these people she thought she could trust could be capable of the kind of be-

trayal, the kind of dehumanization that in fact occurred on that night.

You have heard from the defendants via their confessions in this case. You have heard from several of them that "yes" they had sex with her, and "yes" she was unconscious, but "hey: no harm, no foul," "she didn't know about it, it was no big deal." You heard Krista tell you that when she confronted one of these rapists, and she said, "I want to know what happened that night," he said to her, "If you don't remember, then nothing happened," because that's what he wants to believe. You have heard the tape of one of these defendants saying on national TV, "It wasn't a rape, it was a gang bang." Well—surprise—a gang bang when the victim is unconscious is rape.

You can choose through whatever prejudices you have to ignore all of this evidence, to say this was not rape, to say these were nice young men. You can choose to participate in the betrayal of Krista Absalom by saying "I don't like that victim; I won't consider this a crime." If you do that, you will pay. You will pay by having to hope and pray that it is never you or yours that are in that situation next. You can judge the victim, and defend these defendants. Or you can say what they did is wrong, what they did is a crime, what they did is intolerable.

I ask you to look at all of this evidence, and I ask you to find these five defendants guilty, guilty as charged. And I ask you to find the criminal justice system in this case guilty of an obscenity of a sentence in saying that what happened to her can be fixed with a seven-hundred-and-fifty-dollar fine. I ask you to find the District Attorney guilty: guilty of having betrayed his oath of office, guilty of failing in his fundamental responsibilities to the citizens he is supposed to represent, guilty of betraying all of us.

And I ask you, and this is not normally part of a summation, but I ask you to impose a penalty, the only penalty that we have left to us, and that is to remember their names.

We have in this country a political system that determines who gets to be law enforcement and who gets to be judges. To

the women in this audience I say, we've had the vote for almost seventy-five years. It's time we used it. To all of us I say, we have the power. We will never take the politics out of prosecution. But we can make doing the job a make-or-break issue. We can force them with our intolerance to do what morality and decency and justice requires—give us all our day in court.

After eight months of investigations by two separate commissions, on February 17, 1994, Governor Mario Cuomo signed an executive order appointing a special prosecutor to see if justice could still be served in St. Lawrence County.

As hard fought as it was, Krista's triumph was one of many. In the year since *Sex Crimes* was originally published, the war has continued unabated. For me, one victory shines past all the others: The National Child Protection Act was signed into law.

The act calls for a federal registry of convicted child molesters and abusers to prevent them from obtaining access to children. Oprah Winfrey adopted that idea and introduced and supported a bill that would make it a reality. But it languished for two long years as a victim of national politics.

In July of 1993 Oprah aired an interview on her national TV show in which she talked about her frustration: "There's just a lot of lip service and I don't know how to turn it around." Her guest was Andrew Vachss. He answered her: "The only way to turn it around is with force. . . . If the number of people who watch your show every day, if that many people simply wrote a letter to Congress saying, 'Unless you pass this bill, I'm going to remember your name in two years or four years or whatever it takes.' That's it. That would do it."

In the fall, *Harper's* magazine published a breakdown by category of presidential mail. So many people had written to President Clinton in support of the Oprah bill, that it had its own category. Oprah's interview of Andrew re-aired in December. When the segment about what the audience could do came on, a leader across the bottom of the screen announced: THE NATIONAL CHILD PROTECTION ACT PASSED CONGRESS ON NOVEMBER 20TH, 1993, AND WILL SHORTLY BECOME LAW. Ten days after the interview re-aired, on December 20, 1993, President Clinton signed the bill into law. It is impossible to know how many children will be spared sexual abuse because of that law. And, as Oprah said at the signing, "This is just the beginning."

If I've learned anything in this past year it has been that our greatest impediment to change is not rapists, or their collaborators. It is not a national decline in character or courage. It is our despair. We are slow to forgive a rape victim so paralyzed by horror that she cannot fight back. But we have not fought back either. When I spoke in St. Lawrence County, I borrowed a phrase from my husband: *Remember their names*. From Richard Manning (in St. Lawrence County) to Richard Brown (in Queens County)—they all have to run for re-election. And if 98 percent of the rapes in this country are going unpunished, then we have a *lot* of names to remember.

—Alice Vachss, May 1994

Part One

DREAMS
AND
NIGHTMARES

1

"Y̲ou're dead."

It was said quietly, a fact more than a threat, a postscript to a sentencing. The judge had imposed seven to twenty-one years imprisonment. It wasn't enough—this time bomb would see the parole board in less than a decade.

He would wait.

He told us each in turn—the judge, me, the defense attorney: "You're dead."

I knew it should make me afraid, but what it did was make me angry.

We had all the information we could ever want to convince us that Gary Glenn* needed to go down for the count. But all the criminal justice system could do was keep him breathing hard on his stool between rounds.

The first time he'd been arrested, they couldn't even do that. They let Glenn go. They knew he was guilty, but none of the rape victims could identify him. He took it as permission to continue.

They confiscated a nightstick when they arrested him that first time. He replaced it. He needed it for his work.

Queens Sex Crimes Squad had an "unsolved" series of sexual attacks.

---

*The names of defendants and public figures are real. There is no reason to protect Gary Glenn's identity. We're the ones who need protection from him.

3

It was always the same: the sniper-silent approach, the security guard's uniform, the nightstick, the knife. Each time the violence grew worse. Whatever internal ritual this predator completed when he raped, his gods wanted blood sacrifice. Every morning when the detectives came to work, they checked to see if he had struck again, dreading the inevitable homicide, hoping that somehow he would slip, and fall.

Glenn's final victim was Mai-Lilly Steele, a tiny little thing who couldn't have weighed ninety pounds. She worked as a reservations clerk at La Guardia Airport. On the night that changed her life, she completed a midnight shift and agreed to meet her friends for a drink at the local airport hotel. It all seemed normal, routine. Business was good, promotions were in the air. Mai-Lilly's future looked like dreams come true.

The dreams shattered as she climbed out of her car in the parking lot. Glenn burst out of the night, in full uniform, zombie-silent, stabbing with his knife. There was a split second, frozen in time, of seeing the nightmare.

Then she kicked at him. He stabbed, severing the nerves in one thigh. It excited him, even more than the rapes had. He was in control, winning the struggle, slashing, stabbing, relentless, powerful.

Mai-Lilly could smell her own mortality.

She retreated within the car. She curled herself into a fetal position, her legs drawn up to protect her vital organs. The car door was partially between her and her attacker. People talk about "now or never" . . . Mai-Lilly lived it.

Death was waiting, calling. She summoned the strength to fight, using all her fear and horror to kick out. She caught Glenn off-balance, unprepared—the shove of the car door sent him flying. She followed, tumbling out of the automobile. He fled, but she was beyond knowing that, consumed by her terror-driven crawl to the hotel lobby, trailing life's blood, pounding on the glass doors, pleading for safety, rescue.

Glenn had picked the wrong victim. Mai-Lilly survived.

As soon as she was released from the hospital, they showed Mai-Lilly photos. They knew it was Glenn—so did she. They arrested him; she testified before a grand jury; he was indicted.

Mai-Lilly underwent months of physical rehabilitation. The promotions at the airline came and went, passing her by while she struggled to regain the use of her limbs. She wanted to move back to her home-town—away from the fear. The court case was still pending. She tried to find out what was happening, but no one seemed to know. She started making plans. They were interrupted when a subpoena arrived in the mail.

Glenn sat in a jail cell, waiting.

During the first few weeks I worked as a trial lawyer for the Queens district attorney's office, I couldn't find my case files. On my second or third day there, my bureau chief had handed me a list of over a hundred names and indictment numbers. I went to the DA's record room to retrieve the corresponding files. I was handed only a dozen. Where were the rest? The staff shrugged; files kept getting lost. The ADAs (assistant district attorneys) didn't return them. That's why there was this new policy that the lawyers couldn't keep their own files on their desks. Everything had to be returned to the record room after court.

Other ADAs told me to "chill out." Plenty of files never got found at all. And even those that were found wouldn't help much. They showed me a conference table in the paralegals' room. It was stacked four feet high with motions, transcripts, grand jury minutes. Nobody knew for sure what was in there. There wasn't anyone whose job it was to find out.

The next week I got handed a new list. I went back to the record room to search for those files. The record room staff thought I should have known better by then. "Don't call us, we'll call you."

During my second week there, my bureau chief came to me genuinely upset. He handed me a case file for a hearing scheduled that day—a terrible crime, but the victim was in his office telling him she didn't want to prosecute. Convince her.

It wasn't anything I said that convinced Mai-Lilly Steele—it was finally having a prosecutor assigned to her case.

People who knew me when I was a public defender had predicted I wouldn't last three months working for the Queens district attorney, John J. Santucci. Prosecuting Gary Glenn confirmed my belief that they were wrong.

That first day at the hearing, Mai-Lilly was afraid. She later told me that was why when the defense attorney asked if she was sure Glenn was the man who stabbed her, she had answered, "I guess so." It was the first time she'd seen him face-to-face since the night of the attack. I told her a jury could only be as sure as she was—and they had to be sure "beyond a reasonable doubt." Was it him? Yes.

Other trial attorneys at the DA's office taught me a new phrase: "one-witness ID." Jurors wanted to see more than just the victim. When they get in the jury room, they seem to forget what we all know—that crimes don't tend to take place in front of witnesses.

The jury on the Glenn case never got to hear about the series of rapes Glenn had committed. Only Mai-Lilly testified, and she'd been fighting for her life the one time she'd seen the defendant. During the weeks between the hearing and the trial she'd gained the strength to tell the jury she wouldn't forget that face her whole life. The jury convicted.

Mai-Lilly and I earned the public a minimum of seven years of freedom from Gary Glenn. It was the most we could do. Glenn spent his years stewing in the bile of his hatred, defying the myth of rehabilitation. He was denied parole at his first hearing, but sooner or later he'll be released. He has spiritual brothers to join—all the evil in the night, waiting and calling to him.

2

Until the day I got fired, I prosecuted sex crimes. Once I started, it seemed like the work I'd been destined to do. It was not, however, what I had in mind when I applied to law school. Inspired by a postgraduate spell as a prison counselor, I thought my vocation was on the other side as a criminal defense attorney.

The work in prison was mostly chance. When I graduated from Boston University in 1970, I joined VISTA (Volunteers in Service to America), the stateside Peace Corps. That was what I had wanted to do after high school, and college hadn't changed my goals. Just before I was due to report to Chicago for VISTA project assignment, the dean of my college notified me that I'd won a poetry prize, and I used the money for a summer hosteling trip through Europe. In July I got a lengthy telegram from the government notifying me that VISTA no longer qualified as a draft exemption. They had confused both my gender and my motivation. My impression that the agency was not geared to women was later confirmed when I learned that VISTA required its volunteers to live within strict geographic limits in the "community" regardless of safety considerations, and that this policy had persisted despite the fact that several female volunteers were said to have been raped.

VISTA reassigned me to New York. When I returned from Europe in the fall I chose a project in the South Bronx, working with short-term inmates at Rikers Island Adolescent Remand Shelter.

Training was monotonous, but enlivened by the prospect of finally being about to do something. The regular volunteers were trained along with a more insular group who were about to start their legal careers as volunteer lawyers. It gave me an idea that I tried to talk to one of them about once. I was thinking about going to law school myself—what did she think? She told me not to—it wasn't worth it.

The only useful training session was conducted by a community organizer. He said we knew nothing about where we were going. The thing to do, he said, was not to try to pretend we did, but to ask questions and learn.

I learned about New York City cockroaches. The first place I stayed was so infested that there was no getting rid of them. I learned never to get up in the middle of the night. After dark, I learned to turn the light on and wait before entering a room. When I moved I was determined not to have roaches. I put down so much boric acid that it was months before any of them tested the waters. Then a huge, venomous-looking one staked out his territory in the bathtub. I sprayed an entire can of Raid on him. He flipped over on his back and enacted a death scene James Cagney would have envied. I went to get some paper towels to dispose of him. By the time I returned he'd flipped back over and made his escape. As disgusting as he was, I had to kind of admire him, especially when he had the good manners not to return.

I was assigned to work and live with a female roommate, a blond Midwesterner. I had my overalls and Janis Joplin hair. The South Bronx wasn't what anyone might call integrated. When we walked down the street in the first place we lived, little children would point at us, screaming, *"Mira! Mira!"* And look at us is what people did. We stretched the definition of "community" and found a place to live in the Bronx version of Little Italy, where on Sunday mornings the shops smelled of fresh-baked breads and homemade cheeses. People no longer pointed at us in the street, though there were candy stores where all conversation stopped the second we opened the door.

In 1970, the South Bronx was still a study in contrasts: the fading elegance of the Grand Concourse yielding slowly to the surrounding decay. Even then there were enough burnt-out ruins to foreshadow the neighborhood's future.

To get to work, we had to walk through butchers' warehouses full of rotting, bleeding carcasses. It seemed like a metaphor.

The project's offices were centrally located in an anonymous building in the shadow of the Third Avenue El. Several days a week the volunteers would commute from there to Rikers Island. The Remand Shelter was more modern and linear than I'd expected. For someone who knew that when the gates locked they would again reopen, what was most oppressive was the smell—a dirty, heavy ammonia odor—and the ever-present hazard of fire. When I'd been in high school I'd volunteered at a city hospital children's ward. Most of the long-term patients had been disfigured by burns. It left me with a deep and lasting fear of fire. It was impossible to look at the long, iron-gated corridors of the Remand Shelter without knowing that if a fire started, I would have little chance to get out alive.

I was supposed to be a counselor, but I didn't know much of anything. I'd grown up in the suburbs of Boston. In college I'd joined the women's movement, marched against the Vietnam War, experimented with just about everything, but I hadn't acquired any useful skills, except to value learning. I'd majored in comparative religion, studying Moonies, Native American mythology, and intertestamental literature. No one in the South Bronx was particularly interested in the religions I'd studied, although I did get to learn about Five Percenters, the race-based cult then popular at Rikers Island. No Five Percenters talked to me themselves, but prisoners fascinated by them did. Their "gospel" was intellectualized but the message was clear . . . they preached hate under the guise of pride.

Rikers Island is a jail, not a prison, which means that there are no convicted felons housed there. The Detention Center holds people accused of all manner of crimes, so being on the grounds at all exposed us to the risk of dangerous escapees (a risk that we once avoided only by a matter of minutes). But the only convicts on Rikers Island are short-term prisoners, either adults serving less than a year or adolescents serving less than two years. Our clients were almost exclusively young black and Hispanic males convicted of petty crimes like purse snatchings. It was considered bad form for the volunteers to ask about our clients' crimes.

On a home visit to set up a discharge plan, I found out that the TV was never turned off, the sound never turned down. I got the same message when one of my clients got rearrested. The judge and the public defender were polite to me, but overwhelmingly indifferent to the defendant.

I set up literacy courses and scholarship opportunities. Lyndon Johnson's Great Society was alive (albeit barely), so that was still possible. Having something concrete to offer helped, but not enough. It was hard to escape the feeling that I wasn't qualified to be teaching teenage convicts how to return to the ghetto, or for much of anything else. Frustrated with the idea of counseling as a career, I filled out my own applications.

At that time law schools were just beginning to accept women in significant numbers. Figuring it was my only hope, I cleaned up my lifestyle enough to score well on the Law School Admissions Tests. I had dreams of going to Stanford, but it was accepting only a handful of women each year. My own alma mater, Boston University, was aiming for an enrollment that was one-third women. That's where I went.

Law school was unremittingly boring and I never felt at home with the other students. I went through with it for the degree, not the education or the credential. The uprising and killings at Attica during my first year of law school confirmed my decision that I wanted to be a defense attorney; the individual against the government. It sounded a lot nobler than it most times turned out to be.

It was the summer after my first year of law school that my work started centering on violence.

Massachusetts was trying a dramatic experiment. At that time "deinstitutionalization" was heralded as the solution to a long history of programmatic failures. In New York, this meant discharging the mentally ill from state-run hellholes into the streets, where they eventually became "the homeless." In Massachusetts it meant closing the juvenile "training schools"—the idea was to stop throwing our children into snake pits.

But implementing this logical-sounding plan was jeopardized by the population of young men who had made violence into a lifestyle. It was one thing to release runaways; murderers were a different story. As each infamous training school closed, the juveniles who were too frightening to release were shipped to another until the most dangerous and volatile of them were amassed under a single roof in one sealed wing of a juvenile detention facility.

The Commonwealth created a new institution. Originally it was run by psychiatric social workers as a "therapeutic community"—they named it Andros, Greek for "man." The day a "resident" came heart-stoppingly close to raping one of the staff, Andros II was born.

Andros II addressed precisely what Andros I had ignored: that its population of juveniles was the most violence-prone and lethal collection of underage criminals ever assembled together in Massachusetts correctional history. The new institution had only three rules: no sex; no drugs; and no violence. Their strict enforcement was revolutionary, especially since the training schools (of which the residents were all veterans) had prominently featured all three. For their whole lives, they had been taught that violence was the only card they had to play, and now we all seemed surprised by the vehemence with which they played it.

The juveniles at Andros were not the only ones accustomed to "might makes right" as a way of life.

The staff were mostly ex-convicts. On my first day one of them offered me a ride home. He was the bulkiest human I had ever seen, with more scar tissue than face, and tiny little psychopathic eyes. He flashed a line of broken teeth in my direction—it was his attempt at a smile. You could tell he didn't do it often.

I was relieved to be able to say thank you but I had my own car.

A few days later I got to see The Bulk in action. He walked in on one of the inmates pumping iron. He snatched a dumbbell and threw it the length of the hallway. Then he grabbed the young man who'd been using it and sat him down forcefully. And then The Bulk started to cry and said: "You can lift weights your whole life and you'll never, ever, you'll never be as strong as me. And look at me. I'm nothing. I got nothing." This wasn't the counseling they taught me in VISTA.

Andros II was designed around and effective with young men whose violence was an expression of anger. It succeeded with hair-trigger young killers who everyone else thought there was no hope for. But Andros II failed with inmates whose violence was sexual. It was not equipped to deal with anyone who enjoyed the infliction of pain.

To succeed where it did, Andros II had to create within its walls a community with its own values. Unlike the "therapeutic community" that was the goal of the original Andros, these values had little to do with an inmate's ability to learn the lingo. In fact, they sounded like the old-time convict's code. Instead of earning "points" for good behavior like making a bed, these young men learned an "us against them" loyalty to what Andros II stood for.

There was a sign hanging in the director's office at Andros II that said: IF YOU CAN'T BE COUNTED <u>ON</u>, YOU CAN'T BE COUNTED <u>IN</u>. When I first read it, I thought it was corny. Andros II had political enemies. When the entire staff agreed to resign if they fired the director; when all of us combed the city for three dangerous escapees; when a convict on life parole risked arrest to save a kid . . . I understood it was more than just a saying.

I worked the three-to-midnight shift at Andros II as a floor counselor. It tested my courage every day, and was the most exciting thing I had ever done. To convince the director to give me the job, I also agreed to write a history of the program, a task that continued after I returned to law school in the fall. I interviewed the by then ex-director, the one who had put it all in place and made it work. He was the first truly effective person I'd ever met.

Interviewing him, I learned that when I'd been in the South Bronx, he'd been in Chicago, directing a project that utilized VISTA volunteers. Andros II did what VISTA hadn't—introduced me to what Champion Jack Dupree sang about in "My Real Combination for Love." I didn't know at first that I would marry him but I knew I would keep him in my heart forever.

During the summer after my second year of law school, I worked for the Vermont public defender's office in Burlington. The one judge who handled all criminal matters did not want women in his courtroom—not as witnesses, not as defendants, and certainly not as attorneys. I never got the chance to prove him wrong. When my new boss took over, I had a more immediate battle to fight.

The new public defender was a political appointee. I resigned in protest over his policy of automatically pleading every defendant Guilty the first time the case appeared in court. Burlington was a small town, so I made front-page headlines. After that, the public defender seemed to reverse his policy, so that he never pleaded anyone Guilty. It was my first lesson in the power of the media.

I graduated law school in 1974 and moved to New York, where my future husband had grown up. He taught me a new approach to cock-roaches. When one huge specimen made the mistake of taunting us with his invulnerability to extermination, my future husband captured him and made him a pet. He put him in a fishbowl with a screen over the top and named him Raid. Raid kept trying to charge up the sides of the fishbowl and knock off the screen. We siliconed the sides of the bowl so Raid couldn't get a purchase. He retaliated by trying to eat all the silicone, which worked enough so he could run up the sides of the bowl, but eventually it was what killed him. We got a puppy next, a junkyard dog named Simba who my husband rescued from low-lifes he found drowning an entire litter. Having started out life so hard, Simba turned out to be as tough in his own way as Raid.

I worked on a research project on parole decisions in New Jersey. Most of the subjects were lifers at Trenton State Prison, many convicted of massive, ugly crimes. There was no death penalty then—"life" was the most the state could do to a person. That left the question what to do with these inmates during their incarceration. The possibility of parole was a way to control the inmate population. The research project proved that at the time the granting of parole in New Jersey lacked any sem-blance of predictability. In response to the findings, a new chairman of the parole board instituted far-ranging reforms of the parole grant pro-cess—including a contract between new inmates and their parole officers outlining what rehabilitative efforts the inmate had to undertake to be favorably considered by the board. New Jersey became a model for the country.

I was admitted to practice law in 1975. One of the "lifers" from New Jersey became my first client. At the time, Trenton had converted its death chamber into a lawyer's interview room. The room was poorly lit. You could feel but not see the gun tower outside, mounted on the wall of aging bricks surrounding the country's oldest prison. The guards had left the electric chair in place against the day it would be used again. The chair was wood, with black leather straps still attached, and burn marks etched into the arms. It made for a solemnity softened only by the respect I received from the inmate I was interviewing. At one time he had been destined for that chair himself.

My first real job after admission to the bar was as a public defender in

Manhattan. I was the first person hired after the Legal Aid Society had changed policies in 1975 to a "vertical" system in which lawyers followed the same case throughout the legal process. Several times a month we would work in arraignments where recently arrested people filled the court pens. Anyone who could not afford a lawyer—and that was most of them—would be assigned a Legal Aid attorney.

I found a much lower class of criminal than I had at Trenton. Other Legal Aid attorneys used to laugh at me because I thought there was a major distinction between a guy who hit you over the head and took your money and a guy who took your money and *then* hit you over the head. Gratuitous violence disturbed me more than violence with a rational, if illegal, aim.

Legal Aid was fond of lingo, guilty of mistaking cold for cool. It took me a while to outgrow that and to learn, despite law school and the Legal Aid Society, to speak like a human being. Actually, it was a defendant who first taught me that lesson.

He was a street sociopath who'd stabbed someone just for the fun of it. It was in night court, with its assembly-line justice, and the prosecutor had offered him a sentence he couldn't refuse. He kept telling the judge he wanted the plea, but when the judge asked him what he'd done, he insisted on his innocence. I whispered several times to the defendant, "You have to admit the acts," but he wasn't listening. Finally, out of frustration, he yelled at me, "It wasn't no axe I stabbed him with, I used my knife!" It was enough to be an admission, and to teach me to talk so that people could understand.

Not all the defendants were unlikable. Two cousins who made me laugh also taught me what it meant to be a defense attorney. I'm tall for a woman, so I'm not used to feeling dwarfed. But these two looked like seven-footers, with country accents and an air about them that made me think I heard bluegrass music in the background. They had long criminal records for petty theft. This latest arrest was for stripping an abandoned car. When I interviewed them, each one freely admitted his guilt but insisted his cousin was innocent. They argued about who was going to take the weight.

They were still arguing when the case was called. I had to shush them to keep them from making admissions—it made me feel like a schoolmarm. I made an argument to the judge about a legal technicality—if the car was abandoned, there was no complainant, so the legal paperwork was deficient. The judge must have liked the defendants as well, because he agreed to dismiss. The cousins ducked their heads when they thanked me.

It made me understand that court was a battle between opponents where size and physical strength weren't what mattered.

Sometimes what mattered had to be rewritten to suit the circumstances. During one night-court session a group of children of Holocaust survivors were arraigned on disorderly conduct charges for a protest they'd staged at a performance of a Wagner opera. When the judge let them off with just a warning, the warning was this: "I never want to see you back in my courtroom, never again." Then he winked and repeated himself, in case he had been too subtle: "Did you hear me? Never again!"

I represented a transvestite prostitute whose patron claimed he'd been robbed. My client told me it was a fee dispute. The plea offer from the prosecution was felony probation. I had to ask the defendant to trust me enough to stay in jail three days before I could disprove the charges. We made that agreement. When I kept my word and the case was dismissed, the transvestite thanked me for treating him like a human being. I think it's the saddest thank-you I ever got.

At Legal Aid I specialized in assault cases. They were unpopular among defense attorneys because they involved a lot of work and often went to trial. Unlike muggings, where the line between victim and perpetrator tended to be clear-cut, assaults often involved disputes where both sides had a story to tell. The police seemed to decide who was the victim by who was most seriously injured—the winner of the fight wound up the defendant. And even when there was an obvious aggressor, the circumstances shaded their culpability.

I represented a bartender who stabbed his boss. The injuries were serious enough for the DA's office to want a long prison term. But my client was a hardworking man who had never been in trouble with the law. When I investigated I found out that every day for many years his boss had made his life miserable, bombarding him with insults and racial slurs and even firing him until the union compelled the boss to take him back. On the day of the stabbing, the defendant was cutting up foodstuffs in the sink when his boss walked over and told him he was fired . . . again. In a moment of accumulated rage, the bartender turned, paring knife in hand, and stabbed his tormentor once. The little knife broke from the force of the blow, but it had done serious damage. The bartender was filled with horror. He called 911 for an ambulance and then ran out into the street to flag down a patrol car for assistance. As much as he hated his boss, he was inconsolable over what he'd done.

I thought the bartender should get probation. Eventually he did. After Andros II, nonpredatory violence seemed like fighting back to me. It didn't offend me the way other crimes did.

I represented one diminutive woman in her sixties who had already served a "life" sentence for murder. She was everything Damon Runyon pictured about old-time gangsters. She talked, raspy-voiced, out of the side of her mouth, and she hid a heart of gold beneath a tough exterior.

She had assaulted her boyfriend (also in his sixties, and also only about four feet tall) when she discovered he'd been stepping out on her. After the judge yelled at her while he reluctantly imposed probation, I gave her my limited insight into avoiding domestic violence. We talked about the immortal Screamin' Jay Hawkins song "I Put a Spell on You." There's a line that says, "I don't care if you don't want me, I'm yours." I told her there was a difference between that and "I don't care if you don't want me, you're mine."

Not all of the violence was defensible, and as much as the circumstances could mitigate an assault, they occasionally made it much worse. The most frightening person I represented at Legal Aid was charged with only a minor offense. He had thrown a Coke bottle at a young woman on a bicycle. When I went to interview him, he said, "Yeah, I threw the bottle at her. She deserved it. She was laughing at me. They all laugh at me. Someday I'll make them all sorry." To this day it makes my blood run cold to remember his voice.

My husband coauthored a text on *The Life-Style Violent Juvenile*. After his departure from Andros II, the institution had declined. The one flaw and disappointment of his design was that it was too dependent on the force of his own personality. The book was a way to preserve the principles that made Andros II work when it did. Legal Aid let me take a leave of absence for the last three months of 1977 to assist with the research. It made me remember the excitement of changing things, not just processing them through existing systems. By the time I returned to work, I'd had time to recognize my growing disenchantment with being a public defender.

By the end of 1977, even before New York City discovered crack cocaine, too much of Legal Aid and too much of the court system itself was devoted to narcotics cases. New York had enacted sentencing legislation supposedly designed to take the big dealers off the street forever. Instead it overfilled the courts and prisons with small user/dealers facing mandatory life incarceration for selling tiny amounts of dope. The volume of cases, the stakes, the amount of money in narcotics trafficking, tainted the entire system. Uniformed police officers bitterly resented an anticorruption policy that prohibited them from making narcotics arrests even when they personally observed street drug sales. Because cocaine had become a middle-class party fad, assistant district attorneys would brag about having tinfoil packets in their suit-coat pockets while they recommended maximum incarceration on a drug case. Legal Aid attorneys bragged that "you're not a real lawyer until you can do a stand-up on an A-One felony" (conduct a trial without any preparation whatsoever with the defendant facing twenty-five years to life). Armies of teenagers who had no qualms about informing crowded out the aging group of thieves in their fifties who were the last class of prisoners clinging to a belief in a criminal's code of honor. Defending drug cases was a matter of winning the rat race—whoever got to the prosecutor first got the best deal.

One day when I was leaving court I saw a junkie who had just been discharged from the pens. In the time it took him to make it downstairs and out the door, he had found some way to get high. He sat down on the steps of the old courthouse and nodded off. A shadow fell across him . . . from the courthouse across the street newly erected at great government expense to house the centralized narcotics court parts. It was impossible to look at him without thinking: What was the point?

In the middle of 1978, when I was nearing the end of my three-year commitment at Legal Aid, the union chief came to me demanding that I pay the union dues. I complained that the dues went for political donations to "revolutionary" Iranian students who later turned out to be the shah's secret police. The union guy accused me of just being cheap. When I took a twenty out of my purse, he thought I was going to pay up. Instead, I put a match to it. "I'd rather burn my money than give it to you." He demanded that the Legal Aid Society fire me. I was told not to come to work anymore, but the official record supposedly says that I "resigned."

For financial reasons, I would not have chosen to leave Legal Aid when I did. But I also knew by then I was not going to make Legal Aid—or criminal defense—a career. It wasn't that I had expected my clients to be innocent—out of the thousands of people I represented only a handful of them were. But I had expected to be proud of what I accomplished.

After the job at Legal Aid I took some court-appointed cases in the criminal courts. While I had been a public defender my husband had begun to establish his law practice, and we shared an office for a time. I was no good at charging people for my services. My husband threatened to get me a parrot and teach it to say: "Money in front! Money in front!" I stopped taking the criminal-defense assignments when the only reason I could find to do the job right was professional pride.

In family court, before I knew better, I took a few assignments representing adults. The family courts were more violent and dangerous than the criminal courts, and the accused adults (called respondents, not defendants) were as a class more despicable. Most of the work representing children in abuse and neglect cases went automatically to the Legal Aid Society. For a time I made a mini-career out of representing children in foster care review petitions, which was gratifying but limited. It wasn't my work—I'd have to keep searching.

As national service is supposed to, VISTA had confirmed my belief that what I wanted to do was make a difference. But its methods seemed designed to have limited impact. Andros had taught me that there could be effective alternatives—even if you had to create them yourself. But it wasn't my cause. The years since had taught me skills, but I was still looking for something that felt like mine. I thought about doing something other than law, but I couldn't think of what.

In 1979, a year after I'd left Legal Aid, I heard about a fledgling idea—that rape victims needed their own counsel, independent of a prosecutor, to represent their interests in the criminal courts. I read enough about it to think it might be the work I'd been looking for. But before I went ahead trying to create something on my own, I wanted to make sure I believed in it. I put together a working group to evaluate rape victim representation.

With the help of a small grant from the ARCA Foundation, we held a project conference in 1980. Most of the people who attended were lawyers who functioned in various roles within the criminal justice system. We also invited one woman who had been the complainant on a much-headlined rape case. As it turned out, she was not the only attendee to talk about her victimization. It was a lesson I was to learn over and over again. There were more victims out there than anybody knew about.

The woman whose case had gone to court told us: "There were three young men, one with a gun, and they pushed their way into the apartment . . . and they gathered up my stereo and money and stuff and then one of them said, 'I'm not leaving till I get my nuts off on this little bitch.' . . . They all did rape me and they tied me up and pushed me around a lot and beat me up and threatened to maim me. . . . I think that was the most terrifying . . . the fear of having a knife stuck up my vagina."

Almost as disturbing was her assessment of the experience of prosecuting a case to conviction: "I came to feel that the criminal justice system was my enemy. . . . I felt in a way like I really had no one to blame but these three guys . . . but . . . they were all my enemies, and this amorphous criminal justice system was certainly my enemy." Her words were echoed by other victims.

There might have been some dispute about whether victims needed their own lawyers, but there seemed to be damn near unanimity that they needed a criminal justice system more responsive to their needs. New protocols were being written by law enforcement and the medical community outlining how victims should be treated. The standards seemed so minimal to me that they were themselves an indictment of how things were then being done.

I read and heard a great deal about "sensitivity," and I realized that it was lacking in many instances. But I concluded that being considerate and courteous to the victims of rape was mere gloss unless it was accompanied by a determination to prosecute more effectively. It was a mistake to call for an attitude without also calling for the aptitude necessary to make it meaningful. Victims should not have to trade compassion for competence. Trying to write up the project's finding, these seemed like pretty words, but just words. I decided maybe it was time to step in the ring—this time on the side of the prosecution. Instead of trying to make other people do the job right as an outsider, I wanted to see if I could be on the inside, doing the job right myself.

It was not just that I felt a compassion for victims. The literature in the early 1980s also contained shocking information. One FBI study said that on average someone arrested for rape in this country served less than a year in jail. I knew this average was skewed by how few of those arrested were actually convicted of rape. (A 1976 study in Seattle, for example, said that of 315 rapes reported to law enforcement in 1974, only 6 resulted in rape or attempted-rape convictions.) Even those convicted of rape served on average only four and a half years in prison, despite a Justice Department survey which concluded that the public felt over-whelmingly that a rapist who "did no other harm with his crime" should serve fifteen years.

So I started applying to the various DA's offices in New York for a job where I could prosecute rapists. I was an experienced trial attorney by then, but I didn't have some of the normal prerequisites—I was experi-enced, but not connected.

The number of slots for ADAs was limited according to each district attorney's budget. It was obvious from just reading the newspapers that a certain number of positions were reserved for "nephews" (relatives of someone with sufficient clout to demand a job slot) and for the politically ambitious who would later on need the line "district attorney's office" on their résumés. There was especially heavy competition for the few slots as sex-crimes prosecutors because these cases tend to wind up in the headlines.

Still, I figured that in every law-enforcement bureaucracy some per-centage of the employees would actually have to work, just as in every army some percentage of the soldiers actually have to fight.

Each of the five New York City boroughs elects its own separate district attorney, as do the neighboring counties. Most of them had the same negative answer to give me. Manhattan (New York County) didn't want me at all. Nassau (on Long Island) would put me in appeals but not in sex crimes. Brooklyn (Kings County) agreed to offer me a job but withdrew its offer when I said I wanted to be paid the same as anyone else with my level of experience. In December of 1981 Queens offered me a job.

Queens is the overlooked borough of New York City. Although Queens routinely complains that it is the last borough to receive city services such as snow removal and sanitation crews, it is geographically the city's largest county, and is second only to Brooklyn in population. It is a borough predominated by homeowners, with a large population of children and the city's highest concentration of elderly. Still, it seems to have little sense of self-identity. Those Queens residents with a loyalty to location tend to identify with their own community rather than the borough. People in Manhattan list New York, New York, as their return address. People in Queens list Bayside, or Flushing or Jamaica Estates or Far Rockaway. Queens isn't even mentioned.

As in all counties in New York, crime is a major issue in Queens. House burglaries have always been of particular concern, and have only recently been superseded by drugs as the crime most affecting the county's residents. Still, when it comes to law enforcement, politics seem to take precedence in Queens.

3

I entered a law enforcement community that was still deeply affected by the findings of the Knapp Commission in 1972—while I was still in law school. Most New Yorkers remember the Knapp Commission for its exposure of cops who were "on the pad" (bribed routinely to overlook crime). It was because of Knapp that uniformed officers were not allowed to make street arrests for drug sales. The city's official position was that they could not be trusted to remain honest. But far more controversial at the time was the commission's additional findings—about dirty DAs.

According to the Knapp investigators, corruption was so pervasive that local prosecutors could not be trusted to clean their own houses. The commission recommended legislation to take jurisdiction over corruption prosecution away from the local DAs and give it to a special prosecutor, to be appointed by Governor Nelson Rockefeller. In a rare moment of unity, all five of New York City's elected district attorneys opposed the creation of a special prosecutor. It was a sign of the depths of the brewing scandals that their protests were ignored. By the end of 1973, a year after Knapp, three of the five district attorneys had left office. The Bronx elected a new district attorney, Mario Merola. Manhattan lost the legendary Frank Hogan, Manhattan's DA for thirty-one years, because of a stroke from which he never recovered. Queens's district attorney, Thomas Mackell, retired because of a precedent-setting arrest and indictment—his own. Mackell was so popular a politician that even after his arrest for official misconduct and conspiracy he managed to resist resignation until the governor began formal proceedings for his removal.

When there is a midterm vacancy in a district attorney's post, a governor's appointee serves until a new election can be held. In Queens, Governor Rockefeller appointed as interim district attorney Michael Armstrong, previously general counsel to the Knapp Commission. He was going to clean up Queens.

Armstrong served for only seven months of self termed "lame-duck" reforms. The *New York Times* of August 26, 1973, reported Armstrong's warning that "the [Queens DA's] office would revert to political control if State Senator Nicholas Ferraro, the Democratic candidate, [and] a close friend of . . . the Democratic county leader, was elected."

Although Ferraro won, it was Mackell who continued to dominate the headlines throughout the course of his trial, conviction, and eventually successful appeals. I had finished law school and moved to Queens by 1974. It was impossible not to know who Mackell was. I don't remember hearing of Ferraro until I joined the DA's office eight years later.

In 1974, Rockefeller's successor, Governor Malcolm Wilson, appointed Richard Kuh to replace the ailing Hogan in Manhattan on an interim basis. Kuh had gained recognition ten years earlier for his prosecution of the famed and controversial comedian Lenny Bruce on obscenity charges.

Frank Hogan had been such an institution that for several decades the position of district attorney of New York County had been off-limits to the politically ambitious. In 1974 there was heavy competition for the job. The front runner was Robert Morgenthau, who had previously served as United States attorney in New York. Morgenthau ran on claims of an anticorruption record.

The Manhattan race focused on how the new DA would run his office. One of the major campaign issues between Kuh and Morgenthau was sex-crimes prosecution, which had become central to the politics of prosecution by then.

At this time the country was starting to take a second look at sexual assault. In 1972 a grass-roots organization in Ohio called WAR (Women

Against Rape) had gained national attention. By 1973 New York City's mayor had created an interdisciplinary Task Force Against Rape. WAR came to New York.

As was happening virtually across the United States in response to political pressure, particularly from women's groups, New York's rape laws were under revision. By 1974 the Rape Shield Law was enacted, limiting cross-examination of a victim concerning her sexual history. In increments between 1971 and 1974 the penal law had done away with New York's uniquely stringent requirement of corroborating evidence for even an adult woman to prosecute a sex crime. (Even after the reforms, cases involving children and mental incompetents still needed proof beyond the victim's testimony before a case could even get to court.)

Singer Connie Francis was raped in a hotel room in Nassau County in 1974. (The case was so publicized it opened the floodgates of civil liability—for insufficient security—in rape cases.) That same year Nassau County created what *The New York Times* hailed as the first unit in the country to specialize in sex-crimes prosecution. Kuh applied for special funding and announced his intentions to create a unit similar to Nassau's within the Manhattan DA's office. Morgenthau one-upped Kuh by promising that *his* specialized unit would be staffed exclusively by female attorneys.

Morgenthau won the election.

When I joined Legal Aid in 1975, I didn't know that Morgenthau had only recently become DA. I did know that although people in the courthouse spoke of him with respect, it was not with the reverence and love that they still used to describe Frank Hogan. I only saw Morgenthau occasionally at arraignments, if a high-profile case came through.

In Queens, amidst rumors of ties to organized crime that persisted even after his death, Nicholas Ferraro resigned in 1975 to become a New York State supreme court judge. He had served as DA for only a little over a year. His most notable act as district attorney was to bring his cousin, Geraldine Ferraro, on board as an assistant district attorney. (Later, when she ran for vice president, she described her background before the Queens DA's office as "being a housewife.")

Courthouse regulars always insisted that Nicholas Ferraro's resignation was less than voluntary. His conduct fueled those fires. Even eight years later, when I tried a case before him, Ferraro's resentment of his successor was ill disguised.

But Ferraro becoming a judge gave a new governor (Hugh Carey) an opportunity to appoint a district attorney for Queens. There were several front runners, including a local Queens attorney by the name of Mario Cuomo, but the governor selected John Santucci.

The mid 1970s saw three separate governors appoint interim district attorneys for New York City. And in those same years Queens County had four different DAs.

The position of district attorney is a unique political plum. There is the obvious appeal: the power to decide who gets prosecuted and, almost more significantly, who doesn't. But beyond the obvious, the New York City district attorneys control huge and independent budgets, and they have absolute, unbridled power to hire, promote, and fire hundreds of employees (from law graduates to investigators to "provisionals" who in theory "supplement" civil servants). There are big-figure contracts for everything from paper and supplies to office renovation, and grants for such specialized law-enforcement needs as "witness protection." And there is virtually no review of how a DA's office functions internally.

The scramble over, the post of district attorney for Queens county was about to stabilize. Acting as interim DA, in 1977 Santucci easily got the Democratic nod and ran for office on a "clean government" campaign, avoiding actual issues whenever possible. When crime *was* mentioned during the campaign, organized crime took precedence over sex crimes. Santucci promised to create a specialized unit in the Queens DA's office . . . an airport bureau. Both of New York City's major airports, Kennedy and La Guardia, are in Queens. The airport bureau would be charged with investigating Mafia infiltration of the airports.

After Santucci's election in 1977 and despite his creation over the years of serial "airport bureaus," the media continued to complain that the airports were centers of organized-crime activity. The crimes Nicholas Pileggi exposed in his book *Wiseguy* (the basis of the movie *Goodfellas*) took place in Queens County while Santucci was district attorney. A Queens-based Mafia figure, John Gotti, was dubbed the "Teflon Don" by the press for his ability to evade conviction during the same years.

Santucci was a small-potatoes politician with statewide ambitions and national dreams. With progressive reluctance as the years passed, he settled for being district attorney of Queens County. In 1978 he failed in an attempt to win the Democratic nomination for attorney general of New York. In 1980, he ran fourth out of four for the nomination for U.S. senator. In 1981 he rewon election as Queens DA.

Notwithstanding his reelection, Santucci was never highly regarded within the Queens courts. The day I interviewed with him for the job, my husband had asked me to pick up the minutes of a hearing he had conducted in Queens. I'd searched through small catacombs of dirty, narrow hallways and cluttered offices to find the right court reporter. On my way back to the building adjoining the courthouse I found that other than a security desk and a sign with foot-tall letters that said DISTRICT ATTORNEY JOHN J. SANTUCCI, there was little to distinguish the space occupied by the DA's offices. The security desk sent me to the third floor. As I got off the elevator, it was like I'd somehow wound up in an entirely different building. The hallway wasn't elegant, but it was wide, brightly lit, and clean. The carpeting and lack of activity made for a kind of muffled silence. I passed closed doors with signs indicating various executives. At the end of the hallway were glass doors and a small reception area facing a conference room and surrounded on two sides by secretarial space. The secretaries left me waiting in a padded chair.

With time to kill, I leafed through the transcript I'd just picked up. In heated words the judge was excoriating the Queens DA's office for its incompetence. I closed the transcript quickly and put it back in my briefcase.

I was ushered inside to Santucci's inner office. The room was large enough not to seem crowded despite several overstuffed chairs, a couch, a huge dark wooden desk, and polished bookcases. From the windows there was a view to one side of the Queens House of Detention, and to the other of the judge's chambers in the courthouse.

Santucci was short, with the build of a lightweight who had grown moderately fleshy over the years. He had Mediterranean features, which I later learned passed for sexy among the more fawning of his female support staff. During the interview he asked me if he could bum a cigarette—he said he was trying to quit. Still, he sounded sympathetic to victims when he talked about sex crimes . . . and he offered me the job.

Later on, I pieced together enough from what other people told me to figure out why. After his first election Santucci had created a unit in imitation of Morgenthau's—but along with sex crimes, it handled several other "special" categories such as domestic violence. The Special Victims Bureau was designed more for show than for effectiveness, with sharply limited duties. The unit was charged with "investigation" and indictment (presenting cases to the grand jury so that formal felony charges could be brought in supreme court). Special Victims did not try cases. Rumor had it that its first bureau chief was Mackell's goddaughter—and that she never walked into a courtroom as a litigator. During the ten years that I later spent in the Queens DA's office, I never saw any evidence to the contrary.

The bureau chief they were describing was not the only one to hold that title in Special Victims' brief history. The other chief of the bureau had been Geraldine Ferraro. After Ferraro successfully ran for congress in 1978, her rival at the Queens DA's office was determined to keep her bureau to herself by eliminating the competition. There weren't many women in the Queens DA's office, and most of them were in Special Victims. They were rarely recommended for promotion.

Always media conscious, Santucci was well aware of the limited PR value of a Special Victims Bureau that didn't try cases. By 1981 Santucci wanted the office to at least have a female sex-crimes prosecutor with trial experience. Before he hired me to start at the beginning of 1982, he had none. Santucci didn't hire me because he thought I was a member of any club, and I didn't join his staff because I thought he would be a great boss.

It didn't take me long to learn the setup. Santucci structured his office to be top-heavy. There were a few hundred ADAs, supervised by about twenty-five bureau chiefs. Except in megaheadline crimes, bureau chiefs were strictly administrators, with no caseloads of their own. The rest of the hierarchy, collectively referred to as the Third Floor (where most of them had their offices), included a chief of trials—one step higher than a bureau chief; several executive assistant district attorneys; and a few-odd high-level positions for displaced politicians (like the ex-chairman of New York State's parole board, himself under investigation at the time) who seemed to find their way into the Queens DA's office. There was also a class of displaced executives that the DAs of Queens, Brooklyn, and occasionally the Bronx seemed to trade among themselves based on who was recently elected or who needed to curry favor in a particular community at any given time.

Anyone above the position of ADA set policy. There were times when Santucci deferred most of his authority to the Third Floor. Other times, he rewrote policy for himself. Often it was hard to know what the Third Floor had in mind.

Like ADAs elsewhere, Santucci's legal staff were, for the most part, hired directly from law school. Santucci was actually less rigid in this than the DAs in the other boroughs were—he had to be to accommodate his hiring "exceptions"—but even so, very few newly hired ADAs had any prior experience. They learned on the job.

Queens required law graduates to give a three-year commitment to the job—that being the average amount of time people remained on staff. There was a small population that stayed longer, usually called career prosecutors, although the term referred to longevity rather than skill or experience.

Like most of its counterparts, the Queens DA's office was structured into bureaus according to task. There was even a traditional advancement path according to bureau: Intake; Criminal Court; Grand Jury; Supreme Court; (then, past the three-year mark:) Major Offenses; Homicide Trials. Unlike the other counties, Queens had no regular schedule for promotions. Ambitious young lawyers languished in assignments they'd long since outgrown for months and years without knowing when transfers were coming or whether they would be on the transfer lists.

When I started as an ADA, everyone seemed to presume that I was unqualified. Several people, including one of my first bureau chiefs, openly resented my presence. What did I think I was doing being assigned directly to supreme court trials (in Kew Gardens, no less, which had higher status and a higher profile than the other DA office locations) when so many people had waited so long for such a position? No one seemed to have a sense that Third Floor decisions were part of an overall prosecution design.

Santucci assigned me to a trial bureau, then seemed to forget me. I had been there a few weeks when I bumped into him by accident. He told the executives who were with him to find some rape cases and transfer them to me. They grumbled, but eventually complied. After that, whatever bureau chief I had at the time knew unofficially to assign me sex-crimes prosecutions.

As a trial attorney I was never part of the Special Victims Bureau. I only inherited their indictments. Sometimes it was hard to remember we were supposed to be on the same side.

4

My first lesson about sex-crimes prosecution was that perpetrators were not the only enemy. There is a large, more or less hidden population of what I later came to call collaborators within the criminal justice system. Whether it comes from a police officer or a defense attorney, a judge or a court clerk or a prosecutor, there seems to be a residuum of empathy for rapists that crosses all gender, class, and professional barriers. It gets expressed in different ways, from victim-bashing to jokes in poor taste, and too often it results in giving the rapist a break. The one weakness I discovered in collaborators is that they always underestimate the Resistance.

The first rapist I tried, Johnny Washington, was also the first felony trial for the judge who presided. At the initial conference between the judge, the defense attorney, and me, the judge offered to let the defendant plead to the charges in exchange for a minimum sentence. I objected, but the judge ignored me. It was the defense attorney who turned down the offer, insisting that the victim had consented to the sexual intercourse. But in light of the judge's generosity the defense attorney waived a jury—preferring to let this judge issue the verdict on the guilt of the defendant instead of twelve jurors. Right then, I should have known.

Washington had been arrested for several rapes in which the assailant attacked strangers from behind, covering their heads with a jacket before he threw them to the ground. Only one woman ever identified him. She had declined emergency-room treatment after the rape, so there was no forensic evidence of intercourse. (No semen was found in her vagina or underwear.) That, plus several preindictment prosecution errors that translated into lost evidence, was why no one else had been anxious to try it.

The judge diminished my own enthusiasm by his conduct during the trial.

Carmen was petite, dignified—and terrified when she took the witness stand. She testified that she had returned home from her job as a bank teller at around six-thirty in the evening. A stranger had followed her onto the elevator in her apartment building. When Carmen tried to get off the elevator at her floor, the stranger grabbed her from behind. He told her he had a knife and that he would kill her if she didn't cooperate. At the roof he dragged her off the elevator and over to an electrical shack, where he made her undress and lie down on the gravel. He covered her face with his jacket while he raped her and sodomized her. Then he made her give him her watch and money. After he left her on the roof, she crawled down the outside of the building to her apartment, terrified that he was still on the stairwell and would attack her again. Her sister, a social worker who counseled rape victims, testified about seeing Carmen appear at her door, her clothes in disarray and scrape marks all over her back and legs. They called Carmen's boyfriend, who was a police officer, to take them to the precinct to make the complaint.

Four days later Carmen saw Washington on the street and called the police. That was the man who raped her. Washington gave a phony alibi when he was arrested.

Once he heard Carmen on the witness stand, the defense attorney abandoned his preannounced intention to prove that the victim had consented to intercourse. Still, he'd made his most important defense move when he'd waived a jury.

Unbelievably, the judge decided that because she hadn't *seen* the rape, the victim couldn't be sure of the penetration. He wanted nauseatingly graphic details of what she felt during the intercourse and ejaculation. It still didn't satisfy him (and he was only "convinced" later when the defendant admitted the intercourse in his presentence report.)

I told the judge he was saying that a blind woman couldn't prosecute a rape case in Queens County. That quote was picked up by the media, with two results. The judge still did not find Washington guilty of rape, but he imposed the maximum sentence on him for the lesser offenses, including first-degree sexual abuse; it added up to the same sentence as a rape conviction. And the judge hated me for life.

So did the defendant's mother. She showed up at the sentencing, screaming at all of us for what we were doing to her little boy. The defense attorney opted to rant against me in the newsletter of a local bar association on whose board he sat as a director.

I also angered an executive assistant district attorney, who called me into his office and accused me of having leaked information to the press. His accusation got deflated when he made the mistake of telling me he "knew" my husband was a reporter. When I corrected him—my husband was an attorney who specialized in representing children—he settled for ordering me never to talk to the press again.

There were always enemies to be made. That was the first lesson. But at least Johnny Washington wasn't going to be raping anyone anytime soon.

It didn't take me long to get the reputation of someone willing to take on any rape prosecution. Other trial attorneys "gave" me their sex cases. Mostly what I got were the ones nobody else wanted: cases in which the proof was weak, or the victim unlikable—or simply cases that involved a lot of work.

I was proud to be doing the work. I'd seen enough ugly violence to believe that people have a right to be safe from sexual predators. I'd worked in prisons enough to not delude myself about what they were, or what they could accomplish. But prison can at least contain predators—keeping them away from us.

Lawyers who knew me casually said that I "switched sides" when I became a prosecutor. I did change perspectives—but not convictions. I never believed that prison atrocities were some twisted form of justice. The ugly abuse of power doesn't become less offensive when its victims are less sympathetic. But the violence within our prison systems cannot be an excuse to tolerate violence outside them.

Many prisoners I met as a defense attorney supported my work as a prosecutor. Just one example was an inmate who served decades of incarceration in Louisiana for a robbery he committed as a teenager. Despite impeccable credentials for parole or pardon, he spent twenty years in solitary confinement—while those who could pay the purchase price were freed by a parole system so corrupt that the chairman of the pardon board went to prison for selling releases. That inmate never received any consideration or leniency from our penal system. Nevertheless, he cheered me on every time I took a rapist down for the count. Just as there were hidden enemies in this war, so there were hidden allies.

I wanted to up the stakes for sex criminals. I had a dream about how it could be done, which I expanded with every success and failure during my three years in a trial bureau. It took me almost all the time I was at the Queens DA's office to understand that doing things right was a direction, not a destination. But I think I understood early on that there were no neutral corners to rest in, and that any power I might have to fight came from being prepared, always, to go the distance.

The closest I came to seeing my vision become a reality happened years after the Johnny Washington case. I was chief of Special Victims by then. A woman walked in who made me feel as if anyone I'd ever met could be a secret sexual victim. I don't know that under the old Special Victims Bureau she would have made it past the front door.

5

I've gone over this a lot of times in my head: what went on in those first few minutes of that interview, what it was about Laurie that I couldn't turn my back on and still be able to look at myself in the mirror the next day.

One thing was that even then, even in the midst of it, she looked and sounded like anybody's best friend. She was a slight, pretty, competent-looking woman. She had a sense of humor and sense of the absurd, but nothing that hit an off-key note. She never let you know she was on the edge. A term I read all the time in psychiatric reports—"appropriate affect"—always made me think of Laurie. That was her. I guess it was a skill she developed to survive—because she'd been living in hell for as long as she could remember.

I'd known about Laurie's case for a couple of weeks before I met her. I'd gotten a call from the criminal court deputy bureau chief. A lifelong friend of his, a nurse administrator named Judy, had a nurse working for her who'd just been raped at knifepoint. She'd managed to escape but was "a mess." Prosecution was unthinkable—she was in no shape for that. But Judy had wanted some guidance on how she could help this nurse. Oh, and maybe I should know . . . the rapist was the victim's own father.

I told the deputy chief to have Judy call Special Victims's social worker.

Now here was the social worker at my door, telling me that the nurse, Laurie, and her brother had some legal questions she couldn't answer. They didn't seem like they could wait for a follow-up appointment. The social worker had good instincts for spotting cases that needed legal attention. She also had a talent for understatement.

It was the Friday before the Fourth of July. Special Victims's halls were filled with victims and witnesses; survivors, and supporters. The crimes that had brought them to the DA's office had taken place only a day or two before. There were elderly people with bandages and canes; recently raped teenagers; wives with blackened eyes and defeated postures; frightened, noisy children; impatient uniformed officers.

Sometimes a rape victim would seem unnaturally calm. We had to keep reminding ourselves that it *wasn't* unnatural—it was a warning signal that she was still in shock. No matter how many times you read about rape trauma syndrome, seeing it is disconcerting. Recognizing it as a treatment emergency is even harder. But not recognizing it might mean a suicide.

By noon at the latest all the people filling the corridors had to be interviewed and their cases evaluated; for the ones that required indictment the witnesses had to be prepared to testify; the paperwork had to be completed and approved by me and an executive assistant, the ADAs had to be on line to present the case to the grand jury. If all that took much past noon, we ran the risk that fewer than sixteen grand jurors would be willing to work the afternoon before a summertime holiday weekend. If the "notice of voted indictment" was not handed up on time, the defendant would be released without bail.

I said I would talk to Laurie myself, since I was the only one left to handle a crisis. I warned the social worker we might be interrupted. I was supposed to be helping the ADAs evaluate cases, signing off on prosecution memos for the grand jury.

Laurie only wanted advice. She'd already been told her case was unprosecutable, that no one would believe her, that nothing could be done. She accepted that as an ugly truth—she was used to them. But her father would be getting out of the hospital soon—and he was definitely going to kill her. Wasn't there anything that could be done about that?

The question was matter-of-fact, no melodrama, no hysteria. Laurie patted the bureau's dog, Sheba, quietly as she talked—Sheba liked her. Laurie's brother Thomas, in his twenties and trying to look manly, nodded at the truth of what she was saying. The social worker, her face shining with sympathy and late-stage pregnancy, started to cry.

Laurie just got to you.

I got the crisis-level facts from her that first morning. They took a while to tell. This wasn't an ordinary crisis.

Starting when she was nine (later on, Laurie remembered abuse from when she was much younger), Laurie's father had forced her to have sex with him. She wasn't the first daughter he'd done this to. He'd raped his oldest daughter, Mary, until she was in her midteens. When Mary started to be sexually active with boys, she wasn't "his" anymore, so he'd started in on Laurie. Until the weekend before Laurie came to see me, she'd thought it had been just the two of them.

There were six children altogether: two brothers, Jonathan and Thomas, and four sisters, Mary, Laurie, Dorothy, and Florrie. Florrie was retarded. Laurie had spent her life watching out for Florrie: making sure she was taken care of; keeping the secret to prevent her from knowing what was happening to her sisters; guarding against Florrie ever being alone with their father. Then Laurie found out she'd failed.

Florrie told her that whenever Laurie had avoided or managed to escape their father, he had raped Florrie instead. Florrie didn't put it that way. But Laurie had been so vigilant that, when Florrie started to disclose the abuse, she'd asked *when* it had happened. As Florrie answered her, Laurie was able to piece it together.

All those years, he never stopped raping and sodomizing Laurie. Laurie was thirty-one years old now, and it was still happening. After what he'd done to her as a child, she'd grown up not being able to tolerate being touched by any male. So she was his alone. It had gone on, year after year. What he said later on was a perfect self-portrait. "Before eighteen, it was child abuse. After that it was just incest between consenting adults." He told Thomas, "When you have children, you'll understand. You'll do the same thing to your daughters." But that was *after* it all came out in the open; after he'd tried to kill Laurie and she'd escaped. He said it to try to justify what he'd done.

Laurie's father had special methods of terrorizing her. The one she remembered most vividly was when he took her in his car and threatened to crash and kill them both. He drove onto a bridge, told her; "We're going to die," and floored the gas pedal, stopping the car only at the very last second, and only inches away from their death. She grew up afraid every day.

On the surface, Laurie's life looked almost normal. She went to school. She became a nurse. She was good at what she did and got promotions and opportunities and recognition. It wasn't that strange that she still lived at home at thirty-one; lots of people did these days. It was a little odd that her father dropped her off and picked her up at work each day, that he would call incessantly if she was delayed more than fifteen minutes at the end of her shift. But lots of things are odd. Nobody asked why.

Under the surface, the competing stresses in Laurie's life accelerated out of control. Each day of her life ended another dream she had for escape. Her life was a trap set by her father the first day he raped her.

As much as her father had damaged Laurie, he'd never destroyed her dreams. Ultimately that's what almost killed Laurie—and maybe what saved her. It wasn't big things Laurie wanted. She wanted a night out with a girlfriend. She wanted to go on a business trip. On her braver days, she even wanted to go out on a date. He kept promising he would stop—maybe someday he really would and she could live her life.

Her father saw in Laurie's little dreams a loss of his control. He reacted by tightening the reins. There were battles, emotional ones. His violence no longer resolved their conflicts in his favor, as it always had when she was younger. His victories were temporary. Even when he punched her hard enough so that lumps showed on her face and the back of her head (she told people at work that she'd fallen), it didn't stop her from taking a work-related trip out of the country.

Laurie was even talking about moving out and getting her own apartment. Thomas would help her. Her father knew she never would. He'd done too good a job. She was his. But that she could even *think* of it was intolerable. His response was simple: Escalate the violence.

Laurie knew all the signs for when she was going to be forced to have sex with her father. Her mother (a specialist in cold complicity) would be off visiting friends. They'd be alone in the apartment, or Florrie would be in a secluded part of it. Not that it wouldn't be obvious to an outsider—he slept in Laurie's bedroom most nights—but they had their own pretenses. Even in the house, nobody looked, nobody saw.

He'd say to Laurie, "Tonight's going to be a good night." She'd try to make excuses. He'd insist. She was his. She'd try pleading, but that just seemed to excite him—like when she cried or screamed. She'd try resisting, but that only made him hurt her more.

That night, she argued harder than usual. She even tried to walk out the door. He had to go into the hallway and drag her back. What if the neighbors had seen? Even then she tried to leave again, but Florrie had gotten scared and wouldn't come with her. So she stayed, this one last night.

He threatened to kill himself. She told him she didn't care anymore. He knew she meant it. On the way home that day he'd threatened to drive them off the bridge, just as he had when she was little. But this time she didn't plead or try to stop him. It fired an even greater rage inside him.

After all these years, she knew what happened if she tried to resist. Sometimes twisting her arm or pulling her hair hard and long was enough to remind her. But not tonight. Tonight she needed to be taught a lifetime's lesson. The knife would do it. Put it to her throat. Tell her she's going to die. Watch the fear. Feel the power. There's a good girl. Why do you like it rough? Why do you make me hurt you? The knife will stay under the pillow while you do what I want. While I do what I want to you. While I do it hard. So you remember that you're mine. So you'll feel it for a long time to come. I can always take the knife out again. If you fight, tonight we're going to die. Tonight's the night— since you hate it so much— it'll end, everything will end, we'll end it tonight. If you don't struggle (against the knife), it won't hurt.

Later on, he claimed he had never intended to use the knife on her; that it was just to scare her; that he would have used it on himself; that it wasn't there at all; that Laurie was lying; that I put all these ideas in her head.

Laurie submitted to the threat of the knife, to the sex, to him staying inside her after he'd finished, and after he told her again they were both going to die. She had been taught all her life to live for another person:

for his needs and desires, for what was best for him. Her father had taught her well.

It wasn't a life's philosophy that Laurie could limit to only one person. She worried about everyone's needs and desires disproportionately to her own. Even when death didn't sound so bad, she worried about Florrie. Florrie would hear them. Or if he killed them, Florrie would find their bodies in the morning. What would that do to her? Florrie wasn't that strong. It would destroy her.

After he raped Laurie, they argued—about whether he would kill her or she would kill herself—until he finally fell asleep. She lay in bed, thinking about dying. She'd be damned if he would get to kill her. She'd do it herself. She slipped the knife out from under the pillow. No—wait! Florrie. She had to wait until after Florrie left in the morning. She hid the knife in the kitchen, went back to bed, stayed awake, trying to think.

Florrie woke, knew something was wrong, asked. Laurie tried to say, "Everything is O.K." It obviously wasn't. She finally shooed Florrie out, off to her job in a supermarket. He was awake by then. They argued about the dog, Lucky, who was crying to go out. You do what I say. This is going to be the day. Are we going to forget about last night, or are we going to end it now?

I'll walk Lucky. I'll make you breakfast. It will be O.K.

Laurie did. She talked him into letting her walk the dog. He knew she was his. He knew he'd won. He'd always win.

She put on sweat pants and a sweatshirt. No purse, no money. No way to run. She walked the dog, said good morning to a neighbor; thought about not going back, but what would she do with Lucky? She couldn't just leave the dog on the street, defenseless. She returned.

Down the long corridor to the apartment door. Open the door with the key. Let Lucky inside. Make sure Lucky's O.K. She could see her father from the doorway. He was lying on her bed. Naked. She knew what would come next. What would come next for the rest of her life.

She closed the door softly. Him inside. Her outside. Then she ran; ran for her life and then kept running. Down the streets, past the closest subway stop—he might follow, he *would* follow. Then on to the next stop. Call Thomas for help. No money, no change even for a phone call. Call collect. Thomas isn't there. Ask for Jonathan, (they work together).

Start to cry. Get out enough of it: "Daddy tried to kill me. I'm two subway stops away. Come get me."

Jonathan said something in disbelief and anger, but he came anyway, brought her to Thomas's house. Thomas's wife loaned her clothes. Thomas got her money. They used the wife's maiden name for the airline ticket; sent her to Mary, the sister who'd escaped.

I understood why Laurie had been told by other lawyers that she couldn't prosecute. People believe that if something is unthinkable, it can't be true. I wish they were right. I wish it were fiction.

Laurie told me about lying in bed for days, too sick, too scared, in too much pain from the rape to get up even to go to the bathroom. Thomas filled in the rest: what happened after Laurie left New York.

It wasn't only Laurie who thought of her father as bigger than life, as more powerful than he could possibly be. They all did. It took courage to do what the brothers did; it was the kind of challenge that shows what a person really is. Laurie's father didn't deserve the sons he raised. They were fine people.

He called, Jonathan first and then Thomas. "Where's Laurie?"

"She's left."

"I want her back. Tell her she'd better come back. You'd better tell me where she is."

The brothers shipped Florrie off for the weekend, picking her up at work and not letting her go home. A day, two days of phone calls, him alone in the apartment. His wife was still away. The brothers came for some of Laurie's things. He threatened them. He told Jonathan it was his fault. Jonathan would pay. Jonathan would die. He'd kill him. He called again. "Where's Laurie?"

They weren't listening. He'd teach them. Threats didn't work, he'd use something better—what he'd put inside each of them, his control. He called, said he'd taken care of things. He said he drank some insecticide. They'd all be sorry.

Jonathan later told me he was sure his father waited to actually swallow any insecticide until after he'd phoned, until the ambulance sirens were right outside his door. Too bad they got upstairs so quickly. He survived.

The poison did a pretty fair job on his insides—acid poured into evil—but he recovered quickly. The brothers had him transferred to a psychiatric ward in a good hospital. They paid for it. He was still there. One of the reasons they were in my office, Thomas told me, was that the hospital had almost given their patient a weekend pass.

The "patient" had called Florrie to make arrangements. It was all set up until the brothers found out by accident and put a stop to it. But they couldn't be sure it was stopped for good. Even if it was, soon enough the hospital would want to discharge their father altogether. And then he'd kill Laurie. He'd threatened Jonathan and Thomas too. Thomas wasn't worried for himself, he said, but his wife was. What could they do? What could I do?

While I'd listened, I'd tried to prepare myself for this moment. I knew it was coming. The social worker had said Laurie and her brother had questions. I needed answers.

All right, I'd attack the immediate problem first. They wanted their father kept in the hospital. Could I do that? Well, that depended on Laurie. Was she willing to prosecute?

I startled her with the question, but the answer was yes, if she had to.

O.K., then I will inform the hospital there's a pending DA's investigation. I'll tell them no discharge or even passes without notifying the district attorney. We were planning an arrest.

I'd need some information: the name of the hospital, the psychiatrist, his phone number. What was the patient's name? William Porter.*

I phoned the hospital with Laurie and her brother still sitting there. The psychiatrist assured me his patient would not be released.

I didn't like something in the doctor's voice. I decided to confirm my conversation with the psychiatrist by letter.

I told Laurie and Thomas that between the pressure from Jonathan and Thomas (who were paying the bills) and the DA's office (which could post a police officer at his door if the hospital didn't cooperate), we'd probably bought ourselves a few more days, at least the weekend. But I told them to keep their guard up. I arranged with Laurie to return Monday, to talk more about where to go from here. She looked spent,

*I have created an alias. There is no way to use this defendant's true name without invading his daughter's privacy—another added benefit the system gives to rapists who grow their own victims.

so I promised her she wouldn't have to talk about the crimes during our second meeting.

After Laurie left, the social worker and I talked over what we'd heard. We couldn't believe how "normal" Laurie seemed after what she'd lived through.

The social worker said that she'd gotten Laurie's permission to tell me something else I might need to know. To this day Laurie never mentions this topic unless she has to. It was the hardest part for Laurie, and she'd said she didn't have the strength to tell it twice: Laurie had undergone two abortions.

Laurie's father refused to allow her to use any birth control devices when he raped her. When he impregnated her, she had an abortion. She was a nurse. She knew the medical consequences for incest babies.

After the abortion, Laurie hid from her father the birth control pills she began taking against medical advice. She was one of those women for whom the pill was dangerous. To Laurie, it was a lesser risk.

Laurie lost the medical gamble . . . before her thirtieth birthday she had a stroke. While she was recovering, her father was happier with her than he'd ever been. He took care of her. She was too weak to fight him in any way. To him it seemed like she'd completely given in. Later he told her he was sorry she recovered.

After she regained her strength, Laurie's father impregnated her again, deliberately. He tracked her cycle. He chose the most likely time for her to get pregnant and insisted on repeated sex. She had a second abortion.

Laurie was raised a Catholic. She never forgave herself for the abortions.

After I sent off the letter to Porter's psychiatrist, I went back to running the bureau. There were other emergencies, but none more disturbing than what Laurie had told me. I needed to figure out what more I could do.

It wasn't until Laurie's second visit that we really talked about what prosecution would mean. Before, I'd just needed her commitment. Now it was time to start the planning. Laurie had adjusted to the idea of pressing charges, but she wasn't comfortable with the idea of "sending my father to prison." (Neither was I, but our concepts of what should happen to him veered in opposite directions. Too bad incest is not a capital crime.)

Once Laurie's father was arrested, we would have a little more time to make decisions. I expected that his defense attorney would ask for a psychiatric examination at arraignment. Porter would be brought to court on discharge from a psych ward. Add that to the suicidal gesture and the charges, and the first thing a defense attorney would think of was mental competency. The court-ordered fitness exam would take thirty days. The judge's only bail choices would be release or remand. I thought I could convince the judge to keep the defendant held without bail. If all my strategy worked, we'd have a month in which to make decisions.

If things didn't go the way I expected, we needed an alternate plan. One possibility was to let Porter plead to felony probation, on condition that he spend five years confined to a psychiatric hospital. It would be a rare plea bargain, but given Porter's options, I thought it might be possible to convince a defense attorney to agree to it. We had a first-degree rape charge. If he was convicted at trial, he faced mandatory imprisonment.

Laurie was comforted by the idea of inpatient psychiatric probation. At the beginning it was a tentative goal. It was at least a way to keep Laurie and her brothers safe.

Laurie understood that to accomplish any of this, we needed some weapons of our own. The most powerful weapon we had available to us was to get an indictment. An ordinary arrest had too many risks. The lower courts might not take the case seriously enough. And if a judge released him on low bail, Laurie would end up dead.

A grand-jury-voted indictment would have more impact. That meant Laurie having to testify. She said she would if she had to; whatever she had to do. She was going to learn exactly what that meant.

Laurie and I made a list of what needed to be accomplished. I wanted more details of the most recent crimes, and I wanted a history, so that I could understand the overall context of what had happened. That meant full interviews with Laurie, Thomas, and Jonathan. I would arrange for a good detective from Queens Sex Crimes Squad to take over the police role in the investigation. Laurie understood that she might have to be interviewed by him.

I didn't see why Laurie should have to testify live before the grand jury. I asked her if she was in counseling. Yes, but she didn't like her first therapist. She'd just found one she liked a whole lot better. Good.

Would the new therapist give me an affidavit as to Laurie's state of mind—so that I could ask a judge to permit her testimony to be video-taped? She'd ask.

I wanted Laurie to go for a physical exam by a proctologist, to see if there was old scarring from the times she'd been sodomized. She'd already been examined gynecologically—the doctor had found redden-ing two weeks after the last rape. (It is rare to find medical signs of force even shortly after a woman is sexually assaulted.) I needed the records of that exam, and to talk to the doctor.

I didn't know how much time we had. When I'd talked to Porter's psychiatrist, I'd been disturbed by how sympathetic he sounded toward his patient. He made noises like a collaborator. I didn't like how easily the psychiatrist had adopted his patient's concept that this was just an "affair" between Laurie and her father. It was that kind of thinking that had allowed the legislature to put incest in the same section of the penal law as adultery, and to designate it the lowest category of felony. Some-how, when it comes to incest, there are special tolerances. When it's the four-year-old down the street who's the victim, we're willing to say the offender is a pervert who should go to prison, but when it's a father's own four-year-old daughter, we call it family dysfunction and say he should get probation.

I couldn't rely on the psychiatrist complying with the family's wishes to keep Porter hospitalized.

I deferred any of the investigation that could wait until after indict-ment.

I scheduled Laurie's in-depth interview. To prepare for it, I asked her to come up with some dates for Porter's sexual assaults. I didn't want to deplete whatever was holding her together. But the law in New York said I needed specific dates.

Like that of most states, New York's criminal procedure law presumes that a crime is a one-time incident between adult strangers. Whenever the criminal behavior doesn't fit that mold, as with child sexual abuse or domestic violence, the procedural rules tend to get in the way of prose-cution. Technicalities are glorified to the point where a child can be raped over months or years and the rapist might go free if the child cannot name exact dates. The standard is supposed to be "reasonable-ness"—but it is the courts themselves who have been unreasonable.

I talked to Laurie about challenging the law on her case. She loved the idea. What had happened to Laurie was unusual in how far into adulthood the abuse had continued, and in how violent the force had been. But it also fit all the patterns of child sexual abuse. It raised many of the same issues—but presented by a victim who could explain as an adult.

Since Laurie was an adult, the courts would expect her to be able to name the dates of the recent sexual assaults. The crimes that took place when she was a child, though, might not have that restriction. Because in Laurie's case there were charges to be brought well within the statute of limitations as well as charges from years and years ago, my original idea was to charge all of the crimes and force a judge to rule on the issues both as to the statute of limitation and as to the requirement of specific dates.

It didn't work out that way. It turned out that much of the early abuse took place in Brooklyn, and Laurie had been sixteen before her family moved to Queens. Legal jurisdiction depends strictly on what county the crimes happen in. The jurisdiction problem clouded the statute-of-limitations issue enough to convince me that Laurie's wasn't the right test case. O.K., there were more urgent tasks to accomplish with this prosecution.

(Later on, I did find a perfect test case for the statute of limitations. It marked the beginning of the end of my career at the Queens DA's office.)

I should have known that asking Laurie for dates was a bigger request than it sounded like. But it took me a long time to learn when to take into account Laurie's fragility, how much she'd been damaged, and when to trust how strong she appeared to be.

The term "Post-Traumatic Stress Disorder" is used a lot in sex-crimes prosecution. Laurie lived it. What her mind used for survival was "numbing." If, as one defendant I prosecuted attempted to claim at trial, his past traumas had really made him a rapist, Laurie would be a mass murderer.

Even when we limited the charges to the crimes against Laurie during the past five years, there were more painful memories than she could bear to dwell on. The experience gave her a new perspective on her life. All the time she'd been living the nightmare, one of her goals had been not to think about what was happening to her, to just get through it, stealing whatever moments along the way happened to be her own. Now, thinking about it all was overwhelming.

It would have helped if Laurie had had time to recover before being taxed by the requirements of an alien legal system. In this country we rarely afford victims that luxury.

No one teaches prosecutors how to be therapists, and I'm not sure it's an appropriate role for them anyway. But somebody needs to teach prosecutors how to look at (and out for) the effects on victims of the state's conduct and attitudes. I do believe that prosecution can be empowering—*if* it's done right. But that's a very big "if."

When Laurie and I went over the crimes so that I'd know what to ask her for the videotape, I had her tell me the entire history, including the parts most in her memory, not just the crimes she would describe to the grand jury. Later, when I summarized this conversation for professional reasons—to the detective for the police reports, the defense attorney for discovery, the judge during plea bargaining, I was never able to communicate how I felt listening to Laurie, the total sense of horror. What Laurie said was as close to unspeakable as anything I'd ever heard.

Child sexual abuse often does not include physical violence. The violence is to children's spirits more than to their bodies. A psychological extortion traps children between shame for what is happening to them and the walls of control instilled by their abusers. Those traps are what permits abuse to go on for years and years.

Children are threatened into keeping the secret. They are threatened with huge, child-oriented consequences if they tell. The molester kills a kitten and says the same thing will happen to the child. Or the molester shows a clipping about a mother who got sick and died, and says it will happen to the child's mother. The form of the threats varies . . . the malevolence never does.

The shame is increased by the fact that for the child victim on an elemental level, the abuse may be physically stimulating. Many child abusers do not actually penetrate their victims. They fondle and stroke, they rub themselves against the child's private parts. They often require oral intercourse from the child, but it takes a further degree of depravity to actually want to penetrate such small organs.

I prosecuted one child molester arrested after his four-year-old daughter, being examined in the hospital for a broken arm, pointed to her vagina and asked the doctor: "Do you want to kiss me there, like Daddy does?" When the father was questioned, he admitted to intercourse with his daughter. He added, "I only hurt myself." The therapists thought it was a sign that he was amenable to rehabilitation, that he recognized his behavior as self-destructive. They misunderstood. He was referring to the physical pain he caused himself by forcing himself into too small an opening.

Laurie's father combined the traditional psychological tools of the pedophile with the twisted cruelty of the sadist. Not only did he penetrate his child when she was very small, but he enjoyed the pain that it caused her. Laurie never actually said to me that her father could only reach orgasm if she was bleeding or screaming, but every memory that she had of his finally being satisfied always included one or the other. He enjoyed her being physically hurt, and he enjoyed being the one to do it. If she was too damaged vaginally, he would rape her anally, telling her it was her fault it hurt so much; stop moving; she should appreciate how considerate this was of him.

Much of what Laurie told me she said in a dispassionate voice, like she was dead inside. Only once during that whole session did she show emotion. That was when she was talking about the basement of their Brooklyn home. The other sisters and brothers would be sent outside, being told by their father that "Laurie doesn't want to play."

Laurie would be taken down to the basement, which had been especially fixed up by the rapist with a mattress, soundproofing, a deadbolt door lock beyond Laurie's strength, and special instruments for special occasions. What was most important to the setting was the mirrors on the ceiling above the mattress on the floor—so Porter could watch while he raped his child. It was when Laurie told me about the mirrors that her composure broke.

I asked her why she was crying. I thought maybe naming the pain would diminish it. She said, "These were the people who were supposed to love me."

It wasn't only the rapist who had betrayed the little girl.

In some ways the hardest part for Laurie was not her father's torturing her, but her mother's acquiescence in the abuse. Laurie's mother was an

47

obsessively self-centered woman. That's all there was to her. There is no question that she knew that her husband was forcing himself sexually on his daughters. When Laurie started to be able to look at her memories, she remembered being much younger than nine, and being in bed with her parents. Her father was raping her. Her mother wasn't participating, but she wasn't stopping anything either.

When Laurie did finally complain to her mother, her mother beat her.

Laurie had only one adult in her life that she trusted; her mother's sister, Aunt Peggy. One night when things were so hard she couldn't stand it, Laurie asked her mother if she could visit Aunt Peggy the next day. Her mother asked why. "I just want to talk to her," Laurie said. "I want to talk to Aunt Peggy." She was beaten by her mother for that request as well.

As I listened to all this, it seemed unimaginable that this hell could continue for as long as it did. What I wanted to believe is that if it happened today, someone would stop it. When Laurie told me about her older sister, Mary, I wanted to ask someone: her teachers, her "therapists," everyone: "How could you not have known? How could you have let this happen?"

Of all of them, Mary probably fought Porter the hardest. As much as he filled her life and her soul with poison, he never broke her spirit. She tried every kind of defiance she could. None of it worked.

Porter used other weapons besides his physical strength against his children. Humiliation was one of his favorites.

Every one of the brothers and sisters remembered the first time a boy came over to pick up Mary for a date. Porter walked into the room after the boy had already arrived. He viewed the situation and then walked up to stand in front of Mary. He back-handed her across the face so hard that she fell to the floor. Then he called her a slut and walked out of the room. That was just before her first suicide attempt.

The incest stopped when Mary started being promiscuous. Then, when she became a lesbian, Porter let her move out. She moved down South, far away enough to feel at least physically free of him. But it took a lifetime of trying to be safe from the poisons he had put inside her.

At one point the daughters were sexually abused by a relative of their father's. Laurie's younger sister Dorothy put a stop to this by telling her father. Porter got white-hot angry and barred the relative from the house forever; he wouldn't share his property with anyone.

It may be that Dorothy's telling prevented her from being abused by their father. Or it may be that Dorothy was abused as well. There's no way to know. Dorothy always took Porter's side against Laurie, and does so to this day.

During my third meeting with Laurie, I understood that Laurie's disclosures were bottomless. I couldn't prepare her to testify the way I would a mugging victim. Even as to the individual incidents that would make up the indictment, I decided to get the details of what Porter did during the videotaped testimony. I knew the kinds of atrocities to ask about. I didn't need a script.

What I did need was that court order permitting videotaping of Laurie's grand jury testimony. I wanted to use the part of the law that said some forms of traumatization of sex-crimes victims qualified them as "special witnesses" for videotaping. It was the one part of the statute that Special Victims hadn't used much, until Laurie's case. Child victims automatically qualified for videotaping, but for adults I needed judicial permission.

Laurie's therapist wrote an affidavit about her degree of traumatization, and I attached it to my application. Then I gave it to the clerk to give to the judge, like I would a search warrant or a court-ordered subpoena. I could tell from where I was watching that the judge expected something routine when he picked up my papers. He started to scan them, flipping through. Then he turned the pages back to the beginning. The judge read the thing over about four times before he shrugged to himself, picked up his pen, and signed. To the judge, the application was uncommon but not of major significance. For Laurie, it meant a ticket to a new life.

I still had to interview Laurie's brothers. Tactically, it was important to charge William Porter with the threats against his son Jonathan. Also, the brothers had each had several confrontations with their father during which he'd made admissions. Beyond that, I needed to get some perspective besides Laurie's on her father's lifetime of depravity.

Jonathan and Thomas were at that stage of trauma survival where they were rethinking all of their past perceptions. It may be that some of their overwhelming sense that they *should have known* was most acute just then. But the family life they described seemed so completely incestuous that it was hard for an outsider to imagine that they hadn't seen it.

The brothers were very different personalities. Jonathan was introspective, deadly serious, driven, touching in how much he hurt for his sisters. Thomas was charming, outgoing, a surprising combination of young enthusiasm and mature responsibility. Despite their differences, much of the information they gave me was the same. They had no doubts in their mind that what Laurie was saying was true. It fit everything they knew.

I asked Thomas and Jonathan about the image William Porter presented to outsiders. The brothers used the same words that Laurie did: a real nice guy, a good neighbor, hard-working, always willing to do a favor for a friend.

Porter made a point of being a strict disciplinarian as a father. His sons had to always act like gentlemen. His daughters were not allowed to swear—all rapists worship control.

The brothers' memory of Mary was similar to Laurie's. She was always acting out, always in trouble. Their mother seemed to resent all of her daughters, but Mary most of all. (This last part I had to figure out for myself. Neither brother was ready yet to express open disapproval of their mother. That would come later, when the shock of realizing just how much of a monster their father was had subsided.)

Of all of them, Mary was the only overtly defiant child. None of them would forget when their father hit Mary and swore at her in front of her boyfriend. It was a glimpse of the dark undercurrent to their father's personality that individually and as a family they had pretended did not exist.

Dorothy was different. Neither Laurie nor her brothers seemed to understand her recent behavior. They had trouble accepting that she could take their father's side. She acted as if it was Laurie's fault that he'd tried to kill her. She accused Laurie of splitting the family apart.

Aunt Peggy told me much later that Dorothy was always the one left out. She'd even been left with Aunt Peggy for years when she was a baby before her parents remembered to pick her up. (Being left out was a terror for Laurie and the other children as well.) Eventually Dorothy responded to Laurie's disclosures by quitting medical school only weeks short of graduation and checking herself into a mental hospital. It was her way out.

Jonathan, being older, remembered more than Thomas did about Florrie's youngest years. Florrie had been born with a normal intelligence, and no one quite remembered when she had started being limited. (Aunt Peggy later told me that Porter routinely took his baby girl and shook her until her teeth rattled. Today doctors call that "shaken baby syndrome"—the kind of battering that results in severe brain damage and often death. Back then they didn't have that name for it—but the savagery was the same.)

Trying to find out the extent of Florrie's retardation was difficult. All the brothers and sisters were so protective of her that I couldn't get an accurate take on it. She worked as a cashier in a supermarket and could attend to her own basic needs. The most precise that Laurie and her brothers got was that there was some piece missing from Florrie—she couldn't handle things.

Laurie, Jonathan, and Thomas were too fragile for me to push the issue. My asking to talk with Florrie made them very nervous. Ideally, I would have prosecuted William Porter for the incest of both Laurie and Florrie (with Mary testifying to background of the crimes against her in Brooklyn, if a judge would let me). That scenario would help the prosecution, but not the victims.

When Laurie had run away from her father, she'd run to Mary's home down South. For days she was too heartsick to even get out of bed. Mary was solicitous, loving, supportive, and sympathetic. She was in every way on Laurie's side up until the moment when Laurie decided to return to New York.

Mary tried to talk Laurie into staying. When Laurie turned down that offer, it caused a rift between them. When Laurie later decided to prosecute, that rift became a chasm. Mary might eventually turn out to be a resource at the trial, but right now she clearly wasn't going to be for the grand jury proceeding.

That left the two brothers and Laurie. What I needed from the brothers was testimony about eyewitness facts: Laurie's flight and her condition, the statements Porter had made, his threatening Jonathan's life. I prepared them to testify. They had their own issues.

When William Porter's sons started confronting him, he tried to intimidate them out of their moral outrage. He did it with poison—not the kind he swallowed, the kind he introduced into their lives. He told his sons that when they had daughters, they'd do the same thing.

People know a little bit about child abuse. William Porter's sons knew just enough to worry that their father's prophecy might come true, as if this was a disease. I told them that if their father had really succeeded in corrupting their souls, they wouldn't have reacted to Laurie the way they did. It seemed to comfort them, to relieve some of their fears, but not enough for either of them to risk having children. Their wives understood why.

The brothers told me about other statements Porter had made. While he was in the hospital, Porter had bragged to Thomas about his conquests: He and Laurie were a "couple," they even "did it" in a car; about his control: Laurie would never prosecute, she wasn't strong enough, she would commit suicide first; and about his "progress" in treatment: Someday he would be able to see his daughters naked and turn his face away. To Jonathan he tried to justify himself: He and Laurie were so much a couple that it almost seemed normal. When Jonathan confronted him about the knife, he said it wasn't always like that, he didn't force her—not all the time.

There was one more "statement," the one that was itself a crime. When Jonathan stopped him from getting a pass from the hospital, Porter told him that if it took him twenty years or the rest of his life, he would get out and he would find Jonathan and kill him.

I asked the brothers about their memories of Laurie's childhood. Did they remember ever hearing her scream when she was in another room with their father? No, it wasn't like that. Laurie was her father's favorite. They would be sent to play outside, even in terrible weather. Laurie would get to stay inside. There would be presents for her from their father, and he would be the one to tell them that Laurie wasn't going to play with them. Later she'd be very quiet, but then, she was always quiet—unless she was throwing tantrums. She did that, too. Somehow Laurie always seemed to get her way.

Even when she was young, Laurie was treated more like William Porter's wife than like his daughter. Not that they thought anything was wrong at the time. It just seemed to be the way things were. Their mother was gone a lot. She liked to visit friends. Laurie would prepare her father's meals, and she'd be the one he talked to.

It was difficult to get specifics from the brothers about their childhood. As much as they accepted the *concept* that their father had done terrible things to their sisters, the realities were too painful. When I asked Jonathan about the basement of the house in Brooklyn, he described many of the same details that Laurie did. He was even relieved that we were talking about a physical setting, concrete details. But then he interrupted his description to ask me why I'd asked, and without waiting for an answer continued: "You don't mean? Oh, my God!"

By then I had enough to go with, and compelling reasons to hurry. We scheduled the videotaping of Laurie for one day and the live testimony from the brothers for the next.

The day Laurie testified on videotape was a bright summer day.

Laurie spoke . . . a voice from the grave. What she was saying belonged to a different dimension. I remember listening to her and prompting questions when she got off track or overwhelmed. I was leaning back in a chair, which was propped against the connecting door to my office. I could hear the private line in there ringing softly. I thought it must be a friend calling. Somehow, beyond this room there was something besides pain and courage.

After a while Laurie was no longer in the same room with me. She was back in the basement, nine years old and terrified. She was back on the bed, with the knife at her throat, feeling her father rape her.

I simply asked questions. I had a list of dates I had to get her through, and then it would be over. And I swore it *would* be.

The whole session took up an hour and a half's worth of tape. Most victims' grand jury testimony is five to twenty minutes long.

The process cost Laurie all her strength. People don't understand about re-experiencing trauma. Jurors want to see rape victims emotional, without thinking about how much it costs the victim to show that emotion instead of relating the events by rote. It's O.K. for rapists to be numb, but not victims.

I once read in the newspaper about a jury in Dallas that voted life imprisonment for a rapist. The jurors talked about how furious they were with him, how angry the crime made them. Yet the fact pattern contained much that jurors normally find problematical. The rape took place in his house after the victim had voluntarily accompanied him there during the course of some kind of date—all the sort of things that shouldn't matter to jurors but often does. But this rapist had videotaped the rape. The jury saw rape firsthand. They viewed for themselves that the deliberate humiliation of a human being by force and the twisted imposition of one's sexual will on another are truly ugly. Seen up close, all the questions and hesitations disappeared. There's nothing erotic about rape.

It's as if we make victims create their own videotapes before we believe them.

Well, if that's what it would take, then Laurie and I would create the videotape to convince them.

We managed, with a little assistance. The weekend before, I had been upstate, where I'd found a beautiful garnet-streaked crystal. I'd been looking for some way to make a little magic for Laurie, and as soon as I saw the crystal, I knew it was perfect. It's not that I believe in crystals. But I do believe in people having something to hold on to.

Laurie's reaction to the crystal surprised me. I'd used rocks before, especially with children. At Special Victims, we'd usually give children a stone to put in their pocket while they testified and to hold on to if they got upset. We explained that many other children had carried this stone, and that it had helped them.

When I gave Laurie the crystal, I told her it was a present to help her get through. I sat her down and said, "This is you. This is your strength. It's softly colored and its beautiful, and its as hard as it needs to be to endure." I couldn't tell if that meant anything at all to her except that she appreciated me thinking of her while I was away on a trip.

While we were taping, Laurie did something with the crystal that I'd never seen anyone else do. Everyone else just held on tight. Laurie tossed the rock back and forth, unconsciously, from one hand to the other, arcing it high between her two hands and then rhythmically catching it, not missing a beat. It worried me. I thought she'd be really upset if she dropped the crystal and it shattered. But it also warmed me inside to watch her, tossing her strength up in the air for everyone to see, showing it off during what had to be the hardest thing she'd ever done. Good for you, Laurie. You really are going to make it!

The next day, when Laurie's brothers arrived in my office, they were so nervous they were endearing. What they were doing was unquestionably courageous and admirable. They were standing up to what they feared most—their father—solely because it was the right thing to do. But Laurie and her brothers are real talkers; when they tell you a story, they repeat verbatim what *everybody* said. And that's all I wanted them to do in the grand jury.

The grand jury indicted.

When the detectives went to the hospital with the arrest warrant for William Porter, they read him his rights and took a statement from him. William Porter said what he had said all along. It was an affair. No force. When Laurie was little, it might have been child abuse, but now it was not a crime. It was what they both wanted. As for the incest statute, he'd thought up an answer for that. Laurie was not really his daughter. His wife had had an affair. No one knew but him.

It didn't matter to William Porter what this last particular lie would do to Laurie. I guess on the scale of things it was relatively minor, but it was an accurate summary of his life's philosophy: Say anything, do anything, as long it suits my purposes. And if anyone else gets hurt—well, that's their problem.

At arraignment no defense attorney was willing to take the case.

I'd like to think that Legal Aid ducked the case on the basis of the allegations, that some crimes penetrated their intellectualized refusal to be offended by any malfeasance. That's certainly what the Legal Aid supervisor said to me. They asked for 18B (court-appointed counsel), but the 18B attorney wouldn't take the case. It took three days to get an attorney willing to be assigned this case.

The attorney who took the case chose not to ask for a psychiatric evaluation of Porter at the time of arraignment. My prediction had been wrong.

It scared Laurie and her brothers when bail was set. I had prepared them to expect the fitness exam, a month of remand. The fact of bail was frightening, even though the amount set was extremely high for a nonmedia, nonmurder case.

Since Porter always borrowed money from his children, they had a fairly accurate idea of what his resources were. They could have sat down and added it all up and determined that he couldn't possibly make that kind of bail. But all of them still had this sense of his power, that he controlled everything, that he was bigger than life and that they were still powerless against him. It was an adjustment to think of him as a defendant, as one small man against the legal system.

There were multilevel fail-safe mechanisms in place to ensure that he wouldn't make bail. First, the brothers really did control virtually every source of money for the family. Porter had his salary, but that was it. And for the past weeks he'd been on leave and not receiving even his pay. There was a question of whether he was vested in pension rights, but the defense attorney, in hope of getting a private fee out of the case, was looking into the pension and had put a hold against the funds.

Also, the judge granted my request for a bail-sufficiency hearing. Normally this is a tactic reserved for organized crime figures. Basically it means that if someone is about to put up bail, he has to prove that the money is legally his, and not the proceeds of a crime. It's not that I thought Porter was connected to organized crime—at least not the kind people normally mean by the term. Many pedophiles form affinity groups, but those who limit themselves to incest offenses don't tend to be among them. Porter didn't take Polaroids—he didn't "share." A bail-sufficiency hearing was simply another way to be sure that I'd be notified by the court if Porter was about to be released.

The defendant's commitment papers were marked "Notify ADA Vachss" if anyone offered to post bond for Porter. The papers included both my work and beeper numbers. There was a mechanism so I'd know even in the middle of the night if Porter somehow slipped through all the other systems. Putting the Department of Corrections on notice that an inmate was dangerous to others if released meant they could be sued. Maybe, if efficiency flagged, civil liability would make them more cautious.

The jail agreed to tell me anytime Porter had a visitor—but that was because of a good corrections officer who cared that some lives were at stake. He and I both figured that without visitors, Porter would have a harder time convincing somebody to put up that much bail.

Even with all these measures in place, neither Laurie nor her brothers felt all that safe. It was time for a new plan.

After the arraignment, Laurie and I had a long talk about the decisions that now needed to be made. That first day she'd come to Special Victims, I'd told her she could stop whenever she'd had enough. Laurie understood without me needing to say it that there would be consequences if she decided she had no further strength to do this—the kind of consequences that might end her life.

I didn't tell Laurie that I wanted to try William Porter for his crimes, to roll all the dice on convicting him and then convincing a judge to send him to prison for the rest of his life. Porter was in his fifties; give him twenty-five to fifty and there was a good chance he'd die in prison.

Instead, we reviewed the options. We could continue to aim for inpatient psychiatric probation.

We could go to trial. Twenty-five to fifty was the legal maximum if Porter was convicted, but it wasn't mandatory. Even after a jury trial, the judge still had the power to sentence him to as short a sentence as two to six years. And then there was always the possibility of a Not Guilty verdict.

The other option was plea bargaining.

People think that plea bargaining is a dirty word: an automatic insult to victims and defendants. I guess that's because of the way it's usually done. Prosecutors can plea-bargain for all sorts of wrong reasons that all add up to the same thing: conviction rates. Some of the most obscene pleas I've ever seen a prosecutor take have been done in the name of sparing the victim the hardship of testifying; some of them with the victim in the courtroom trying to protest . . . with no one listening.

The penal law that defines offenses even encourages betraying victims with leeway for prosecutors like "sexual misconduct," which amounts to misdemeanor rape (and a maximum sentence of one year instead of twenty-five.) And incest, being the lowest grade of felony (making it an automatically probation-eligible offense), invites even more abuse. Defense attorneys have their own reasons for selling out their clients. And because plea bargaining is so often badly motivated, citizens whose cases are pleaded out can never be sure if they've gotten justice.

There's something else that I find offensive about plea bargaining—the negotiations become a fish market. Lawyers whine: "*Why* can't I have this plea?" or "I have too many other cases too try, why can't you be *reasonable*?" They make personal, sexist remarks: "How can such a pretty woman be so hard?" They manipulate and cheat and lie to get the judge on their side in the debate. There are bidding wars:

"I want four to twelve."

"He'll take two to six."

"I'll go down to three to nine if you come up."

"No? then it's five to fifteen."

Lawyers try to chip away at prior offers: "I know I said last time that if you offered it, I'd take the three to nine, but now it seems like too much."

There are even some unspoken rules for what a case is "worth." The numbers vary among jurisdictions, but the considerations—the degree of proof, the likelihood of conviction, the sentences judges tend to impose after trial—rarely vary. It's the way societal prejudices are incorporated into the entire system, not just the trial cases.

Plea negotiations are what they're called: bargaining. It's very easy to lose sight of the case itself, to lose sight of anything other than the bargaining. When that happens, both sides get the best bargain they can, but they often forget about justice and dignity. Defense attorneys at least have the minimal control on their bargaining of having to sell the plea to their clients. Prosecutors, who allegedly "serve the people," have no such restrictions, although they do occasionally have to sell their pleas to the media.

With all these faults, the plea-bargaining process still offers victims some tangible benefits. Most obvious is that the victim does not have to testify at trial. Also, a plea is a guaranteed result. Going to trial *is* rolling the dice. If the defendant pleads, then there is no chance of acquittal. And there is no chance that even if the offender is convicted, some judge might impose a lower sentence than he deserves.

If the plea bargain includes the waiver of the right to appeal, then a plea also offers finality. When a defendant is convicted at trial, he still has the right to go to a higher court and try to argue for reversal (and either dismissal or a new trial.) Sometimes such appeals are successful. A trial can not offer the victim the same finality that a plea does.

Plea bargaining can be worth it *if* it's done right. That's exactly what I told Laurie. We could come up with a sentence that would satisfy us. We could put a time limit on that offer and refuse to lower it. We would treat the case at all times as if it would definitely go to trial, and not get on the emotional roller coaster of counting on a plea before it happened. We would not participate in a fish market or give up any shred of our dignity to get a plea. What I explained, and what made sense to Laurie, was that if we plea-bargained that way, there was no way to lose. Either we got the plea that we wanted or we went to trial. We didn't give up anything.

The plea offer Laurie and I settled on was six to eighteen years. Eight and a third to twenty-five was the maximum Porter faced unless a judge was willing to impose consecutive sentencing for the different crimes against Laurie. (Consecutive sentencing, one prison term imposed after another, is always an extra to hope for—over and above giving a defendant the maximum.) Anything less than five to fifteen years didn't seem long enough. Six to eighteen would give Laurie a guaranteed six years (before Porter saw the parole board) to reorganize her life and make sure she was safe from her father's revenge.

After we decided on the plea offer, I asked Laurie for one more decision. It was a choice I gave all victims. Did she want to know the details of how negotiations were progressing, or just the bottom line? Her answer was "just the bottom line."

The first time the case was conferenced in the assigned court part, I communicated the plea offer to the defense attorney. I didn't put a deadline on it then. I just said that it was a firm offer; we wouldn't go any lower. (That's a position prosecutors often claim, but courthouse regulars get to know pretty quickly which ADAs mean what they say.)

The lawyer said he thought the offer was way too high. Maybe he also thought he hadn't put in enough billable hours yet to be considering a plea at this early stage. Since he was a court-appointed attorney, his fee depended strictly on how much time he put into the case. He had said he wanted this judge because the judge always approved the vouchers the lawyer submitted for payment.

We scheduled and completed the pretrial hearing about the admissibility of Porter's statements to the police when he was arrested. Since Porter had put into his statement his claim that Laurie wasn't his daughter, I wanted that cleared up before trial. Laurie's mother (who had originally claimed to be offended at the idea that she'd had an affair) started "admitting" that Laurie wasn't William Porter's daughter. I wasn't buying it, but I figured that would be a distracting issue for a jury. And I wanted as straightforward a trial as I could force Porter into.

With Laurie's permission, I asked for blood tests to determine paternity. Originally the defense attorney promised he would consent to the blood tests. But then he started stalling. Delays are a time-honored defense technique. The theory is that the passage of time is bound to hurt the prosecution. The attorneys who make conventional wisdom a religion rarely take into account that this rule may not apply to all prosecutions. Some victims, particularly children, get stronger every day they are free from abuse. It never occurred to this defense attorney that Laurie's ability to prosecute might *increase*. He took his time.

When I decided I'd waited long enough, I filed the motion papers on my own. I wanted the standard blood test for paternity, called HLA. I also wanted DNA analysis, the new genetic testing.

Special Victims had been a leader in introducing DNA evidence in sex crimes, but enough problems had come up with DNA analysis by then that I wanted some more information on it. Paternity was a lot more straightforward a test procedure than rapist identification was. And Laurie's case was the ideal one for experimentation. Also, I would have HLA results, which are admissible in every court in New York. I believed both kinds of tests would come out the same, but if they didn't, I would learn a lot about DNA without creating a risk to Laurie's case. I could prove if I had to that HLA was a more accepted procedure than DNA.

The defense attorney thought he was making life difficult for me by insisting that he have his own DNA paternity testing done by an independent lab. He got his hard-driven bargain—and I got two double checks of DNA testing instead of one.

By the time the blood was drawn for the paternity testing, Laurie had gained significant strength and clarity about prosecution. The lab that drew the blood did its best to undo that progress.

The lab was located in Brooklyn. The blood needed to be drawn from Laurie and from her biological parents and shipped on the same day. It was easy enough to arrange an afternoon appointment for the detectives transporting William Porter to and from jail. The detectives agreed, too, not to deliver their prisoner to the lab until they'd gotten telephone clearance from me that Laurie was out of there and safe.

It was also easy to get Laurie the first appointment of the day.

Sandwiching in Laurie's mother midmorning, so that Laurie wouldn't have to see her, was trickier. We left a couple of hours' leeway. But the lab was slow getting started, and Laurie started worrying that the timing wouldn't work.

She tried to get assurances from the lab receptionist (who'd already been told by the DA's office that it was imperative that there be no contact between the three people whose blood was being drawn). The receptionist had her own agenda. In answer to Laurie's questions, the receptionist told her a story about a "friend" of hers who had quarreled with her own mother; mother and daughter didn't speak to each other for a long time. The mother died suddenly, and the friend regretted the rift for the rest of her days. The story and its message hit Laurie like a body blow.

Laurie finished doing what she needed to do at the lab. That was always the deceptive part of her personality: You could never tell how upset she was from what she accomplished.

Afterward she wandered aimlessly around Brooklyn for hours. Then she drifted into a church and sat in the back crying for as long as she could stand it before her heart broke. She prayed for God to give her a reason to want to go on living. The seed of belief in herself was still so delicate.

People want to believe that families really are what Hallmark cards promise. That makes it hard enough for victims like Laurie to escape their situations. But then, if they find the strength to free themselves, there are people like that poisonous receptionist making them feel guilty for taking the first step to survival. No wonder Laurie wound up an incest victim past her thirtieth birthday.

When she'd run from her father's bed and knife, Laurie had found some elemental, adrenaline-driven strength to survive. It had been a tremendous first step. But since then she'd needed to draw on reserves within herself she didn't know she had.

I remember Laurie calling me just after one of her worst times and telling me about praying for just one whole day of feeling at peace. It was as if depression and guilt and fear were so tangible that they were suffocating her. All the pain that she couldn't afford to feel while the abuse was happening caught up with her once she'd escaped. It damn near defeated her.

Laurie felt guilty about everything: how much trouble she'd caused, even how bad things were for her father. She told me she thought about him in a cold, damp cell, with his terrible asthma. I listened. I didn't question her feelings. But I reviewed her options.

I knew that Laurie needed to trust me. What I hadn't understood before then is what that need was made of, what would happen to her if she didn't.

During the months that the blood-test results were pending, nothing happened on the case other than formalities such as the pretrial hearing. The defense attorney seemed to believe he could build a defense on lack of paternity. I was sure that the tests would prove that Porter was lying, but it didn't matter—it was still incest and rape, no matter what Laurie's bloodlines were.

At first Laurie was offended by what she believed was another one of her father's lies. When her mother "admitted" the affair, Laurie started to have doubts. Maybe she wanted doubts. I remembered once hearing a therapist describe one of her incest victims' recollections: "I used to lie in bed at night and pray that I would somehow find out that he wasn't really my father."

The tests finally proved irrefutably that William Porter was Laurie's biological father. But there was one last obstacle Laurie and I hadn't known about. It almost destroyed the fragile balance between us.

When the tests came back, the defense attorney and I had our first serious conference with the judge over plea negotiations. I repeated our offer: "B" felony (top count); admit the forcible rape; six to eighteen years imprisonment. Take it now, or it won't be offered again.

The defense attorney whined that his client denied the forcible rape. All he would admit to was the incest. (Big concession—it was in his confession and all his statements.) The judge pointed out that there were three counts of incest on the indictment. Even if the jury acquitted on forcible rape, he could give him two to six on each such count, "consec" it on the three counts, and come up with the same six to eighteen. The defense attorney counteroffered five to fifteen. He'd talk his client into it.

I said, "No. No fish market." We set a firm date for trial. I wanted to wait until after the holidays. (No prosecutor wants a Christmas jury. They sometimes give acquittals as gifts.) Afterward I called Laurie and explained what a firm trial date meant: better than probably, less than definitely. She asked about the plea. I told her only that Porter had turned down the six to eighteen. No details. It was what she'd said she wanted.

I was uncomfortable not telling Laurie everything, but I also didn't want her to get her hopes up. She didn't understand that if we said yes to five to fifteen, the defense attorney would return from his "talking his client into it" with an offer of two to six, looking for three and a third to ten. It was a greasy slide.

Maybe I should have told her what had happened, despite our agreement. Maybe I should have figured out that it was unrealistic to try to spare her these uncertainties. One thing was clear from what happened later: What I did say didn't work.

Laurie and I had talked enough by then that I think she knew I wasn't telling her everything. I'd described all the other court appearances in much more detail. This one I bottom-lined in a couple of sentences. She sounded hesitant, but she didn't pursue it.

A few days later Laurie called, sounding at the end of her rope. I could hear it in her voice: She didn't believe I could say anything to fix what was wrong, but she had to ask. She didn't say that. She just talked about having a bad time. We'd talked about the bad times before, but this sounded different. Finally she got to her question. William Porter had called Jonathan. He told Jonathan he wanted to do the right thing, to plead guilty and get this all over with. He told Jonathan he'd been willing to take a ten-year sentence. But I'd said no. I just wanted a conviction. I didn't care about Jonathan or Laurie at all. Only he did, only William Porter. He'd tried to do the right thing and had been stopped by a ruthless, ambitious prosecutor. Now this was going to have to go to trial and tear apart the family. Think about what it was going to do to their mother and to Dorothy, who was back in the hospital. And it was all my fault. They'd been fools to trust me. Look what happened.

Laurie said it wasn't that she believed her father. It was that she didn't know. Why hadn't I told her what was going on?

I told Laurie exactly what had happened in court, word for word. I explained minimums and maximums to her, that what William Porter meant by a ten-year sentence was three and a third to ten. I reminded Laurie that we'd agreed on six to eighteen.

While I was talking, Laurie's breathing started to get better. Her voice gained some strength. She told me about all the doubts she'd had in the past twenty-four hours: about herself, about me, about prosecuting, about ever being free of William Porter, ever being able to trust anybody; about any of this being worth it. She told me about thinking of killing herself; about the plans she'd made, the darkness of her depression, the physical sensation of suffocating, of struggling to get through each day hour by hour. After a while, she was talking just to be sharing.

If Laurie had been less fragile, I would have objected to being a life-support system. That's not what prosecutors are for. But I couldn't say that to her. I was the one who had told her she had the strength to do this. It was only fair that sometimes I had to help her find it.

But I'd learned the lesson again: Don't overestimate Laurie's recovery. She had thirty-one years to undo. Porter had had a lifetime of twisting her spirit into knots. She'd had only a few months to start untangling them.

I started the intense preparation that's only possible when a firm trial date is set. The most important component of that is mental. A case starts out being just assorted facts. It's got to end up shaped into a picture of the truth—whether that truth is one flash of time or thirty years of torment.

I wanted to avoid having the trial look like *Family Feud,* with Laurie, Jonathan, and Thomas on one side; William Porter, his wife, and Dorothy on the other; and Mary and Florrie who knows where. Some of that took care of itself. The closer the trial got, the more Dorothy chose to be out of the picture. She was always back in the hospital, or "in crisis" or some other kind of leave-me-out-of-this posture that made it unlikely she'd be a witness.

I wanted to talk to Mary before the trial, but it had to be timed right. I knew what I wanted to say: She was a hero. She'd defeated William Porter in her own way. This trial was the final victory for her. She'd shown Laurie the way. I didn't know if it would convince Mary to testify, but I knew she had earned the right to hear those words.

Florrie was an easier issue. I wasn't going to push Laurie and her brothers about her. I still thought about Florrie's victimization as a potential prosecution as a last resort if William Porter was acquitted. But I wouldn't even mention it to Laurie and her brothers unless it came to that. It was too painful for them—it shifted the focus and the roles of everyone too much to be a subject for discussion at this point. On the other hand, William Porter knew what he'd done to Florrie, and he probably knew that she'd disclosed his crimes. He couldn't afford to put her on the stand. If he did, I'd make my decisions question by question, without harming her if that was possible.

Eliminate Dorothy, Mary, and Florrie, and that left William Porter one witness: his wife. I already knew she was willing to lie to get him out of prison. She proved that when she'd gone along with his story that Laurie wasn't his blood. This was a mother who had lain in the same bed with her husband while he raped their daughter. It didn't seem realistic to expect that she'd draw the line at perjury.

Even if I couldn't keep her off the stand, there was a way that I could at least keep Laurie's mother out of the courtroom for the rest of the trial. Put her on the witness list (on the extremely remote chance I might actually call her as a witness), and she'd be excluded from the courtroom for anyone else's testimony. Except for the defendant, no one, not even the victim, is allowed to hear the other trial testimony before taking the stand.

I figured William Porter would have to testify. Maybe he'd call character witnesses. I wanted ammunition.

There are specialized evidentiary rules for all this, but if a defendant takes the stand, or if he calls witnesses to talk about his good moral character, there are ways that a prosecutor can sometimes contradict that with evidence of prior misconduct besides the crimes on trial.

William Porter's fingerprint record was not extensive. He had a twenty-year-old assault arrest for which he'd served a few months in jail. He'd told his children that the man later died from the assault. He'd told Jonathan that he'd gone to jail to save his son's life, that he'd come to blows with the man protecting his little boy. I didn't find any proof of that. I suspected Porter had just been building the myth. The records had him serving short time, pleading the case out to time served and a minor conviction.

I needed more than that.

I interviewed Laurie and her brothers. Once they understood the questions I was asking, they were embarrassed. This was the man they'd told me had a great public image, who everyone thought was a nice guy. Now they were describing him stealing tools and valuables from an elderly widow who'd hired him to do menial labor. They told me about Porter cheating on his income taxes, trafficking in stolen property, years of petty criminality they had come to just accept. It was the information I wanted. All of this conduct had something in common: It was all the behavior of someone whose personal desires were more important to him than law or morality—the credo of a rapist.

I talked to my other witnesses—the doctors, the detectives. I made Laurie finally get the proctological exam—something she'd been avoiding for months. I subpoenaed the records and found the token clerk who'd worked the day Laurie had run to the subway station. I got the weather reports, a photo of the dog. A hundred little pieces needed to be put together. Trial preparation, that's a big part. But the main part is always the victim.

When we get to be a civilized nation, sex-crime verdicts will no longer depend on how much the jury likes the victim. But we're not close to that today.

As horrifying as what had happened to Laurie was, I knew a jury was going to have problems with a lot of what she had to say.

One of the times Porter had raped her was hours after she'd had her first abortion. That was how she'd remembered that date for the indictment. When Laurie talked about the night Porter had almost killed her, she had said that while he raped her, she thought it was God's punishment for her having had an abortion. If I wanted to put those facts into evidence, I was going to need a prochoice jury.

I was worried about the jury hearing about all the privileges and favors Laurie had gotten as her father's "favorite." It wouldn't fit their image of a Good Victim. Although people never blame POWs for not trying to escape, Porter's jury would expect Laurie to have fought every second of her thirty-one years.

For several of the incidents, the force used wasn't what a jury would expect in a rape case. That last night, he'd used the knife, but there were incidents on the indictment when she'd submitted after he'd pulled her hair hard or grabbed her by the neck. The jury might not understand that the force for any single rape was a cumulative effort, that years of torture made her submit to individual incidents.

Even the morning she'd walked Lucky before she fled, Laurie had said good morning to a neighbor. Her years of coping, of keeping up the façade, the pretence of normalcy she'd used to survive—it would all be used against her at trial.

I couldn't change the facts; I would have to explain them through Laurie and any experts on the topic of incest that the judge would let me call. I wasn't worried about Laurie being articulate and presentable. She was unquestionably both of those. I was worried about any unresolved issues she herself had about her victimization.

I did something experimental when I prepared Laurie for testimony. I had a joint session with her and her therapist. I couldn't think of anything wrong with doing that, and it had a lot of advantages. I'd just never heard of it being done before.

My husband had taught me years ago, when he was cross-examining a cop: Attitude is everything. My husband was the defense attorney. The cop had translated the interrogation into and out of Spanish. The prosecutor was arrogant and insulting to the cop. My husband didn't try to get the cop to say anything, didn't suggest what testimony he was looking for—it wouldn't have worked. He just pointed out to the cop how the prosecutor was treating his police witnesses—as if they were garbage. The testimony came out the way my husband wanted it to.

Too many prosecutors think witness preparation is giving the witnesses the answers, that testifying can be converted into a memory test. I do warn witnesses about what the defense questions might be, and I tell them how various answers might sound to a jury. That's part of the job—but it's not the end of it. Witnesses need a perspective, a framework on how to answer the questions they haven't been told about.

With Laurie the framework was complex. She'd been an incest victim for so long that William Porter had planted his self-protective seeds deep within her soul; somehow it was all her fault, somehow "telling" was the biggest sin.

I understood how much guilt Laurie felt. But I couldn't let her communicate to a jury that the incest might somehow be her fault. According to the incest statute, she was as complicitous as her father—force wasn't part of the definition; incest was any act of intercourse between blood-close relatives. Even in the forcible-rape statute, consent was a defense. I needed Laurie to be clear-minded that only her father was the villain, that she'd done nothing to cause what he'd done to her.

I wanted all the hard issues out of the way before she testified. Maybe therapy can't conform to that kind of timetable, but I intended to raise all these issues and see how far therapy had progressed for Laurie.

The session with Susan, Laurie's therapist, didn't go the way I'd expected it.

I explained that I understood that for most incest victims—not negating how terrible it is—there are some pleasurable aspects to what goes on. The child is singled out, given special attention, privileges, gifts, and status over the other children in the family. Even the sexual acts themselves can contain elements of pleasure. Children feel the taboo, but they also respond to the physical stimulation itself. When it is not painful, their bodies can feel pleasure.

I was walking softly, waiting for reactions with each sentence. I couldn't say, "Look, Laurie, on some levels you liked this. And that's O.K. It's no less a crime. It's just part of the damage he did." But that's what I wanted to say. Just more gently, more acceptably.

Susan and Laurie didn't see this as any kind of problem. It must have come up already in treatment and Laurie had conquered it enough to be comfortable with what I was saying. Maybe it made it easier for her that so much of what William Porter had done to her had been painful. Maybe it was just that Susan was a good therapist.

The session wound up centering on William Porter's power, or lack of it. They loved me talking about him as "the defendant." They loved the idea that it was Laurie who was in control, that it was her decision and her strength that was keeping him in a prison cell.

The session accomplished what I wanted, but it turned out a lot lighter than I'd expected. I was a new perspective in their discussions. Somehow in this therapist's office William Porter had stayed larger than life until I called him "the defendant," until I talked about him being in prison. They started to ask, so I answered. He was in jail, his life controlled by guards. He didn't decide when to get up in the morning. He didn't have his choice of food. He didn't get to say what clothes he wore. If he wanted to wear a suit for the trial, his wife would have to bring it and he would have to ask the guards for permission to change.

It wasn't a discussion about revenge. These small humiliations for

William Porter could never approach the unspeakable pain he'd inflicted on Laurie. It was what incest always is, about power and control. His was over. There was relief and pleasure and strength in that concept. Laurie needed these kinds of details. She needed to shrink him in her mind.

It's ironic that Porter is actually a slightly built man. For court, he perfected a sad-sack image. There was nothing physically intimidating about his public image, no Manson-like force of madness that dominated more space than he actually occupied. He was hunch-shouldered, trying for pathetic, whining about his asthma and how damp prison was.

What was powerful, about him was his unlimited devotion to himself. There were no boundaries to his willingness to sacrifice anyone or anything else. But that wasn't something you could *see* by looking at him.

The "firm" trial date came and went. Porter had gotten himself medically excused from coming to court. I guess he didn't like how things were going.

I did what I always did with defense adjournments: I resolved to use the extra time against the defendant, to make him pay for stalling. Even if he didn't know it, I would.

The timing now gave me an unexpected worry. The trial was scheduled for a few weeks before a *Parade* magazine featuring an article about me was slated for the stands. My picture was on the cover with that of three other women, under the headline THESE MAY BE AMERICA'S TOUGHEST PROSECUTORS. As much as I was proud of the recognition, who knew how a jury would react? If it came down to it, I would have to tell the judge, have him instruct the jury to avoid that magazine, or sequester them if he thought it was that much of an issue. Meanwhile, I couldn't let it interfere with the flow of the case; it was more important to keep up the pressure.

When Porter showed up in court on the next adjournment, I had all the pieces in place. My witnesses were all lined up. The documents I would need were organized. I'd planned all my jury-selection questions on incest and families. Susan and an incest expert were on tap if the judge would let me call them as witnesses.

Laurie was in my office for another witness-preparation session—or at least that was my excuse for getting her in. I also had some sixth-sense tinglings, but there was nothing to be gained by mentioning them.

Instead we talked about why Laurie seemed so upset. Lately she'd been making rapid progress, gaining strength every day. But now that the trial was finally about to happen, she looked like a deer paralyzed by headlights on a desolate road. We talked about her fears. It wasn't too late to back down. No, she said, she'd find the strength. As soon as I came back from the courtroom, we'd get to work on reviewing her direct testimony.

Even before Porter was transported from his prison cell to the court pens, his attorney was talking plea again. Wouldn't I reconsider the five to fifteen? No. Laurie and I had paid too high a price for saying no the first time to give up now. I told the defense attorney I wanted a trial, wanted to max his client on everything, see if he could outlive twenty-five to fifty.

Once Porter arrived in the courthouse, the defense attorney brought the topic up again. I asked the judge to send for a jury panel. He did, arranging one for the following day. But the judge also told me I should reoffer the six to eighteen. It was a good plea. I told the judge, "No fish market," no bartering back and forth. The judge told the defense, bottom line: six to eighteen. Take it now or go to trial. I handed the defense attorney my potential witness list. It was a small gesture of where I wanted this to go. He got the message.

Even when Porter decided he wanted the plea, he tried through his defense attorney to whine his way around it. Did he really have to admit to *forcing* Laurie to have sex?

Yes.

But it wasn't force.

Then let's go to trial.

O.K., O.K. But he can't plead to the sex crime.

Then he can't plead.

Look. Be reasonable. You know what it's like in prison for child molesters.

Yeah, the same as it is for everybody else. (I hate this stupid myth that prisoners somehow give child molesters a bad time. That's only when the child molester is weak or unconnected. And they'd give just as hard a time to a weak, unconnected bank robber.)

The judge chimed in. He too thought that this "Short Eyes" myth was real. He asked me if I wouldn't take the attempted murder second-degree. (It was the same level felony as rape.) I said no. Then the judge and the defense attorney made a joke about the defendant deserving whatever he got. (And I'm the one who's supposed to be so cold-blooded.)

It went on like that for a while. Testing me. Seeing how far I'd move in any direction. Me just saying, "Let's go to trial." I'd already reoffered a plea I'd had no intention of reoffering. I'd done it because that was what Laurie wanted. What I wanted was a trial. Drop him for the count.

Porter finally pleaded guilty. He admitted the forcible rape, but even then it was only after my questioning. He'd tried to weasel even on the allocution—the part where he was supposed to finally admit what he'd done. He wanted to say it wasn't force. I wanted to say it wasn't a plea. So for a few moments of time, on the record in a court of law, William Porter told the truth about himself.

After the plea, the judge and defense attorney wanted to do a postmortem, the kind of discussion lawyers have from the distance of a disposition, when the case has ended in a plea or verdict. They wanted to talk about just how vile William Porter was. To his credit, the defense attorney had never tried to say anything different, even in plea negotiations. At least he spared me from having to listen to the usual offensive, justificatory speech about how the perp was just sick, or how the victim was precociously seductive, or how this wasn't *really* a crime of violence.

I got out of this particular postmortem as quickly as possible. I already knew how vile William Porter was—what I really cared about was that Laurie was in my office, waiting to continue with the trial-preparation discussions. I had the news of her lifetime to give her.

The courtroom was on the fifth floor. The wait for the elevator was endless. I took the stairs. I burst into my office breathless and full of the need to tell Laurie, to see in her face that I'd made the right decision.

She wasn't there.

I ran into where the secretaries were. Where's Laurie? Did she tell you she was leaving, where she was going, if something was wrong? Had it finally overwhelmed her, just when it was almost over, just when I could tell her she'd won, she was safe, she was free?

I was frantic. No one knew where she'd gone. The ironies were too much for me. I could picture her sitting alone in my office, patting Sheba. I could see the moment when she'd reached her limit. I imagined her walking out, wandering around like she'd done that day in Brooklyn after the lab tests, looking for a church, looking for a god to help her.

What had she said before I'd gone to court? She'd been upset when she came in, but I thought she felt better after we talked. Who did I think I was to make these judgments? Who trained me to know these things, to play with people's lives like this? I should have known I was pushing her too far, asking too much.

By the time Laurie walked in, I was a wreck. She'd gone to get a cup of tea at the diner across the street. There'd been a long line for take-out. What's wrong, Alice? I'm sorry I left. I didn't know when you'd be back, and I didn't see the harm.

No, its all right. I just overreacted. It was nothing. It was fine to go. I just didn't know where you were. But put the tea down. There's something I need to tell you.

What, what's wrong? What happened?

Nothing's wrong. He pleaded guilty. Six to eighteen, like we wanted. It's over. It's finally over.

I didn't know how she'd react. I guessed some mixed feelings. But there was nothing mixed for Laurie. No tears—only pure happiness and relief. She hugged me as hard as she could. She glowed with the news of it, getting happier each second that it sunk in. It was over. She was free. He was in prison where he belonged. He would have to pay for stealing years of her life with years of his. It was over. She'd won. We'd won.

For that time, in that dingy little office room in the basement of the courthouse, there was a little bit more justice in this world. It had been a long trip for Laurie. She'd run from her father as he lay naked on the bed, waiting, knowing she was his, she would always be his. Every step she'd taken had brought her to this. Justice. Safety. Freedom from him. It was finally over.

She sent me flowers the next day, with a card that said: "WE DID IT!"

There were still procedures to finish on the case: the sentencing, the details. We kept in touch. She and her brothers contacted me when William Porter started writing threatening letters from Attica. (I forwarded them to the institution and the parole board.)* Sometimes we kept in touch just to be doing it, just for the sake of friendship.

I did finally get to meet Aunt Peggy, the same day I saw Laurie's brothers again. It was the day I danced with Aunt Peggy at Laurie's wedding.

*Despite institutional warnings and penalties, William Porter never stopped sending his hate mail. The last of his letters arrived before Christmas in 1993. He died in prison in early 1994, only months before he would have been entitled to his first parole eligibility hearing.

Part Two

TRIALS

[Before the rape] I felt good. My life was in order. I was getting ready to get married. [Afterward] everything changed. I kind of lost who I was as a person. . . .

I asked him, "Didn't you have a wife or a girlfriend that you can do this with?" He said, "I like this better. I like it better this way."

—Victim testimony, trial transcript, *People* v. *Eric Barnes*, Kew Gardens, New York, July 6, 1984

1

All of my dogs hate squirrels. For the most part, they have shown remarkable incompetence translating that reaction into action. My dogs range in deadliness from the feral intensity of Simba the junkyard dog to the huge, indomitable bulk of Gussie, the Neapolitan mastiff. When it comes to protection work, their abilities are legendary, awesome. But one squirrel can reduce them to comical ineptitude: the junkyard dog spinning in frustrated circles of fury beneath a telephone wire supporting a safe and taunting squirrel; Bruiser the Rottweiler so engaged in the chase he literally overruns his astounded quarry, Honey the pit bull's joy when a miscalculated jump literally landed the squirrel at her feet—only to be liberated by the captor's dance of celebration. They all let something get in the way.

The one exception was Sheba, the Special Victims dog. Sheba hated squirrels as much of the rest of them. But as old and slow as she was, her wolf instincts would still surface when she saw one. Motionless, she would study the squirrel, absorbing its rhythm, understanding its essence. Then she would start to sway slowly from side to side, homing in on some fundamental kinetic truth about her prey, until the exact right moment when it was time to fake right, flash left, and arrive at where the squirrel was going before it got there.

Sheba had generations of encoded knowledge, to help her attune her mind to her enemy's movements. I had to learn about rodents by watching and studying.

First I had to learn what sex crimes were.

From the beginning, I never had a caseload made up solely of sex crimes. I found out that not every rapist got charged with sexual assault. And there were kinds of evil so akin to rape that it was hard to tell the difference. Rapists always knew what I had to learn: There is more than one way to penetrate a victim. People who think rape is about sex confuse the weapon with the motivation.

Robert Roudabush was charged with attempted murder. It was Christmastime. He was supposed to take his wife, Maureen, shopping for gifts. Instead he got drunk and stayed late at his office Christmas party. When she complained, they argued. He decided he knew how to settle it, once and for all. He went into the bedroom, stripped down to some long underwear, and assembled a minor arsenal on the bed—two rifles, a shotgun—but he still needed ammunition. He went down to the basement, rummaging around until he came up with a few hundred rounds, then came back upstairs. He disabled the kitchen phone, then returned to his bedroom to load his weapons.

While she had been waiting for her husband to come home, Maureen had taken the children upstairs to a neighbor's apartment, where the local Girl Scout troop was holding its Christmas party. Her two-year-old had fallen asleep, and Maureen left her with the neighbor while she went downstairs to speak to her husband. She took her one-year-old with her.

After the argument dead-ended, Maureen took the infant into the kitchen to prepare a bottle for him. She was standing at the refrigerator with the baby in her arms when Roudabush spoke from behind her: "Don't move, I'm going to kill you." As she turned instinctively toward the sound, he shot her. The first bullet lodged in her neck, near the spinal column. She and the baby both went down. That was why the other shots missed them. Roudabush kept firing until the rifle jammed.

When he let her, she screamed for the neighbors to call 911. They took her in an ambulance. They took him in a police car.

It ought to have been over then, with Maureen and her children safe. But Maureen was about to find out that safety was something she would have to build for herself. She decided it was worth the fight when, after a few days, her mother brought the baby to the hospital. He had a black eye and a huge lump where he'd hit his head when they both went down from the first shot.

Maureen later told me she had had to keep phoning from the hospital, insisting her husband be prosecuted. The DA's office—the old Special Victims Bureau—told her not to bother pressing the complaint. Her husband would never be convicted. Besides, sooner or later she would drop the charges.

Instead of indicting her husband, they made Maureen testify in a preliminary hearing, adding an extra useless and dangerous step to the job of prosecution. The judge believed her. He kept the defendant in jail.

Even after they finally had her testify before a grand jury and Roudabush was indicted, things didn't improve. Special Victims was no longer on the case, and Maureen couldn't find out who was. And no, she was told, there was "no mechanism" for her to be notified if the defendant was released on bail. But my husband is going to get out of jail and kill me and my children. Sorry, lady.

Maureen called Santucci himself, insisting she was going to stay on the phone with his secretary until someone assigned a prosecutor to her case. When nothing political superseded his concern, Santucci could be genuinely sympathetic to victims, particularly to women. His intercession was unsophisticated but a major improvement over indifference. He had the case file marked "no plea offer," prosecute "to the fullest."

My bureau chief told me this complainant was an annoyance—do something about her.

No matter how successful prosecution was, there was no chance, under these charges, that Roudabush could be imprisoned for life. Ordinarily, given how frightened Maureen was, I would have tried to negotiate a plea that guaranteed that Maureen would have time to relocate with the children, reorient her life around her safety against the day her husband was released. "No plea offer" meant eliminating that option.

Even after I started pushing, Roudabush's case stayed pending for almost a year while his Legal Aid attorney stalled the trial. Maureen got divorced, moved in with her mother, waited. Legal Aid went out on strike (a periodic occurrence), and the trial got put off for another several months. Maureen and I talked before and after each court appearance. I started each conversation telling her the bail status hadn't changed. She needed to hear it. Like I later did for Laurie, I put systems in place for her safety, but she still lived in fear.

Roudabush wrote to Maureen while he was in jail. He tried all the angles. One letter would declare his love and repentance and beg her forgiveness. The next letter would be full of threats. Some letters would tell her he'd found God. When none of these worked, when Legal Aid ran out of stalling time, we went to trial.

There was more proof against Roudabush than I was used to having. Maureen was young, pretty, and distraught, with her Irish-rose face radiating credibility. At one point during her testimony she broke down in tears. I talked to her on the break and she said, "I'm so scared of him. He's sitting *looking* at me, and I'm so scared the jury's going to let him go and he'll kill me." The jury seemed to understand her feelings. In addition, there were recovered weapons and ammunition, a confession, and injuries serious enough for a jury not to discount the crimes as "only" domestic violence. The People's case was persuasive, powerful— it felt like a conviction.

The defense called a neurologist as a witness. Because of what the judge later ruled as defense misconduct, the doctor's testimony came as a complete surprise to me.

The neurologist was eminently qualified to make his diagnosis. He had studied Robert Roudabush and confirmed his findings through interviews with the family. The defendant had a history, from birth complications through childhood epilepsy, that together with a lifelong propensity toward sudden violence led to a diagnosis of "episodic dyscontrol." The doctor conceded that the attempted murder being tried was not an isolated incident—there had been a long and escalating course of domestic violence. Because of a brain malfunction, Roudabush had "fits" during which he could not control his anger. Some people called this "limbic rage." The popular media was starting to write articles about it.

According to the doctor, Roudabush did not "intend" his crimes. His episodic dyscontrol meant he had irresistible urges to commit violence— episodes of rage beyond his own control.

Because the testimony came as a surprise to me, the judge gave me the weekend to prepare my cross. I needed every minute.

What the doctor had said sounded logical, but its consequences were devastating. Roudabush wasn't pleading "not guilty by reason of insanity"—he was challenging the "intent" element of the crimes of assault and attempted murder. If he convinced a jury, he simply went free, the

Not Guilty verdict carrying with it a built-in defense to any murder he might later commit.

That Friday night was one of the lowest times for me that I can remember during a trial. What if the neurologist was right? What if this was an accurate diagnosis?

While I was worrying the problem to death, I had a moment of simple perception that felt like it applied to a lot more than this one trial. If I was right about Roudabush's guilt, if I'd understood the central truth about this crime, then what the neurologist was saying had to be wrong.

I spent the weekend researching episodic dyscontrol. I reviewed everything Maureen had told me about Roudabush's violence. She said he would get angry and become a different person—all dangerous, dark rage, out of control. But that didn't mean he was compelled to do what he did. Maureen had enough injuries and threats of violence to qualify as a battered spouse. But when Roudabush had started threatening to harm the children, she'd found a way to draw a line. And recognizing it, he'd decided not to cross that line. The only injury to either of the children had been the night she was shot. Protecting them was her doing, not his, but he'd *chosen* not to be "compelled" in that direction.

Roudabush's violence was by choice, an ugly choice about power and control—just like any rapist's, and no less a choice.

Monday morning I cross-examined the neurologist for several hours. Then I delivered the payload question. If Roudabush suffered episodic dyscontrol, how come the only victim of his violence was his wife? How come he never had these fits at work or driving his car, but only when he was in the safety (for him, not his victims) of his own home?

The jury convicted. Roudabush did ten years of a six-to-eighteen-year sentence before being paroled out of state. He hasn't had any incidents of "episodic dyscontrol" since the trial.

Once I understood that rape was a choice, I started looking at the quality of that choice. It was a serial rapist who taught me that criminality could be completely unencumbered by normal moral constraints, that rape could be as uncomplex as: want it . . . take it.

That prosecution included eleven first-degree robberies, twelve first-degree rapes, nine first-degree sodomies, seventeen counts of either gun possession or gun use, two first-degree kidnappings, and seven other unlawful-imprisonment counts. In all there were twenty-two indict-ments . . . against one defendant, Shelvie Harris. He was a police-department caseload all by himself.

If you didn't look too closely, Harris didn't look that dangerous. He was fiftyish, acne-scarred, with not only his hair but his skin graying. If you got your image of physical power from televised athletes, you wouldn't notice the hard edge to his knuckles, or his ready-for-violence stance. You might even miss that his eyes were the soft, wet, nobody's-home eyes of a psychopath. Harris would prefer you didn't know how lethal he was until he found the opportunity to prove it to you. He knew the value of predator camouflage.

Over two-thirds of Harris's adulthood had been spent behind bars, including a "life" sentence down South, for a half-dozen different con-victions escalating from car theft to armed robbery. He'd been released from an Alabama prison a little over a year before he was arrested as a serial rapist in Queens (and for a series of nine armed robberies of boutiques in Nassau County). As I investigated, it seemed to me that Harris must have raped or robbed every day since his last release.

While he was being sought, Harris was dubbed "The Stalker" by the press because in many of the rapes he followed his victims to make sure they were alone before abducting them at gunpoint in his car. But that was only one expression of his criminality. It would be a mistake to call Harris's crimes a pattern. There *was* no pattern to what he did. He was a predator who seized whatever criminal opportunity he found. The rape victims ranged in age from fourteen to sixty. He raped a bride on her wedding night when she ventured into the hotel hallway to the ice machine. He raped a woman he trapped entering her car in her own driveway at nine o'clock in the morning on her way to work. He raped a schoolgirl on her way home from classes. He raped a pedestrian in an isolated park. He stuck up stores from auto-tire shops to clothing bou-tiques. He always had a gun. He would very calmly tell his victims that if they didn't cooperate, he would kill them. No one ever doubted that he meant it. One young woman did tell him that he was going to have to kill her—she wasn't going with him. He pistol-whipped her into submission.

Harris's rapes were different from other sex crimes. Not that they were any less harmful to victims, but they were rapes of opportunity, not of the dark rage that I saw in other cases. For most rapists the act of deliberately humiliating another human is integral to what they do. When they rob, they look for that same opportunity to degrade and control—forcing the victim into acts of compliance as part of the theft. Humiliation is their foreplay, control their dose-related drug. With Harris it wasn't dark rage—it was the dark psychopathy of his personality to take whatever he wanted, with his gun.

Reading the case files on Shelvie Harris, I felt a bone-deep chill.

I didn't get all twenty-two cases at once. The Special Victims Bureau indicted them piecemeal, skipping anything inconvenient. There was one time Harris had almost been caught in the act. He had managed to escape, but had had to leave his car and gun behind. Special Victims indicted him on the attempted rape the police had interrupted, but didn't think it was important to charge him with gun possession. They agreed to indict at my insistence—but didn't understand why I was "bothering," or what I meant by how it would look to a jury at trial.

It was a massive amount of work to prepare all these cases for trial. But having this many crimes together was an opportunity to finally put Shelvie Harris behind bars for the rest of his life—natural life, not the kind Alabama had imposed.

The defense attorney knew the ropes. There were too many cases, too little defense. He asked me about a plea. I asked him if he'd seen a psychiatrist lately. He said no, he was serious . . . we should talk.

Harris's record meant he *could* be sentenced as a persistent felony offender—maximum sentence twenty-five years to life. But because of a twist in the sentencing law, the judge had the option to not find him a persistent felon at all. I could go to trial on every single one of the twenty-two cases and still wind up with a sentence of six to twelve years. New York's penal law virtually always preserves the option for a judge to be lenient to a rapist. The defense attorney offered to plead guilty for a promise of twenty years to life. It was too much guaranteed time to turn down.

The victims, the defense attorney, and I agreed to the plea. The trial judge where the cases were pending, Judge Joseph Asserta, was pleased. All we had to do was collect all the indictments together and it was a done deal. It was normal procedure for one judge to handle all of a defendant's cases but it wasn't written in stone.

On their way to being sent to Asserta, some of Harris's indictments appeared before Judge Decatur—the one who had earlier bench-tried the case against Johnny Washington. The defense attorney and I told him we had agreed with Judge Asserta they should be transferred to him. Judge Decatur wanted to know why. Judges get credit on their productivity records for the number and kinds of pleas they take. When Decatur heard about twenty-two top count felony pleas he didn't even ask what the specific charges were, or anything about the defendant. He told the defense attorney that *he* would give Harris fifteen to life instead of twenty to life if the defense would just get the indictments all sent to him. As usual with this judge, I objected—he ignored me. I had nothing to say about it. He had the legal power to make this deal over the prosecution's objections.

I told Asserta what happened. He put a stop to it, using his seniority to insist that all the cases be sent to him. To assure the defense attorney's cooperation, he agreed to the same deal the other judge had offered. I went ballistic. I even asked Santucci's chief of trials to try to intervene, but Asserta didn't care. Too bad for me. He didn't need my permission, either. And apparently he wanted credit for these pleas more than he wanted to please the DA's chief of trials or to keep the stalker off the street for another five years.

I fought the plea every inch of the way. Give me a trial. Give me twenty-two trials. I was ready. The answer was no.

If I couldn't stop the judge, I could at least make a lot of work for him. I made the defendant plead to every count in every indictment and then still refused to put on the record that I was legally satisfied with his admission of guilt. On every count, I argued, begged, pleaded for the judge to reconsider. Asserta was upset by my vehemence, but he didn't budge. Shelvie Harris got five years off his minimum sentence, and the likelihood that he would be paroled again in his lifetime, as a gift from the judiciary.

2

While I was learning about rapists, I also had to learn how things worked, how the criminal justice system "manages" sex-crime prosecution. The first course in that curricula was judges.

Back then indictments started out in front of a central "complex judge" and stayed there for the preliminaries such as bail arguments, motion papers, and plea negotiations until both sides were ready for trial. Then they were sent, supposedly in a lottery-type system, to the next free trial judge in one of Queens's three courthouses for supreme court trials. (To make everything more disjointed, the three courthouses were miles apart.)

There were two complex judges I worked with most often. The first was Judge Asserta. This was before he was reassigned to be a trial judge, before Shelvie Harris. Even then he was a crusty, obstinate old man, but we got along. His version of approval was to yell at the other ADAs for not being more like me. That was when he still liked it that I was willing to answer "ready for trial." Once he was sent to a courtroom that was a trial part instead of a complex part and I fought him on Shelvie Harris, he stopped being quite so taken with me.

A few days after Harris's sentencing, the chief of trials visited Asserta on a different case. The judge threw him out of the courtroom, saying he never wanted to see him again and adding, "That goes for *her* too." Everyone knew he was talking about me.

It was another six months before any cases of mine wound up in front of Asserta for trial. Then, we almost avoided the trial when the defendant wanted to plead, and this time I wanted to go along with him. The one impediment was that the top charge was defective, and the DA's office, out of some illogical rigidity, refused to permit me to dismiss it. We went through the charade of trial proof—during all of which I waited for the judicial explosion Asserta had promised me if I ever darkened his court-room door—until the judge had no legal option but to dismiss the defective count. As soon as he did, the defendant offered to plead guilty to the rest of the indictment. Asserta asked for my position. I reminded him he didn't need my approval. He answered, "I know that. But if I take this plea and you don't like it, you'll be mad at me." All this time I'd been afraid of him, he'd been more afraid of me.

It wasn't long afterward, on a case that had nothing at all to do with me, that Asserta created his own downfall. He retired shortly after a racial remark he made hit the newspapers. There were two perpetrators, but only one defendant had been arrested. When the defendant, a black man, was sentenced, he insisted he'd acted alone. The judge tried arguing with him and said, "I know there's another nigger in the woodpile." When the remark exploded in the press, the judge's defense was that he hadn't meant it "the way it sounded."

By contrast, my second complex judge was the picture of dignity and decorum. He was white-haired, charming, always a gentleman. And he was subsequently convicted and imprisoned for corruption.

As I had with Asserta, I got along with this second judge while he was in my complex. I didn't expect that to last. He was notoriously lenient in his sentencing. I expected that sooner or later I would offend him with my plea bargaining. He surprised me.

I learned how wrong I was during a bench conference. The defendant had already beaten murder charges and then a rape indictment (when the victim refused to testify against him), and now all that was pending against him was a one-witness third-degree robbery case. Even after conviction, he would be eligible for a minimal sentence.

Plea or trial, I wanted the defendant sentenced to the most I could get—the maximum for the crime charge. I told the judge that. He knew I wasn't being reasonable. "What kind of a plea bargain is that?"

I told him, "Look, this is a bad guy. I know you could let him plead to the charges and give him a lot better deal than I'm offering. I'm asking you not to do that. I'm ready for trial. Let me have my shot at him." The judge agreed to send the case to a trial part. No plea. Trial. Conviction. More time at sentencing than I ever could have gotten on a plea.

When the complex judge was prosecuted for corruption, I kept hoping he was innocent.

Judges don't only affect pleas. They can change verdicts. Because the bottom line in our criminal justice system is a jury verdict, rapists depend on public prejudices to insulate themselves from consequences. Juries are always looking for permission to bring those prejudices into play. The person they turn to most for such permission is the judge.

Plenty of judges let a jury know their personal opinions one way or another. Or they make all their rulings so biased against the prosecution that it's impossible to get a conviction regardless of guilt. Prosecutors can't appeal an acquittal, so there isn't the same kind of restraint on a judge who wants to be completely defense-biased as there is on one who favors the prosecution. And then, of course, there are the collaborators.

Most often when bad judges send the jury a message on a rape trial, it is about the victim. In one trial of mine, the judge spent all her time during the victim's testimony shaking her head in disbelief. The victim was a teenager, a hard home life exacerbating the rebellion and unhappiness that went with that territory. The defendant was someone she'd met on the street, talked to, hung out with in a school yard at night. The case had taken over a year to get to trial. By the time she testified, the victim was eight months pregnant. She'd been placed in a home for unwed mothers, and with some serious support from the counselors there, she was just beginning to emerge from the depression the rape, and her own family life, had caused her. She had enough belief in herself, at least, to walk into a courtroom and tell a jury that it was wrong for her to be raped. The judge, sitting behind the victim, judgmental, told the jury by her conduct that that wasn't true.

The teenager testified about meeting the defendant that night and hanging out with him. As they talked they wandered around, eventually winding up in a deserted school yard. She told him her problems, her secrets. Later he used them against her at trial, but at the time he had sounded sympathetic. All that changed when he wanted sex and she didn't. She screamed. Someone called the police. By the time they came, it was too late.

I was the one who had to phone the victim and tell her that the verdict was Not Guilty. The next day I got a call from her counselor. The victim had run away. Did I know where she might have run to?

I wish judges had to receive phone calls like that, not just prosecutors. Maybe that judge would have learned not to sneer during testimony. But that's dreaming. She got the kind of phone call such judges get: She's no longer a trial judge; she was promoted to the appellate bench. It was hailed as a move forward in the advancement of women in the courts.

The way it works, trial judges get their positions either by appointment (by the mayor or the governor) or by election. The process of decision making for appointment is not open to public scrutiny. Theoretically the elected judges, who at the trial level are one step higher in status than the appointed ones, have to answer to the public for their positions. But there are so many subrules to their nominations that, at least in Queens, election is dependent on endorsement by the local Democratic party. There have been repeated media exposés about the power of the clubhouses in selecting judges . . . but no effective reform.

Even the judges who can't get elected wind up sitting on felony cases as acting supreme court judges. The judge who tried Johnny Washington and who undercut the plea offer on Shelvie Harris was one of them.

Queens did seem to have more than its fair share of bad judges. Maybe it was because they found the county a safe haven. When I complained once to Santucci's chief of trials about a shockingly inept judge, he told me to write a memo, and that it would be added to the file the DA was keeping on the judge. From what I could tell, that's as far as the memo went—into the file. I learned to solve such problems for myself.

Lawyers are not allowed to overtly judge-shop. But there are ways to at least position yourself to wind up in front of the right jurist.

Because I got along with the complex judges and their court personnel, they accommodated me when they could. If I was already on trial and a ready case of mine appeared in the complex, as long as my trial judge agreed, the complex would send the case to the same courtroom as a "back-up." It didn't take me long to figure out how to stay where

I was if I wanted to. All I had to do was find a good, hard-working judge and try a string of cases back-to-back.

I wound up trying several strings of cases before Judge Julie Soleil. Most times she sat in Long Island City in a beautiful old courthouse that was routinely used for period-piece movies. The corridors and court-rooms had high ceilings, white walls, mahogany and marble. The top floor, where Judge Soleil sat, even had a huge stained-glass domed skylight. As lovely as it was, ordinarily I would have avoided this court-house. It was inconvenient to get to, security was deficient, and it was dangerous. After dark the area was urban-desolate, and there were peri-odic jail escapes. It was worth all of that, though, to get a good judge.

Soleil was ladylike, with her lace collars and pearls showing above the neckline of her robes. Even when she imposed a lengthy sentence, she spoke softly and kept her head down, as if she'd rather be doing some-thing else.

What I liked about Judge Soleil was that she was willing to listen to legal arguments and to base her decisions on what she thought the law required. That may sound like a minimal standard, but only to outsiders.

Early on, Judge Soleil presided over a trial that would have been a preordained acquittal in many of the other courtrooms in Queens County.

The victim was a big, homely, unlikable teenager—just what every-one I know thought of themselves when they were adolescents. She had a crush on one of the popular boys, a handsome athlete; he was every-thing she wasn't and wanted to be. One night she ran into him in the neighborhood. Probably she would have been willing to do anything he asked of her. Instead he forced her to have sex with him and his friend. If the term had been fashionable then, it would have been called "date rape." He did it to be doing it, because he could, and who would care?

Even her family didn't care. Her brothers yelled at her for getting raped. Her mother wouldn't interrupt her bowling night to take the girl to the police precinct.

The victim had it in her to go to the police anyway. One of the rapists, the friend, was arrested. He went to trial, with a consent defense. The jury didn't like the victim. She wasn't very likeable, sullen where she could have been sympathetic, unresponsive in cross-examination, even when the attorney raised points she could have answered. She didn't expect a jury to believe her. She just needed to do this for herself. It made me angry to think that she wasn't entitled to justice. I tried the whole case angry.

The jury convicted. One of the jurors told me afterward that he'd sat as a juror on a homicide case, and that rape cases were harder.

It was over a year later before the codefendant was found and arrested. I contacted the victim. She'd built a life for herself, met a man, had a son. She was still willing to prosecute. I put together enough of a case, including the threat of testimony from his codefendant, so that Mr. Popularity pleaded guilty. When I told the victim *both* rapists were in prison, she was happier than I thought she could be. She said when her boy got older, she would tell him.

What I wanted to tell him was that his mother taught me something about bravery.

Even before I started doing this work, I'd heard enough times that anyone could be raped so that it wasn't an adjustment for me to understand that victims were human beings. I liked some more than others. People could be manipulative or annoying or hostile . . . it didn't mean they hadn't been victimized.

What I hadn't known was that being a sex-crimes prosecutor meant eyewitnessing courage. It was the one common denominator among the victims I had the privilege of accompanying into a courtroom to testify that they had been raped.

Other ADAs in the office insisted on more common denominators than that. They wanted their rape victims to fit a certain image. How the jury responds to a victim is an enormous percentage of the verdict in any sex-crimes trial—which is why prosecutors want Good Victims.

In New York City, Good Victims have jobs (like stockbroker or accountant) or impeccable status (like a policeman's wife); are well-educated and articulate, and are, above all, presentable to a jury: attractive—but not too attractive, demure—but not pushovers. They should be upset—but in good taste—not so upset that they become hysterical. And they must have 100 percent trust and faith in the prosecutor, so that whatever the ADA decides to do with the case is fine with them. The criteria for a Good Victim varies with locale. In the Bible Belt, for example, the profile would be a "Christian Woman." But the general principle remains the same.

Such attitudes are not only distasteful, they are also frightening. They say that it's O.K. to rape some people—just not *us*. Old-time convicts spell *justice* "just us"—prosecutors aren't supposed to. Sex-crimes prosecutors are supposed to understand that the only way to keep the wolf from our own door isn't to throw him fresh meat but to stop him the first time he darkens anybody's door. Rapists progress—often they start with people they know before moving on to strangers. They become emboldened by success with easy prey. They start believing we're *all* prey.

People do say with some facility that anybody can be raped, that rapists don't discriminate. It is true that rape victims include among their ranks heiresses and nuns and great-grandmothers. But they also include crack-heads and dope dealers, junkies, whores, thieves, and liars. Rapists certainly do discriminate—they look for whatever vulnerability might insulate them from capture and punishment. Sometimes that means raping a child, because we seem as a country to doubt the word of children who say they've been raped. And sometimes that means trying to sell the rest of us on the concept that it isn't really rape if the victim is someone we don't like.

Like any predator, rapists want easy prey. For some stranger-to-stranger rapists, that can be as literal as seeking out a short woman or someone blind or drunk—in any way more defenseless. The institutionalized elderly and handicapped are recurrent targets of sexual assault. Even child molesters (who by definition seek out vulnerability) discriminate so that children who are learning-disabled, especially young, or particularly emotionally delicate are more frequent targets. Many white pedophiles choose nonwhite victims—recognizing the racism within the criminal justice system. Rapists trust prejudices to protect them. They invented the concept of "She deserved it," trusting collaborators to reinterpret that concept from "She was too vulnerable" to "She was too sexy."

Rapists tend to go to trial more than any other kind of criminal, believing in their souls that all men, including those on the jury, would rape if they only had what it takes. They are supported too often in this belief by the fact that what the defense puts on trial is the victim.

I learned it *is* possible to send a different message to rapists. Two defendants arrested on a gang sexual attack of a local high school track star taught me that lesson. Because their actions fell short of rape, and because the victim had been partying with them immediately before the assault, the two defendants were granted bail. They smirked at the court delays that lengthened their pretrial freedom. Shortly before the trial, they were arrested as part of a gang who kidnapped and raped a woman in their van. The van rape case made all the headlines because the assault was interracial and extremely brutal. Even with bail revoked, these two defendants insisted on trials.

The van rape case was assigned to one of the Major Offense Bureau ADAs. I tried the original case. The two defendants were gratified to see the track star tormented by their attorneys on the stand. She'd been drinking. She was black like them. The jury was mostly male. The defendants were visibly arrogant in their self-confidence, even laughing at the victim when she left the stand. You could see the shock on their faces when the jury convicted. The verdict was brand new information. Soon after, they entered guilty pleas on the van rape case.

So much depends on not getting diverted. And it is in response to victims that juries most often do.

Even the term for complaining witnesses is controversial. I call complainants "victims," not "survivors." I understand why women who have been raped would want to redefine their status. But on the front lines before a jury, they are *all* victims. It is a way to take back focus.

Judges who are complicitous in putting the victim on trial can make it impossible for justice to prevail in their courtroom. Sometimes that complicity is as simple as failing to stop a defense attorney—something that prosecutors are often guilty of as well. While judges and prosecutors are better positioned to betray victims, what victims tend to worry about most is the defense.

I have to admit that the defense attorneys I admire most are those who refuse to represent rapists and child abusers. Unless they're public defenders, who they represent is their choice. Those who are skilled certainly have the right, and maybe the obligation, to make ethical judgments about whom they serve as clients. Despite the image of the defense bar, I have had the privilege to meet many such attorneys.

There *are* some defense lawyers I respect who represent sex offenders professionally and effectively. None of them share their clients' attitudes toward victims, and none of them feel that putting a victim on trial is a winning strategy.

Then there are the lawyers who identify with their rapist clients, who seem to enjoy the opportunity to degrade a woman that cross-examination might offer them. I learned about such lawyers in front of Judge Soleil.

It was one of the few times I saw her truly angry, but her anger, unlike mine, was not directed at the defense attorney.

While the defendant, Wendell Nance, was in jail, he'd joined a cult. They called themselves "Black Jews" or "Black Hebrew Israelites," worshipers of Yahweh. Later they were simply called "Yahwehs." They were recruiting at the local jails—a number of rapists had joined them. Apparently, it was a socially acceptable crime among the cult.

During the first day of trial proceedings, about twenty Yahwehs were in the audience. They all wore white turbans and were dressed in imitation of the Nation of Islam. I've never met a Black Muslim who wouldn't have been offended by them.

The Yahwehs were very noisy. Mostly what they did was call out religious expressions, but discreetly timed. Whenever a ruling went against the prosecution, there was a whole round of "Praise be the Creator!" It annoyed the judge a lot more than it annoyed me. I didn't think a jury would like the Yahwehs much at all. (Years later, I found out I was right, but that was when they were defendants in a child-torture case.)

After we'd gone through the endless pretrial arguments and Wendell Nance had been placed back in the courthouse pens, Soleil called the cult up to the bench. She instructed them that they were welcome in the courtroom (defendants have a constitutional right to a public trial) but that they would have to remain silent once jurors were present. They responded that they "had to praise the Lord." The judge wasn't going for that. They had words back and forth. The cult mistook soft-spoken for weak. They thought they could intimidate the judge. She thought she could reason with them. They were both wrong. Soleil threw them out of her courtroom, issuing orders that barred their return for the rest of the trial.

But the Yahwehs were not done yet. While the trial was progressing, they held daily ceremonies in and around the Long Island City court-house. Some of it I got to observe, but mostly I heard secondhand about whatever they were up to.

I wound up with a detective-escort for the duration of the trial, and I had to sneak my witnesses in and out of a side door for them to testify—as if my victims weren't already scared enough. Eventually, the cult held a public ritual in the park across from the courthouse, placing a curse on the judge, and me, and the building itself. Then they dis-banded, reportedly fearing to be in the vicinity when the wrath of their god struck. I had my own ideas of what God wanted out of this trial.

During the time when there were still daily "services," the defense attorney did something so gratuitously hurtful to one of Nance's victims that it shocked me into back-burnering the Yahwehs.

Antoinette was a scrubbed-faced little girl/teenager, indulged and trea-sured by her family. She was also overwhelmed by the hardships of prosecuting. If it hadn't been for her mother, Daisy Bayard, there is no way Antoinette would have tried to prosecute. Daisy Bayard was one of those vital, juicy, sexy women in her mid-forties who have their own handle on the world. The only thing Daisy loved more than nice things and good times was her daughter. But even with Daisy Bayard surround-ing Antoinette with affection and support, no one knew if Antoinette had within her what prosecution demanded.

Some people just don't. One of my bitterest memories is of a nurse in her fifties who had reached the age when she'd fooled herself that she was safe from rape. When some stranger stole that treasured belief, he took away a vital piece of her strength. She'd always told me that she couldn't testify at trial. The prior ADA had promised her she wouldn't have to. I talked her into at least making an attempt at a pretrial hearing, to see if it might be less terrible than she thought. She broke down after fifteen minutes and couldn't go on. The rapist walked out the door, freed on a dismissal by the judge. The defense attorney thought he'd won. The defendant thought he'd learned a good lesson: If he did enough damage, he was safe. If he picked someone vulnerable enough, or he *made* them vulnerable enough through his crime, he could do whatever he wanted to them.

Nance's defense attorney tested to see just how damaged Antoinette was.

We did opening arguments. I said "the People call Antoinette Bay-ard." She walked into the huge courtroom pale-faced with terror and looking even smaller than she usually did. She took all the long steps past the jury and the defendant and sat in the witness stand—a tall leather chair that dwarfed her. She stood almost immediately to swear to tell the truth, and then sat down again, more frightened every moment by the formality of what was happening.

I got as far as saying her first name when the defense attorney inter-rupted for legal arguments. At the bench he filibustered, raising already-settled issues, stalling for time, amusing himself with his ability to monopolize the court's attention, testing Antoinette.

By the time he wound down, Antoinette had shrunk almost into her chair. The wait had stripped her nerves. Now it was just a matter of getting this over with. No introductory questions to calm her down. She was past that. I tried a little, experimentally:

Q: Antoinette, how old are you?
A: Fourteen.

The judge interrupted to tell her to speak up, and she repeated:

A: Fourteen.

I could hear it in her voice. This wasn't going to get better. Just do it.

Q: Were you home on October 25, 1981?
A: Yes.
Q: Can you tell us what happened that night?
A: Yes, I heard a knock on the door—

Then it all came crashing in on Antoinette, what she was going to have to say, how hard it was going to be. She did what a little girl does to escape a bad situation:

I don't feel well right now. . . .

We took a break. Antoinette was oatmeal-colored, past trembling, and as close to catatonic as she'd been since the rape. Whatever strength she had to even keep her upright was gone. Daisy Bayard hugged her daughter, held and patted her while she cried. When she'd given her enough time, Daisy took Antoinette by two hands. She made the little girl look her in the eye. She told her daughter, "You can do this, I know you can. You have the strength. I know you do." She said over and over, "I love you. I believe in you. I know you can tell them, baby. Just tell them the truth."

Sometimes strength is almost visible, especially when it's poured from one person into another. Daisy made Antoinette whole enough to go back on the stand and try again.

Antoinette had a little girl's nightmare to tell. This time, she managed to tell it.

She'd been home alone. She must have been warned a million times what to do when her mother was at work at night and she was left by herself in the apartment. She tried to follow those rules. Someone knocked. She took her little dog with her and went to the door. She asked who it was. He mumbled something, and she thought it was her mother's boyfriend. She opened the door and saw a stranger there.

She tried to slam the door shut, but he put his foot on the sill. She struggled and pushed, the little dog bit at his foot and ankle. But he was so much bigger and stronger than them. He shoved his way in.

He had a machete. He forced sex on her, several different ways and positions, in different locations. She bled a lot. Then he forced her to go through the house looking for valuables, making her separate the real jewelry from the junk. He made her lie on the bed beside him—an endless stretch of terror—while he watched TV and they waited for her mother to come home. When they heard her mother at the door, he shoved her inside the bedroom closet.

On the witness stand Antoinette unfolded the layers of darkness to her nightmare.

You couldn't doubt Antoinette. It was only a question of whether she could say it, not whether it was true. The jury knew she'd been burglarized and raped, sodomized and imprisoned, robbed and tortured and terrorized—the victim of a monster. All that was left to do was to prove that the monster was Wendell Nance.

The details had taken most of the morning session to get through. In the afternoon, after a lunch break, the court officers rigged together a microphone, so Antoinette could whisper out her story and still be heard. By then, she'd gained the strength of having gotten this far:

Q: **Antoinette, you were telling us at some point this person told you to get in the closet, is that right?**

A: **Yes.**

Q: **What did he tell you, what words did he use?**

A: **He told me to get in the closet in a nasty way.**

I tried to get Antoinette to describe "nasty," but there were no words from her short life that fit death threats, so I moved on.

Q: **At the time that he told you to get in the closet, can you describe what the bedroom looked like at this point?**

A: **The bed was messed up, filled with blood. It was . . . my goodness. It looked like a ransack.**

Maybe I'd have better luck with "ransack."

Q: **Can you describe what made it look like it was ransacked?**

A: **The bed was messed up, things were all over the place and clothing were on the floor.**

Q: **What clothes were on the floor?**

A: **My clothes, and that's it.**

Q: **Where did the blood come from; do you know?**

A: **It came from here?**

Antoinette gestured toward her body. When I asked again, she pointed a little closer toward her vagina. It was the most her modesty would allow.

Q: **When did you bleed?**

A: **After the incident in the living room [the first place she was raped].**

Q: **You mean when you were [on] the bed [hours later], you were still bleeding?**
A: **Yes, I was.**

Now it was time. The jury had as much of a picture as Antoinette could paint.

Q: **And this person that you talked to [during the hours of imprisonment], that did all these things to you, do you see him today?**

We held our breath. The judge, the jury, me, the two defense attorneys. This was the final moment; either she would have the courage or she wouldn't.

A: **Yes.**
Q: **Can you point him out for us?**

She stood up. (People who speak so fluently about being a "stand-up" person should have been there—to *truly* know what it means.) She looked as small as I'd ever seen her. She turned her whole little body toward the defendant. She raised her arm, slowly pointing a trembling finger. To say it, she turned her face away, squeezed her eyes shut.

A: **Right there.**

After that it was easier. Antoinette added a few more details, about when she'd looked at him, the lighting conditions, what lawyers unemotionally refer to as her "opportunity to observe," then she continued with what happened:

Q: **Antoinette, after you got in the closet, what else did you see or hear that night?**
A: **I heard my mother scream.**
Q: **How long was that after you got in the closet?**
A: **About a few minutes.**

Q: **Did you hear or see anything else?**

A: **Yes. He opened the door for my mother to see me. She asked where was I and he showed me to her.**

Q: **And when he opened the door, did you see him and your mother?**

A: **Yes.**

Q: **Was the light on in the bedroom then?**

A: **Yes.**

Q: **Did you see or hear anything else while you were in the closet?**

A: **I heard my mother call the dog and then I heard her scream, and then afterwards she got hysterical when he told her to take her clothes off.**

Now that she was talking, Antoinette was saying things she'd never told me before. She was painting a picture of her mother that was different from Daisy's self-description, more vulnerable, less in control. I asked:

Q: **Antoinette, did you actually hear this?**

A: **Yes, and she was wondering where I was. Then he showed me to her.**

Q: **And what else, was there anything else that you heard or saw after he showed her?**

A: **No, after that my mother opened the door and she told me to get dressed. That's after he left.**

There was a little more after that, and all of the cross-examination. There was nothing in that testimony that changed anything . . . but the cross made me angry.

For Antoinette, testifying was a marathon. The closer she got to the finish line, the stronger she felt. The defense attorney deliberately blurred the mile markers, trying to bleed the heart out of her.

He knew that the sex crimes were the most upsetting topic for Antoinette, so he lulled her into thinking he was past asking about them. As soon as she relaxed, he caught her off-guard with a question about being raped. Once she was sufficiently upset, he asked her about the identification. It was his method. He repeated it each time she got too strong on the stand. As painful as this was for Antoinette, it didn't change her testimony any. He hurt her heart—he never touched her credibility. It was calculatingly cruel. Nance must have loved it. It was not effective.

Because there was no pattern or chronology to the cross, it seemed like it ended abruptly. No redirect. Antoinette had done fine, and she'd had it. There was nothing I needed to ask enough to give the defense attorney a second shot at her. Suddenly, the long day's testimony was over.

I told Daisy she would have to come back tomorrow, but that Antoinette's testimony was finally over and she'd made it through.

When Daisy Bayard returned to court for the second day of the trial, she was more herself. I guess that's one definition of love: It was harder for Daisy to watch Antoinette in pain than to feel pain for herself.

I have to admit that most prosecutors probably would not want Daisy feeling more like herself. She was unconventional: too sexy, too flaky, too melodramatic, too defiant, not the Good Victim in any way.

Daisy was my idea of a survivor. But she didn't want anyone to see how much she'd overcome to get there.

Although Antoinette had given us a glimpse of Daisy out of control and hysterical, Daisy never did. Daisy wanted us to see a woman who had talked a machete-wielding monster out of killing her and her daughter. She didn't want anyone to see a woman who had been vulnerable and afraid. It would have been easier if she did, but that wasn't Daisy. I didn't try to change her. She had a truth to tell, and she had to be herself to tell it.

I don't mean that I didn't shade Daisy's being herself to show it off as best as I could. I did sew her into her blouse just before I put her on the stand, since I didn't think her tendency to pop the buttons down her front every time she heaved a big sigh would go over all that well with the jury.

What I wanted was for the jury to see enough of who Daisy was and what she'd gone through to understand that she was her own kind of hero. Hell, mine too!

Daisy Bayard had come home that night from her job running a bar to an apartment she thought was safe, and to a life she thought she controlled. She had walked into chaos and disarray; furniture all over the place, blood on the couch in the living room, the bedroom a mess, jewelry scattered, blood on the crumpled bed sheets—and her daughter missing. She was grabbed from behind by a man with a three-foot-long machete who told her he'd been watching her and waiting for her. She cried out, "My baby, my baby, where is my baby?"

He opened the closet door. Antoinette was crouched, fetal position, on the bottom of the closet. She looked up at her mother with no expression in her eyes—not even a hint of recognition. He closed the door.

Daisy made a decision. All that counted now, for her and her daughter, was surviving. She pretended to like the monster. She stroked and sweet-talked him. She put on fancy lingerie and submitted to sex with him, promising him more. She'd meet him the next night. She'd do and be whatever he wanted. Only please leave now before her boyfriend came home. Only please don't kill her and her daughter.

When he was finished having his way, imposing his will, he left. Daisy called her boyfriend and her brother-in-law the state trooper. She got Antoinette dressed. Someone called the police. They came, asked questions, dusted for prints, took her and Antoinette to the hospital for tests. She tried to transfuse Antoinette with her own strength: Just get through this, baby.

Daisy must have thought about killing her daughter's rapist. She must have thought a lot of things. Somewhere during that night she might have even have had time to think about the fact that she, too, had been raped. But not a lot of time.

I don't know what conversations Daisy had with her boyfriend or her family. I never asked. I do know what was on Daisy's mind. When she first reported the crimes, she hadn't said that the intruder she'd found in her apartment was someone she knew from the neighborhood. Maybe she was afraid. Or maybe she had other plans to consider for him. Sometime on the way home from the hospital, she made the decision to tell the police that she knew him, that he wasn't a stranger like she'd said. She had her boyfriend drive her back to the precinct.

Between what she herself already knew and what she found out by asking around, Daisy was able over the next few days to give the police

a street name, an address, a real name, places where Nance hung out—
more than enough to find him. Six long months went by. She and
Antoinette finally viewed a lineup. It was him.

Daisy told the jury all of it. I believed every word she said—I didn't
know if the jury did. Juries want a conventional victim, fighting against
the act of intercourse even when not fighting is the only way to survive.
That wasn't this crime . . . or this victim.

Some of Daisy Bayard's "being herself" did present serious problems.
She was incapable, even on my direct examination, of answering a
question simply and to the point. She had her own way of saying things
that had nothing to do with the rules of legal evidence. Much of the
testimony was more awkward and interrupted than it would have been
otherwise.

On direct examination, I asked Daisy about knowing the defendant
before the crime:

Q: **Mrs. Bayard, you said that you recognized the defendant.
Where did you recognize him from?**

A: **From the neighborhood. He always is around the place
where I work. Always. He comes in and has a beer sometimes and he's always around. All these teenagers hang
around on the side, on the corner in the summer. They are
always there. There is what they call a hangout spot outside.
In fact, well I know him from the neighborhood. I never
knew his name; I know the face. Always a lot of teenage
kids. I really don't know the names. . . .**

At this point the defense attorney objected, and Daisy was instructed
again by the judge to just answer the questions.

On cross, the defense broached the same topic:

Q: **You know Mr. Nance from your bar, is that correct?**

The attorney had already made the point offensively often that Daisy was
a barmaid—as if that was a morally acceptable defense to rape.

A: Yes. Seeing him around.

Q: And you served him in the bar?

A: Yes, I served him. He don't drink, really; take a beer very seldom. Selling this, that, and the other thing. Peeking in the window mostly. He's on the bike and you also see his face peeping in the window.

Q: He is the only person that peeks in the window?

A: No.

Q: Other people do that?

A: Yes, yes.

Daisy understood that the defense attorney was being snide. It was dripping from his tone of voice. This was one of the few times she showed signs of impatience on the stand. She was trying her best, but she would make the attorney pay for being nasty.

Q: How many years did you know him?

A: Years he's been in the neighborhood.

Q: Well, would you say you knew him four years?

A: For years, years he's been in the neighborhood. I saw the face in the neighborhood. I almost killed Mr. Nance in the neighborhood.

The defense attorney was skilled enough not to miss a beat with his next question, even though he had no idea what Daisy was talking about. Later he would go back to standard defense fare—taking advantage of the fact that Daisy had misunderstood him and thought he meant "*for* years" not "*four* years." In the meantime:

Q: You almost killed Mr. Nance in the neighborhood?

A: Yes.

Q: Have you ever told that to anybody before?

A: Everybody saw it.

Q: I didn't ask you that. Have you—

A: Yes.

Q: —ever told this to anyone before?

A: **Yes, of course.**

Q: **That you almost killed Mr. Nance?**

And then she finally let everyone know that it was just Daisy's way of expressing things, not so bizarre after all.

A: **Accidentally. He almost ran before me but another car hit him instead of me. I did everything I could. Stopped there [to keep from] hitting him.**

There was more, a lot of questions from the defense attorney and from me on redirect, so that the jury fully understood that years before the rape the defendant had run in front of a car Daisy Bayard was driving, and that she'd braked just in time. That was Daisy, that was the way she was going to tell it. I did want Daisy Bayard to be herself . . . but not so much this part of it.

After Daisy's testimony, I said, with a little more emphasis to the words than I normally gave them: "At this time, Your Honor, the People rest." It would almost have been worth it just to see the looks of disbelief at the defense table.

Conventional wisdom is that prosecutors "wave the blue"—call police witnesses to put the police department's, and the state's, imprint of approval on the prosecution, to impress the jury with the weightiness of "the system." One of the problems with this theory is that, at least in Queens County, "the system" may not be all that impressive. Queens is a county where, within the memory of most jurors, the district attorney, the chief administrative judge, and a significant percentage of an entire precinct were indicted and convicted of felonies: corruption, perjury, torture. Waving the blue presumes an era when, if the public did doubt its "system," a juror was at least reticent to admit that to his fellows. Conventional wisdom presumes a lot of things I never had in my cases.

There was plenty of police activity in the case. Had I wanted to dress up the testimony of the victims with a parade of other witnesses, I certainly would have had the bodies to do that. The problem was that I would have also created opportunities for the defense.

The Crime Scene Unit had lifted "partial prints," which didn't belong to Nance and hadn't been compared to those of anyone else at the scene. It took months before anyone made the effort, and even then, they didn't come up with a match.

Plus, at one point when they were searching for him, the police had mistakenly arrested Nance's brother (who used the same alias), then voided the arrest once they realized their error. They were never even sure which was his real name, Wendell Nance or his AKA of Wendell Williams.

Everything was explainable, but these were just the kind of little fiascos that the defense could use to smoke-screen themselves up a "reasonable doubt." They were counting on a jury disapproving of Daisy. More than a defense, they wanted to give such a jury an *excuse* to acquit.

If you believed Antoinette, there was undeniably a burglary/rape, and if you believed Daisy Bayard, it was undeniably Nance who did it. Nothing any other witness had to say could change that.

It would have been powerful evidence to bring in the bloody bed sheets vouchered by the responding officer, or to call as a witness the desk officer Daisy Bayard told that she knew the rapist. But I couldn't pick and choose with the police testimony. Either I introduced it all, including all the problems inherent in the arresting detective's testimony, or I called only the victims and argued to the jury on summation that the whole case was Antoinette and Daisy.

The defense put on what seemed like an endless case. There were days of testimony just on the issue of the partial prints that didn't match Nance's. It took hours of testimony from the defense to explain what fingerprints are, how they can be matched, what a match is, what partial prints are, where these prints were found, what the term "elimination prints" means. It took five minutes of cross-examination from me to establish that the prints could have been there for years before the crime or that they could have been left by the investigating police officers at the scene; that the prints were noplace that the rapist was known to have touched; and that the partial prints were therefore no proof of anything.

The defense case was long, but it wasn't strong.

Trial lawyers never really get to know what goes on in the mind of opposing counsel, so I could only guess that it was a sign of cowardice when the lead defense attorney chose not to sum up in this case. He'd done the cross-examination of both complainants. He'd been *the* defense attorney at every significant point of the trial. He certainly did not have a reputation for the kind of generosity that would have inspired him to defer a winning summation to a younger colleague.

When the trainee defense attorney rose to give the defense summation, my reaction was "It went better for us than I thought." I hoped the jury saw it as weakness.

I don't mean that the defense summation was so bad. Trial lawyers always flatter themselves that summations are the highest form of their art. I guess they can be. Occasionally there are truly brilliant summations—although I still don't know how much influence they really have on a jury's ultimate decision. For the most part, though, even an incompetent trial attorney can give a passable summation. Given the chance to speak as long as they want to a captive audience, almost anyone can make a few good points.

My own summation was what my summations usually are: emotional, briefer than anyone expected, and more a commentary on the nature of the crime and the truth underlying it than a recitation of the proof. I told them, "When that beast came out of the night into that apartment, he came with a plan, a plan not just to do these evil and perverse things, but a plan to use that fear to strike terror . . . so no one [w]ould . . . say, 'That's him. He's the one.' " I had to make them see this monster, feel his power. Maybe I did. I'll never know.

The jury was out a long time. After the first few hours of deliberation they sent back a note: "Time will not resolve our differences." It was the most poetic announcement of a hung jury I'd ever heard.

It was too soon to declare the jury deadlocked. The judge sent them overnight to a hotel and told them in the morning to resume deliberations. The next day, a Thursday, they got no further. Friday morning dragged.

Queens judges tend to declare a jury hung and a mistrial after three days of deliberation, and they rarely permit jurors to deliberate through a weekend unless the jurors themselves request it. The prospect of having to put Antoinette and Daisy Bayard through this all over again in a retrial loomed over that third day.

Later, the jury foreman—who I liked very much, and who apologized to me for the eventual verdict—explained how he finally got the jury to agree on a vote.

The foreman, a salesman by occupation, spent the three days arguing for a conviction on all counts. There was too much disagreement. Finally, around lunchtime on Friday he took the jury-room pitcher and poured some water into a glass. He said to the rest of the jurors, "Look, we can spend from now until forever arguing whether that glass is half full or half empty. What we've really got to decide is if it has *enough* water in it to convict this defendant beyond a reasonable doubt."

I wished I'd said that on summation. But it was too late by then to worry about what I hadn't done. Besides, what I hadn't done was all I'd been thinking about during the three days of deliberations.

Friday afternoon the jury sent the note saying they had a verdict. The parties were assembled. The jury filed back into the courtroom. Something was wrong with the way they looked. They looked solemn enough for a convicting jury, and they wouldn't meet the eyes at the defense table. That much was good. But they wouldn't look over at me either.

The foreman stood to deliver the verdict. As to the first count, did they find that Wendell Nance had raped Antoinette Bayard. Yes. Thank God—whatever else they'd done, Nance would go to prison a rapist. The reading of the verdict continued.

In the end the jury had compromised. Even though it probably did not affect the ultimate sentence, that compromise was obscene. They found Nance guilty of the crimes against Antoinette, but not guilty of the crimes against Daisy Bayard. Daisy was just not their idea of a Good Victim.

The defense attorney agreed with them.

He said as much at the sentencing, arguing for leniency, trying to minimize the crimes. He mentioned Daisy, pointing out that the jury acquitted on these charges and using these slime-coated words: "She doesn't strike me as the kind of woman who would be particularly affected by these events."

I'd intended to limit the topic of my sentencing arguments to Nance himself. The fact that he stood convicted of the machete-point rape, robbery, and burglary of a defenseless little girl spoke for itself.

I answered the attorney more because I was offended than because I thought the judge would consider his words in her sentencing. I reminded Judge Soleil of Daisy, walking into her apartment, finding chaos and blood and a machete-wielding stranger looming over her and grabbing her from behind, her crying out, "My baby, my baby, where is my baby," looking down at her daughter huddled in the closet, catatonic and bleeding.

The judge gave me one of those restless gestures, like she didn't need to hear this. She wasn't disagreeing with me, but she didn't particularly want me to be saying it right then. She was required by the verdict to sentence the defendant only on the crimes against Antoinette. She didn't want the record to suggest that she'd considered the acquitted charges. There was no place left in the legal system for it to recognize the monstrous acts against Daisy Bayard.

I returned to my original arguments. I said that because there was no mitigation, nothing about Nance or the crimes that entitled him to any leniency, the only appropriate sentence was the maximum. It was an approach the judge's law secretary had inadvertently suggested when we were talking just after the verdict. She asked, "What could be worse?" She was right. When the legislature designed a range of sentences for rape, did they have in their mind some more unspeakable act of rape than what was done to Antoinette?

The judge sentenced Nance to the maximum, eight and a third to twenty-five years imprisonment.

The Yahwehs showed up at the sentencing to "praise God." Court appearances were one of the services they offered their constituents. Years later, when most of the local temple were arrested, they never missed a court date. There were fourteen of them (at the outset) produced from the prison pens—enough to make a jury—and the rest of them in the audience, white robes, white turbans, indignant that the state could say it was impermissible to stone their own babies, to whip them and pour hot sauce into the wounds.

Nance filed a *coram nobis,* an appeal based upon incompetency of counsel. As offended as I was at some of the attorney's conduct, he had actually worked very hard for his client. Being accused of incompetence wasn't fair, but it was justice.

Too many defense attorneys feel "bonded" to rapists at trial . . . they don't know their own clients. Put most defense attorneys alone in a dark room and they will reach out blindly until they feel the walls. It is a basic human need to know one's boundaries. Put most rapists alone in that same dark room, and all they will do is hug themselves. They have all they need within themselves.

Lawyers who find common cause with rapists are simply worms. Their clients are snakes. Both crawl on their bellies. But worms are just slimy—snakes can be lethal.

3

B asically there are only three defenses to rape:

1. It never happened;
2. She consented; or
3. It wasn't me.

Defense attorneys cold-bloodedly select which of these three is most likely to fly in their particular case. Legal Aid is so cavalier about these choices that they developed their own acronym for one of them: the SODDI defense—Some Other Dude Did It.

To make their decision, defense attorneys first look to the victim. If a woman is abducted and raped at gunpoint at four-thirty in the morning, the lawyer is going to want to know what she was doing on the street at that hour. If she is a nurse on her way to an early shift, the defense will be identification. And if she is a prostitute on the stroll, it will be a consent defense.

Next, lawyers look at what forensic evidence is available.

The protocol in New York is that the police are supposed to take rape victims to a hospital emergency room, where a superficial physical examination is conducted and a "rape kit" is prepared. Rape kits are evidence-collection kits that contain various slides, swabs, scrapings, combings, and articles of clothing taken from the victim. So many of them are prepared in New York City that the policy of the police lab is to refuse to test any rape kit until it has received notification from the police department that an arrest has been made.

If the slides come up positive for sperm, it is harder (but not impossible) for the defense to argue that no intercourse took place. If there are injuries noted in the medical report, then it is more difficult for the defense to argue consent. If there is forensic blood typing or pubic-hair analysis supporting the victim's identification, that issue is less readily challenged. Essentially, the goal of a good investigation is to make all the defense choices as hard as possible.

The choice depends on the prosecution's proof. If the complainant is not a Good Victim, and there is no evidence of the crime outside her word, then it never happened. If there is evidence of intercourse, then she consented. When there is evidence of force, they might switch to an identification defense if the two are strangers. If not, they may stick with consent, and argue "rough sex" to a jury.

Often the defense is merely a transparent vehicle to legitimize prejudice. As Nance's attorney did with Daisy Bayard, the real strategy is to make sure the jury doesn't like the victim. Concepts such as "identity" and "consent" become devices—they function to permit an acquitting jury to justify saying, "We wanted to see more." The "more" they claim they wanted to see is evidence . . . but what they really mean is that they wanted to see a better victim.

Some defenses, however, are sincere. There was one case in which everyone except me and the victim was convinced that we had the wrong man.

It wasn't a claim I could dismiss lightly. Victims do make mistakes in eyewitness identification—maybe not as often as *60 Minutes* always makes it seem, but it happens enough to take seriously.

The bare facts made a misidentification possible. The rape took place in the very early morning hours. The victim was forced by a stranger with a knife to the landing leading up to the roof of her building, where she was raped in a darkened, deserted hallway. Six months later she saw the defendant—I'll call him Ronald*—on the street and called the police.

---

*I used an alias for this defendant, to be consistent with the other choices I later made about him.

Ronald was tall, awkward. He dressed for court in a nice suit, clean and pressed, but with the sleeves and cuffs too short for his growing limbs. He was seventeen, mildly retarded, and had never before been arrested. He was polite and presentable, a gangly adolescent who looked confused to find himself facing a trial.

Ronald's home was in a part of the city far from the scene of the crime. He traveled a limited route to and from his special classes at a Catholic school. Several of the nuns at the school were ready to testify about what a wonderful boy he was.

Ronald lived with his mother and grandmother, who doted on him, in a house where they'd fixed up the basement especially for their charge. At night when they went to sleep, they locked the basement door, with Ronald safe inside. There was only the one doorway and a small window that was boarded shut. The grandmother would testify that she remembered unlocking the basement door early on the morning after the rape. She found her grandson asleep in his pajamas, looking perfectly normal.

I told the defense attorney I would investigate.

There was no forensic evidence in the case, no fingerprints, no search warrants, no comparison of body fluids—no proof other than the testimony. I knew even if there *had* been an investigation, it might well not have panned out—investigations often don't—but the old Special Victims hadn't even tried. By the time I got the case as the trial ADA, it was too late. The serology lab at the police department told me that any samples were way too old to test even for something as unsophisticated as blood type.

I would have to go on what I could piece together. Start with the victim, move to the defendant, focus on the crime, and try to make everything fall into place—or watch it fall apart.

The victim, Miriam, was an extraordinary person. Certainly she would have failed the Good Victim test. She wasn't tame enough. And she was difficult to pigeonhole. After a while, I figured out that she didn't want people to know how intelligent she was or how kind a heart she had. She wanted people to think of her as "street-smart" and cool. Her lifestyle matched her self-image more than it matched my image of her. But underneath was a perceptive person who didn't settle for easy answers, with the type of heart I admire most in people: courage and empathy all mixed together.

Miriam's account of the rape was detailed: what she did beforehand, what time she walked home from the place where she had been hanging out. She lived in Rochdale Village, a low- to middle-income private housing complex in a dangerous part of Queens, with high-volume crime and a security force that we (the trial attorneys at the Queens DA's office) cringed at the thought of ever putting on the witness stand.

Returning to her building, she had some sense a predator was lurking but thought she had made it safely to the elevator—until the rapist cornered her and forced her to that landing. He had a knife. He talked a lot. She said she thought he was faking an accent, pretending he was Jamaican or from some other part of the West Indies. While he was raping her, he told her to "love me like you love your boyfriends."

After the rape, she called Security. They found a guy wandering around the grounds and brought him to her, but he wasn't the rapist. She told the police pretty much what she later told me. She looked through pictures—mug-shot books—a number of times, but she didn't find the rapist. Then one day about six months later, she was shopping with her boyfriend in a different part of Queens, and she saw Ronald. She thought it was him, but she wanted to be absolutely certain. She had her boyfriend walk over and ask directions. As soon as she heard Ronald's voice, she was sure. She and her boyfriend went and found a cop. Ronald kicked up a fuss, so one of the charges was resisting arrest.

Miriam had answered all my questions except one. I still had to decide if she had identified the right person.

I rechecked a report in the file. Early on in the case there had been a court-ordered evaluation of Ronald's mental competency to stand trial. The finding was that he was somewhat retarded but fit. There was a note in the psychiatric report, sort of an aside: When the defendant was under stress, he assumed a West Indian accent that sounded phony. When asked about it, Ronald had said it was just a habit. He wasn't from the West Indies.

Miriam had told the police about the rapist's "Jamaican" accent months before the psychiatric evaluation.

I thought about Ronald locked up in his basement at night.

There was more. The first time I met Miriam face-to-face was in my Kew Gardens office in the summertime. After that I talked to her by phone, but not in person. The following winter I was on trial in the

Jamaica courthouse. It was snowing hard and blowing cold, and I was piling down the street on a lunch break when I heard my name being called. Although I was bundled up from head to toe, I still didn't want to stop in that weather. When I reluctantly did, a pretty, snow-covered young woman was standing in front of me, laughing at my confusion. She introduced herself. It was Miriam. Later I checked my calendar. It had been about six months since I'd met her that one time.

Without forensic evidence, I needed some way to judge the accuracy of Miriam's identification. Unless we are willing to say that no one is capable of accurate identification (in which case most stranger-to-stranger rapists would go free), there has to be some means of assessing a victim's capacity to identify. This sort of detail was my way. It convinced me Miriam was right.

It did not convince the defense attorney. During the bench conferences, when the judge and defense attorney and I debated the merits of the case, I tried to ask, "Why do you think they locked that boy up in the basement every night? What do you think happens to a retarded young boy's sexuality when he's surrounded by female relatives and nuns who close their eyes to biology? What if he *is* guilty, what are you going to do about it? Why does he fake a West Indian accent when he's under stress? Could he have been sexually abused as a child by someone West Indian?" But no one was listening to anything that started with the premise that Ronald might be guilty.

There *were* plea discussions. The system is too invested in dispositions to avoid them; they are standard in virtually every case. But given Ronald's insistence on his innocence, these particular negotiations weren't the ordinary back-and-forth "bargaining."

I talked with Miriam from the very beginning about what we would offer as a plea. I needed to know what she wanted. If it was doable, she had a right to get it.

Because the defendant was seventeen, he was eligible for "youthful offender" status, which meant that the judge had the option of sentencing him to anything from probation up to eight and a third to twenty-five years imprisonment without "Y.O."

Miriam wanted to give Ronald a chance on probation. I'd known other rape victims who felt that way. It always made me cautious. One of the most damaged victims I've ever met (who had been subjected to hours of unspeakable torture by subhumans who enjoyed every moment of her degradation) told me how guilty she felt to "be responsible" for them having received life imprisonment. (This crime was in another state. In New York it is only in the rarest circumstances that a rapist can get "life.") Not wanting to "feel responsible" was just another part of the rape-induced guilt that had wormed its way into the soul of that victim. It was a sign of all the damage that had been done that she couldn't even be angry or hate her tormentors.

What Miriam said was different. She told me, "I know there was something wrong with him. It's not like I forgive him. But he kept wanting to pretend like I was his lover. I don't know how to say it. Maybe there's some kind of program for someone like that. I don't know. I know plenty of people who belong in prison. Like my cousin. He's just a thief. You can't stop him or help him. He's just a junkie thief. But this guy, there was something wrong with him."

I knew plenty of people who belonged in prison too. Usually, they were rapists. Thieves I could forgive. But Miriam was trying to tell me something, and I was trying to listen.

I did offer Ronald "felony" (five years) probation, with therapy, on a plea bargain. The defense attorney turned it down.

Prosecutors want to think that only guilty people plead guilty. That's nonsense. Given what's at stake, plea bargaining presents many more difficult choices for an innocent defendant than for a guilty one. An innocent man has to give up the chance at vindication. A guilty defendant just has to get the best deal he can. Very few guilty people ever turn down the chance to avoid prison.

When Ronald turned down probation, I was the one faced with difficult choices. I could try to convince my supervisors to approve a lesser plea, like misdemeanor (three years) probation, which would guarantee "youthful offender" treatment. Or I could try to convince my supervisors to approve a dismissal on the grounds that I believed we had the wrong man.

Or I could go to trial.

I was convinced that Miriam was right. I was also well aware that the chances for conviction were minimal. Even forgetting the "locked-room" defense, this was a one-witness identification six months after the fact for a crime no jury would convict on lightly. In front of the wrong judge, the case would be unwinnable. Even if we got someone fair, Miriam was going to have to go through reliving the crime on the witness stand for what? For the one chance in a hundred that we could pull this off?

I talked it over with Miriam before I made the final decision. A detective for whom I have a great deal of respect once described to me that moment when you get to see what courage looks like. "You ask her to do something difficult, like view a lineup, and you can see her chin quiver when she thinks about how hard it's going to be, and then she looks straight at you, and with tears still forming in her eyes, she says, 'Yes, I'll do it.' " That detective was talking about a different rape victim, but he could just as well have been talking about Miriam. She wanted a trial.

I had my own reasons for agreeing with her. It wasn't only that Miriam had a right to her day in court, but also that accepting the lie that Ronald was innocent scared the hell out of me. I had a sense that this young man was not a monster . . . yet.

With those rapists who had fully crossed the line, all I could do was to try, as much as the law and an imperfect judicial system would let me, to keep them away from the rest of us. But with Ronald there was still a chance. As ugly as this crime was, there was some piece missing from it: that kind of power rush rapists get when they realize that they have total physical control over someone weaker; that joy at degrading and terrorizing another human being for the sexually expressed thrill of it. Maybe I overanalyzed Ronald because no one else was looking at him at all. Or maybe I just followed Miriam's lead. But I couldn't join in that lie. I couldn't pretend that Ronald was the wrong person and wait for him to rape again, when it would be too late to change him—or to stop him.

For once, both sides needed a trial.

The complex found us a judge, and this time the People came up lucky. It probably helped the odds that the judge wasn't in great demand for trials. Most attorneys didn't like the pace in his courtroom. He *was* slow and deliberate. But he was also neutral and evenhanded. If he had his doubts about my case—and he must have—he kept them to himself.

That was just the way he was, but it didn't raise his status any within the administrative hierarchy; he was not an "in-favor" judge.

The courtroom they found for us was an out-of-the-way cubbyhole in Borough Hall right next to the Marriage License Bureau. All through the testimony, as a counterpoint to the image of violence within, scenes of just-married couples were visible through the windows. There was so much rice scattered on the ground outside that the overfed courthouse pigeons waddled from obesity.

The day Miriam was scheduled to testify at the trial she showed up an hour late. Every other time I'd seen her, even in that snowstorm, she'd been perfectly made-up, polished and put together; now she looked like a dishrag. I called over to the court and told them we'd be late.

I talked to Miriam for a long time about what trial testimony was like. "The hard part won't be the cross-examination, but there'll be some time during the testimony when you won't just remember what happened, you'll relive it. Once you get past that moment, it will all be easier. You just need to be yourself. Let the jury see who you are, and they will have to believe you. You've already lived through something much worse than the testimony could ever be."

Miriam looked up, half-smiled, and said, "It's just words, right?"

I told her to go wash up and put on her makeup and then we'd talk a little more. That's when she told me. "My boyfriend said not to. He said if I wore makeup, the jury might not like it."

Maybe it was not my most tactful statement to a rape victim, but what I said was, "Your boyfriend's a jerk." Although I'd never met him, I'd thought that before—when he'd refused to testify at the trial as a witness to the identification. But I'd kept my mouth shut and not pushed it once Miriam explained that he was white (Miriam is black) and that they were worried about how a jury might react to that. This time I couldn't keep quiet.

Miriam did beautifully on the stand. I know it shouldn't be that people need to be articulate and intelligent to get justice from the court system—but too often it is. The combined weight of Miriam's dignity and the details she was able to summon up a year and a half after the crime made it difficult for the jury to ignore what she had to tell them. And what she told them, unequivocally, was that Ronald had raped her.

Miriam's testimony didn't, of course, go perfectly. Nobody's testimony ever does. When she was on the stand, I started to ask her about the snowstorm day, but the judge stopped me. Practically, it proved something, but legally, it wasn't admissible. The jury also didn't get to hear about the doctor's notation about Ronald's accent, since psychiatric reports are privileged.

Whether to put the arresting officer on the stand was a difficult decision. I made the wrong choice. Earlier, in my office, the cop had described Ronald's struggling and screaming and flailing his arms around when he was cuffed. It was good testimony. I didn't want the jury seeing Ronald as the gray-suited, shy-looking, overgrown boy he seemed to be in the courtroom. I wanted them to picture him angry and having a fit. On the stand, the way the cop described the arrest, Ronald had "moaned" once or twice. Nothing else. All the cop's testimony really showed was his own resentment.

The defense attorney was a former cop. Maybe that's why the arresting officer was so dead set against me. Or maybe he didn't like it that Miriam had a white boyfriend. Or maybe he was just antivictim, or prorapist. It wouldn't have been the first time I'd seen those attitudes in a police officer.

I knew the arresting officer had prejudiced the jury. I tried to thaw the chill the cop created by his tailored testimony with the "immediate outcry" witness.

In New York, the prosecution is allowed to prove that the victim immediately told someone of the attack. It's an age-old tradition designed to show that she really *was* raped. In recent years the courts have even allowed expert testimony explaining delays in reporting of sex crimes. Both policies are premised on the misassumption that if something as horrible as rape happened to a person, the victim would tell someone right away. The truth is that there are so many reasons to tell or not to tell that's it's really the reasons themselves, not the timing, that say anything about a victim's credibility.

I knew the jury had no doubt that Miriam was raped. But I wanted to personalize what she'd told the jury, to make them see and feel what had happened to her for themselves, to break through that barrier, that distance that lets a jury acquit. I used the immediate-outcry witness to try to do that.

Miriam had testified that when she fled the roof, it was only a few hours short of dawn. She ran down the stairs to the top floor and pounded on doors, asking to be let in. No one answered. She ran down another flight and tried again. Finally she reached the apartment of people who knew her and let her inside.

Miriam's neighbor testified that she'd been home on a quiet summer evening . . . her rest disturbed suddenly by frightening sounds in the night. She heard a woman on the floor above, beating on doors, begging, pleading for help at apartment after apartment, with only silence for an answer. Then the neighbor heard the banging at her own door. She was afraid, but she cracked the door open. Miriam rushed in—desperate, beyond terror.

The neighbor followed helplessly behind as Miriam stumbled the length of the apartment to the farthest corner of the farthest room. "What is it? What's wrong?" she asked. No answer. When there was no place else to run, Miriam slid down the wall until she was crouched on the floor, arms clasping her knees, shivering. She started to cry. At first it was unintelligible. Animal whimpers. Then she sobbed out that she'd been raped. The neighbor and her daughter called the police. It was all that they could do—and more than anyone else had done.

The defense called all the witnesses they'd promised.

Ronald's defense had a hidden strength. It was clear that his lawyer, his family, the defense team seemed to genuinely believe in his innocence. Of everything that happened in front of the jury, that was the most difficult to overcome. The witnesses themselves weren't half so effective.

I'd consulted people in my office about having to cross-examine nuns. After the general eye-rolling and jokes, the consensus of opinion was not to. One woman, raised Catholic, did give me some useful advice. "Ask them if they know anyone they think capable of rape. Nuns aren't allowed to think bad of anyone. They'll have to answer no." I'm not sure that reasoning was totally accurate, but I got the general idea, and it did work. The cross-examination suggested that maybe nuns weren't the best experts on who might be a rapist.

Through the nuns the jury also got to see that Ronald's life was entirely surrounded and controlled by women—the last women on earth he would feel free to talk with about sex.

The grandmother testified about the "locked room." I asked her why she kept Ronald locked in the basement, but she never really answered me. Most judges won't let attorneys get away with "why" questions (they call for the "operation of one's mind," not facts), so there was a limit to how much I could push it. I hoped the jury understood. The defense wanted to make it seem normal to lock someone in the basement at night. It just wasn't.

The grandmother also testified to being dead certain of the times, not leaving room for Ronald to have completed the rape, returned the long distance home, and been in bed when she claimed to have found him. But there was a limit to how credible exact-timing testimony could be when the first occasion she would have had to think about it was six months after the fact.

The jury seemed to react most in summation when I talked about the people Miriam had *not* identified: the guy that Rochdale Security had brought back for the show-up; the mug-shot photos she'd looked at. I told the jury Miriam hadn't wanted to pick out just anyone—she wanted to pick out the *right* person. And she'd waited all that time to do it.

The deliberations were tense. Later on, one of the jurors told me that she could literally see my heart beating when the foreman got up to read the verdict. By then, I felt that way—like my rib cage had to stretch, or crack.

There were three days of deliberation. None of the courthouse "regulars" thought I'd succeeded. They told me to be satisfied with keeping the jury out this long on such a weak case.

All the third morning we waited for a jury question, anything—but there was nothing.

I was afraid to go anywhere in case the jury suddenly wanted us. They didn't. I couldn't remember when I'd last eaten. Finally, mid afternoon, I ducked out and bought a hot dog. I was just unwrapping it when the clerk called with the message that the jury had a verdict. I rushed across the street, knowing even as I did that I'd have to wait for the judge, the defense lawyer, the court reporter, even the defendant.

The last twenty-five minutes were the longest. I paced the courtroom and the hallway. Waiting. The court officers were distant and noncommittal, but not out of coldness. They believed I couldn't possibly get a conviction. They didn't want me to get my hopes up.

I'd had a clean shot. If the jury did acquit, I'd have no one to blame but myself. No, that wasn't true. I'd also blame the jurors. Maybe everyone was right—this was a difficult identification issue. But no one would have been have so sure of a Not Guilty verdict if this wasn't a sex crime.

I rechecked, making sure I had Miriam's phone number with me. As soon as this was over, as soon as I knew the verdict, I would have to call her and tell her. I had been vague about when the deliberations would start, when we'd have an answer. I didn't want Miriam going through this waiting.

Ronald returned to the courtroom, surrounded as usual by female relatives, fussing and protective. I knew I should have known better, but even to me he didn't *look* like a rapist.

The court reporter called in to say that she was on stand-by as soon as we were ready. The defense attorney still hadn't appeared. There was a call in to his office.

It figured that we'd have to wait for him. It was the kind of thing he would do.

I knew that was petty. The defense had actually conducted itself with dignity throughout the trial. But some of the lawyer's casual gestures reminded me that he used to be a police officer and still assumed the privileges that went with being "on the job." Throughout the trial he'd parked in the DA's parking lot.

I wasn't one of those prosecutors who worshiped the police, although there were plenty of quasi-cops in the DA's office. (Those lawyers made me suspicious—I didn't want to be a pseudo *anything,* I wanted to be a sex-crimes prosecutor.) Normally I didn't harbor animosity toward police officers either. But this trial had brought out all my resentment of the "brotherhood."

I tried to imagine what had gone on in the jury room. By accident, the night before I'd seen a message that one of the jurors had the court officer call in to her home: "They're keeping me here." Two nights sequestered in a hotel was a lot to ask of them. Still, all that mattered was whether they'd done the right thing.

The defense attorney walked in. He looked nervous, apologetic. The clerk called for the court reporter. She was away from her desk; the second she returned, she'd get the message.

I tried to read in the defense attorney's face how worried he actually was. Until the judge formally accepted the jury's verdict, it wasn't too late for Ronald to plead guilty. Ordinarily I would never even consider a plea bargain at this late date. But with Ronald it was different.

The lawyer said nothing to me. I'd never had any choice except a trial. Now, if there was an acquittal, it would vindicate the defense decision. But it wouldn't change mine.

If the verdict was Not Guilty, I would have to make Miriam understand somehow that it was only the identification that they doubted, not her.

Two extra court officers walked in. The clerk must have called for added security. It was a professional thing for a clerk who expected an acquittal to have done.

The court reporter walked in, set up. The judge entered the courtroom from his chambers.

It was finally happening. The foreman stood and faced the defendant. The defendant stood and faced the foreman. This defense attorney, at least, had enough class to stand up when his client did.

The clerk asked, Has the jury reached a verdict? Yes. As to the first count of the indictment, rape in the first degree, how do you find the defendant, Guilty or Not Guilty?

Guilty.

The defendant started to cry. The truly bad ones, the irredeemable ones, don't react at all: stone-faced; absolutely self-contained. Maybe they nod, but nothing more. Ronald, though, was just a kid. The defense attorney, his mother, the nuns, and his grandmother had told him so often he wasn't guilty that he'd half believed them—until the verdict.

It was unsettling for me to have sympathy for a rapist. But this time the defendant needed the truth of that verdict almost as much as the victim did.

The case was adjourned for sentencing. Ronald was so upset he could barely answer the "pedigree" questions—address, true name, date of birth. There were official processes and decisions yet to come.

I borrowed a courtroom phone and called Miriam. She started to cry too. She'd been prepared for the worst.

Afterward I talked to the jurors. It had been hard on them to watch Ronald break down in court. I told them about the fake accent, the snowstorm day. They'd had a tough decision—I wanted to reassure them they'd made the right one.

The jurors wanted to talk. They were worried I would be upset that they acquitted on the resisting arrest charge. I wasn't.

They told me that one of the things they'd puzzled about during deliberations was the "locked-room" defense—how Ronald could have gotten out. During cross, I had tried to find some leeway about the locks, but the grandmother had been much too rigid to budge. Everyone on the jury had a different theory. It was like an old-time mystery novel. In the end, though, they simply decided that a boy left alone that much and motivated enough would have found a way, even if they couldn't figure out what it was. It wasn't the major issue—it had been more like a diversion when deliberations were getting nowhere.

There were the inevitable (in this case) posttrial motions based on the defendant's being innocent. I know it was naïve of me, but I thought after the verdict that the family would finally have to face the truth of what Ronald had done. All they did was change lawyers.

Miriam still thought probation was a good idea, but she wanted that left up to me. This was a hard one.

Because he was a youthful offender, even after a trial conviction, the judge had the power to sentence Ronald to whatever he wanted. There was an unwritten rule that dictated: Go to trial, go to jail. My impression was that the judge would not impose probation unless I recommended it. In the end, that's what I did, insisting that it be coupled with extensive therapy. I thought, more than ever, that Ronald was treatable.

I know it was probably against "Office Policy" to recommend probation—with or without counseling. During his term, nearly all postconviction press releases in Queens County contained the language "District Attorney John J. Santucci will demand the maximum sentence." It was virtually word-processed into the press-release copy, combining the fiction that the district attorney actually appears in court with the hype about how tough he was on crime. (In fact, the only time I remember Santucci making a personal recommendation on a sentence was when he asked that a corrupt Nassau County politician receive probation instead of jail.)

There were no written guidelines saying the ADAs had to demand the maximum. Maybe Santucci never thought that was necessary. Anyway, this conviction was mine. I had the right to make my own decision as to what justice required. The judge imposed probation with treatment. I don't know what happened to Ronald after that. I only heard about it if they got rearrested.

He didn't.

4

R onald crossed a line that he didn't understand was there. Other rapists sought out the line to cross. People seem to have this idea that rape happens when a male gets so overcome by his sexual desire for a woman that he loses all self-control. That's not what I saw in the crimes I prosecuted. It wasn't that rapists were oversexed. If anything, they seemed to have an unusual amount of difficulty getting or maintaining an erection, or reaching orgasm. All the prostitutes who are in their graves because they laughed at a John's lack of performance learned the hard way: These were crimes not of excess hormones, but of power and control.

It was my Rottweiler who actually showed me the difference—the day he hit puberty. When Bruiser was a puppy, I used to let him run off-leash in Forest Park. My husband warned me that he was probably getting too old for that, but I didn't listen until it was too late. There was a six-foot stone wall around the park—what could go wrong?

At the exact moment that his hormones kicked in, Bruiser sniffed a female Doberman who lived across the street from the park. His nose told him she was in heat. Bruiser's idea of courtship was to dive-bomb an innocent passing male Great Dane from the height of the stone wall. The Dane didn't know what hit him—until he sniffed the air himself. At the time about the only one who thought Bruiser's display was entertaining was the female Dobie across the street. She knew Bruiser was just a buffoon. He sort of had the idea right—that in the wild he and the other young studs would slug it out for the right to mate. But his good-natured dive bomb in the middle of civilization wasn't going to get it.

What Bruiser did was certainly animalistic . . . but it wasn't ugly. He didn't skulk in shadows. He wasn't a sexual predator. The fact that he let his hormones get in the way prompted me, when I got a pit bull, to get a female (and name her Honey). But I didn't like Bruiser any the less for what he'd done—he was just being his own doggy self.

What I prosecuted, that was different; something *against* nature to be stopped. I prosecuted rapists ranging from dentists to street monsters, from teenage boys to middle-aged women. They are a tribe. They have things in common that aren't cultural or economic. What they share, though, does seem limited to our species.

It was the pattern rapists where you could hold up a mirror and see the dark side.

After Shelvie Harris pleaded guilty, a couple of years passed before I got another chance to try a serial rapist.

In New York City, a "pattern" is identified when the police determine (from the facts, the descriptions, the locations, and anything else they piece together) that three or more rapes have been committed by the same person. Ironically, Eric Barnes just barely fit the minimum of this definition. There were three known rape victims.

My own definition of a pattern rapist has more to do with the ritualized, consistent, predatory nature of the crimes than it does with an arbitrary number of victims. By my definition, Barnes was prototypical. From the moment he was discharged from the army into New York City, just a few months before his arrest for the pattern, Eric Barnes haunted the streets of a small, middle-class section of Queens behind the Kew Gardens courthouse known as Briarwood—waiting, watching.

Shelvie Harris had preyed on anyone who crossed his path. His victims ran the full range of age and description. Eric Barnes picked only conventionally pretty women in their early twenties who lived within a few blocks of his target area. Once Barnes selected his victims, he studied them carefully, noting their habits, picking his opportunities. The stalking was part of the power rush.

I think Barnes started out just roaming, watching, maybe peeping. I don't have any proof of this, but it makes sense from what I learned later.

Barnes was first arrested for a criminal trespass in the early summer of 1983. He had tried to climb in an apartment window. The man who lived there had returned to the darkened living room to secure it for the night and surprised Barnes in the act. Barnes fled to the rooftop. A rookie cop (who'd just transferred from Emergency Medical Services to the police force) caught him up there.

It was the rookie who ultimately solved the pattern. When he had told Barnes what he was arrested for, Barnes had laughed and said, "I'm no *burglar*." The victim had told the rookie what had bothered him most about the crime: The burglar had to have known someone was home. His wife had been at the window—apparently alone—until just moments before.

The criminal justice system didn't have time for sophisticated perceptions. Barnes was released without bail. Nobody thought to treat it like an attempted burglary. As far as the courts were concerned, it was a minor offense, a first arrest, and the defendant was a recent vet. The case was on its way to dismissal.

Barnes took the arrest more seriously. With his subsequent victims, he made sure he knew precisely who was in the apartment before he struck.

What Barnes didn't know was that a gang of subhumans in Nassau County were about to up the stakes. Until the spring of 1983, there was a little-publicized law on the books that said that no matter how much time a judge imposed in consecutive sentences, the maximum any inmate would actually serve for a series of first-degree rapes was fifteen to thirty years' imprisonment. Then a gang of shotgun-armed teenage predators invaded a restaurant in Nassau County, robbing and raping dozens of patrons. When the rapists were caught, the public was shocked that they could be out so soon. In response, the legislature raised the maximum to twenty-five to fifty years (twenty-five years before the inmate saw the parole board, fifty years—less good time—before he must be released). The new law went into effect on May 31, 1983.

In early June, Barnes selected two roommates to watch. They were sharing their first apartment after college, a ground-floor location but in a safe neighborhood. Still, after less than two weeks, they were starting to get uncomfortable. It felt like someone was haunting them. It was nothing they could name, but it was there, an uneasiness.

The night of the attack, they each had family over. One roommate had been celebrating Father's Day with her dad. The other had been at a cousin's wedding with her brother and sister-in-law. When all their company left, they washed and got ready for bed in their separate rooms. A few moments after the last light in the apartment was turned off, Barnes was standing over one of the roommates, knife in hand, telling her, "If you scream, I'm going to kill you." He put the knife to her throat and raped her.

When he was done, he asked her who else lived in the apartment. He said he'd been watching. He must have known. She was afraid of the knife, of getting mutilated, or killed. She said she'd do whatever he wanted. He made her put his shorts back on. Then she brought him to her friend's room.

Barnes kept the first roommate on the bed, held there by the force of her terror, while he raped the second one. This one refused to act like she was going along with him. He was more violent. It seemed like he stayed forever, but when he'd taken enough, he left.

Nothing happened. No one came in the night to arrest him. He'd gotten away with it.

It wasn't long before Barnes found another young woman to stalk. Barbara lived in a studio at the opposite end of a quadrangle from the roommates. There was a courtyard outside Barbara's apartment. The roommates' apartment backed onto it. So did the apartment of the first couple Barnes had stalked. And so did Barnes's.

One hot August night a neighbor stopped by to visit Barbara. After he left, she decided to take a bath. When she left the bathroom to retrieve some cleanser for the tub, Barnes was standing in her living room. She tried to make a run for it, but Barnes grabbed her. He got himself a kitchen knife. He told her he'd been watching her. He threatened her. He bragged that he'd already raped two other women in the neighborhood by crawling in their window.

She tried to talk her way out of it. She asked him, "Don't you have a wife or girlfriend you can do this with?" He told her, "I like this better. I like it better this way." While he raped and robbed her, he demanded: "Tell me I'm a man, tell me how big I am, how much you like it big."

While Barnes was looking for new targets, another pattern took over the headlines. The Flushing Meadow Park Rapist was stalking lovers' lanes at gunpoint, robbing, abducting, raping. One young man, trying to protect his girlfriend, had been shot and nearly killed resisting the gunman. Even with police stakeouts all over the park, the rapist was striking at will.

Besides the airports, Flushing Meadow Park is what Queens is known for. The landscaped park sprawls, bordered on one side by Flushing Bay and spilling over on another side into Queens's other landmark: Shea Stadium, home of the Mets. The park still sports the 1964–65 World's Fair Unisphere. That summer the city was even talking about moving the Forest Hills Tennis Open to Flushing Meadow Park. Now it belonged to a rapist.

There was heavy pressure on the police, especially the Queens Sex Crimes Squad, to find the Flushing Meadow Park Rapist. The Briarwood Rapist was getting hardly any press at all.

The rookie who'd arrested Barnes couldn't forget him and move on, like he was supposed to. He checked the precinct reports for rapes in the neighborhood. He tried calling Queens Sex Crimes to tell them about Barnes's criminal trespass, and what the husband and the defendant had said. The first few times the cop called, no one listened. The third time he called, the rookie said he had information on the Flushing Meadow Park Rapist. Maybe now they'd listen to him. The rookie got a detective who, by coincidence, was assigned to both patterns, Flushing Meadow Park and Briarwood.

That same morning the detective had sent the latest Briarwood victim to look at mug shots to see if she could identify her rapist. While he was on the phone to the rookie, he got a note. Barbara had picked out a photo. The detective asked the rookie to repeat the name of the burglar he'd arrested. Yes. They both had the same name. Eric Barnes.

The detective showed the roommates a photo spread with Barnes's photo. Then he put Barnes in lineups. Barbara and one of the roommates picked him out. The other roommate picked out a stand-in. Still, it was enough to make the arrest on all three cases. One man had raped them all.

By themselves the roommate rape cases would be tough. The roommates were so traumatized by what had happened that there were huge memory gaps and inconsistencies in what they had to say. The facts they did remember weren't typical enough for most juries. Plus, one room-mate had misidentified the defendant. The other roommate had seen him in near-total darkness, with only the light of a street-lamp bleeding around closed venetian blinds to see by.

Barnes's third rape victim was a much stronger witness. Barbara was the one the detective had been talking about when he described what courage looked like. Prosecution was very hard on her, but that never stopped her. She was also the witness who tied the two incidents to-gether. Between what Barnes had said to her about raping two other women and her own inherent credibility, she might be able to carry the whole pattern.

I had another reason for wanting the three rapes tried together. That summer was one of the times when racial tensions were particularly high in New York City. To capitalize on it, the defense bar was looking to make race an issue, especially in sexual assault cases, especially when identification was the defense. The third victim was a black woman. If I tried the pattern together, I'd have to worry less about black jurors dismissing the identification by white women. And with the roommates being white, I'd have to worry less about white jurors not taking black-on-black rape seriously enough. It would have been nice not to have to consider any of this. But I had a rapist to convict, and I didn't want racism getting in the way.

Because it made their statistics look better, the old Special Victims Bureau always indicted each incident separately so there were multiple indictments. I made the motion to have all of Barnes's cases tried to-gether. The judge split the difference. He granted my motion to try all three Barnes rapes together and denied the same motion on a different pattern I was prosecuting with virtually the same legal issues. The two patterns wound up with radically different results.

In the spring of 1984 I did the pretrial hearings on both cases. I couldn't complete the hearings on the other pattern because one of the victims was out of the country. The case stayed where it was until she could be flown in for testimony. The Barnes case was transferred for trial to a better, stronger jurist than the split-the-difference judge. The trans-fer came because the court system was being modified experimentally, with the more experienced ADAs assigned to specific judges.

I found out a little about what my new judge was made of during the bail application in the Barnes case. The defendant had been held on high bail, fifty thousand dollars. The head of a national civil-rights organization came to court to request that Barnes be released into his custody; he said that Barnes was his cousin. The new judge denied the application. He wasn't intimidated by big names, not when it came to a predator. No release pending trial.

Barnes got tried almost exactly a year after he started his patterned march of invasion and rape.

The summer of 1984 was a slow time in the courts. Barnes was one of the few trials I did at the Kew Gardens courthouse, where I had my office. What with its accessibility, the lack of competition, and the interest generated by any serial rapist, the Barnes trial had a much larger audience than I was accustomed to.

Mostly the trial was attended by the younger ADAs and Legal Aid attorneys. (Legal Aid defended this rapist.) There were a few retired people in the audience who spent their time court-watching. The rest of the audience was made up of law students who were working for the DA's office as summer interns on the school break.

Several of the interns were women who, in addition to observing, accompanied and supported the rape victims during testimony. They were such a presence in the courtroom that whenever the jury was out of view Barnes entertained himself by staring them down whenever they looked his way. They weren't used to going head-on with a rapist. Barnes always won the staredown.

Barnes got carried away with this game. He tried it on all the spectators in the courtroom. One day he tried it on a male intern. The intern stared back at him. Barnes accepted the challenge, and they locked eyes. The intern took a finger and scraped it across his neck, in a "you're dead" gesture. It was one of my favorite moments in the trial. I just wished it had been a woman intern who'd done it.

The victims' testimony went about like I expected.

The two roommates were problematical. By the time the trial came, there was palpable unspoken tension between them. The one who'd been victimized first was the one who'd made the identification. She envisioned herself as the "strong one" and had always played that role with her friend. Her roommate couldn't adjust to the idea that the "strong one" had led the rapist to her room. The rapist had responded to each roommate differently, being much more violent with the second one. Neither roommate could figure out why, or leave it alone. Both were so devastated by the crimes that they had little place in their hearts to share the other's pain.

The "strong one" worried me. I'd never seen her cry, or heard that she had. She held all that in check. When she talked about being raped, she expressed anger but nothing else. I do believe that righteous anger makes a person stronger, but this was different, more self-destructive.

I tried to prepare the "strong one" for testimony. She wouldn't say what most victims do: "He raped me"; and she wouldn't say it the clinical way: "He put his penis in my vagina." She insisted on saying: "He fucked me." We talked about that—it was going to be a problem. I explained how it would sound to a jury. She said she understood. When she testified, though, she used the word *fuck*—it was important to her. The jury reacted about as I'd predicted.

The other roommate did a little better than anyone expected. She wasn't consistent on cross, but since she'd made no lineup identification, there was little damage she could do.

I'd prepared the jury not to like my victims. It wasn't just that the two roommates presented problems. I always laid this groundwork for jurors. I asked during voir dire (jury selection): "As you sit here right now, do you have a picture of what the victim in this case is going to look like? Or act like? I'm not saying anything at all about the victim in this case, but supposing when she walked into court you said to yourself: 'She's really ugly!' Would you think that no one would rape her? Or supposing you thought she was really pretty. Would you say to yourself, 'She must have been asking for it?' Do you understand that anyone could be raped? Supposing you were selected for this jury and you listened to all the testimony and at the end of the entire case you thought, 'I can't stand that victim.' If you were convinced the defendant was guilty, would you still vote to convict?"

I had enough problems with the case without giving the jurors permission to bring all their prejudices into the jury room with them. I probably overdid it. I emphasized the issue so much during voir dire that when the jurors actually heard the roommates, they seemed surprised that there weren't more problems with their testimony.

The third rape victim's testimony was as powerful as I'd hoped. She was strong and credible and sure it was Barnes. During my direct examination, it was going great. The statement Barnes had made to her about the two prior victims would tie the cases together.

Then the judge made a ruling that crippled my case.

I suspect because of what the judge considered racial overtones (but for no reason I ever really understood), he wouldn't allow the third victim to repeat what Barnes said during the crime, that he'd already raped two white girls in the same neighborhood by crawling in their window. There were no legal grounds to exclude the statement. The judge ruled it was "too prejudicial." The jury wouldn't know now that all three rapes *had* to have been committed by the same man. Now I had a one-witness identification trying to carry another case where the victims had split on identifying the defendant.

I added what I could to the lineup identifications.

During the pretrial investigation, I'd sent the rape kits to the Criminalistics section of the police lab. (The slides and swabs in rape kits are automatically tested by the police lab as soon as the police officer or detective notifies Serology of an arrest. The combings of head hair and pubic hair aren't tested without a specific request to Criminalistics.)

I came up lucky. One of the pubic hairs from Barbara's rape kit looked like it wasn't hers. I sent her for combings and got a court order for combings from Barnes as well. The lab did comparisons. The hair was consistent with Barnes's. They couldn't say it was a match, but it could have been his. It wasn't much, but it was something.

Juries want something more than a lineup identification. This is what I had to give them.

I also had the three victims identify Barnes's voice in court. With the nonidentifying roommate, the defendant at first refused to speak and then tried to fake a nasal voice when he finally did. His evasion and deception were more incriminating than the victim saying it was him.

I put one of the roommates' fathers on the stand. After the rape, the roommate had called home. Trying to protect his wife from being disturbed, her father answered on the second ring of a too-late-at-night phone call. His heart ached even before he heard his daughter's tearful voice: "Daddy, Daddy—" He waited, not breathing. "I've been raped."

When I prepped his testimony for trial, the father cried repeating the conversation. He told me that he would never forget that phone call as long as he lived. He made sure that the jury didn't either.

The victims' testimony had been emotional. The father's testimony upset the jury almost as much. One of the observers in the courtroom told me, by way of friendly advice, that I was "overtrying" my case. I'm not sure there is such a thing. But I agreed with him enough to fore-shorten the rest of the immediate-outcry testimony. It was enough.

I put on the detective to describe the lineups, wrapped up the details.

On the defense case, the attorney called the stand-in from the lineup who'd been identified by one of the roommates. Whatever the strategy was, it backfired. Not in the lineup photo, but in person, the stand-in looked remarkably like Barnes. Seeing the two in the same courtroom, the jury understood how the misidentification had happened.

But as much as the defense was identification, that issue wasn't what I was most afraid of.

That trial was the first summation I did without notes. I had no choice. At the beginning of the summation I told the jury I'd typewritten out what I wanted to say. I held up the sheets of paper so the jury could see. Then I put the stack face down and told them that I wasn't going to use notes, that if the verdict depended on "my ability to put two words together, then there's something wrong with our criminal justice system."

It was a dramatic gesture to get their attention. After I'd done it, though, I had a moment of thinking to myself, "What the hell am I going to do now if I can't think of anything to say?"

The moment passed. It came to me.

You heard from the victims in this case.

I listed them.

And they told you about being robbed and burglarized and raped and sodomized. And they told you that that's the man who did it.

I pointed to Barnes.

If they can't convince you, ladies and gentlemen, nothing that I can say can convince you. I want you to ask yourselves this, ladies and gentlemen: What is it that you want? If not the testimony of these three victims, what is it that you want? Do you want this defendant to come into court with a black hat and wear a snarl on his face and have dramatic music come up every time that you see his face? That's not going to happen. You can't tell by appearances.

Appearances were lies. Barnes sat in court looking sweet-faced and well groomed, submissive—waiting for another chance to stalk the night.

As long as I was on the topic of appearances, I threw in an issue of my own. It had been on my mind during the trial. The defense attorney was female. It offended me that the fact that a woman was representing this rapist might lend credence to his case. She had to be as afraid of this nightmare as I was, as any other woman I knew was—of being alone in the dark, awakened by a stranger with a knife, a rapist. Yet by her physical presence next to him, the defense attorney was saying to the jury, "See, there's nothing to be afraid of here." I wanted to put the lie to that silent message.

When I was a Legal Aid attorney, I remember an old war-horse of a public defender explaining to us the "Lifesaver" theory of defense. You sit next to the defendant throughout the trial, he said, and whenever the jury is in the room, you feed the defendant Lifesavers. That makes it look as if you like the defendant, and he won't seem so intimidating to the jury. When I first heard the theory, I thought it was funny and clever. It lost its humor when applied by a woman defense attorney to a rapist.

I warned the court officers before summations what I was up to, so they could arrange the chairs and make sure of security. Now I walked over to Barnes, put a hand on his shoulder, and tried not to grimace while I said:

You can't tell, ladies and gentlemen, just because defense counsel is willing to go up to Eric Barnes and to be seated next

**to him, just as I am right now, you can't tell, ladies and gentle-
men, that that's any kind of doubt that he's a rapist.**

Barnes shuddered when I touched him. The feeling was mutual.

**In this country, we don't decide if somebody is a rapist based
on their appearance in the courtroom. We decide based on
only one thing, and that one thing is evidence. And the evidence that we have in this case is from the victims.**

**What do you want? What are you going to require beyond
them telling you that he's the man who did it? Are you going
to require that every rape victim have an Instamatic during the
rape so she can show you a picture . . . of her rapist? Or are you
going to take their word for it? You can say to yourselves,
having heard the evidence in this case, you can say to yourselves that there's a possibility. There's always a possibility of
something. . . . I want you to look to see if you have a reason
to have a doubt.**

Then I went through all the issues that the defense attorney had raised
during the trial and her summation and explained why they were not
reasons to have a doubt. It is easy for a jury sitting as outsiders, watching
the trial like it was a TV show, to intellectualize a "reasonable doubt."
It's especially easy when the defense is based on identification. No one
wants to believe they're sitting "up close and personal" with a rapist,
even in a courtroom with court officers all around.

As always, I was more worried about the issues the defense hadn't
raised but may have tapped into—the pool of excuses, sympathy, and
tolerance for rapists that was more dangerous than any single perpetrator.
I tried to confront them.

The courtroom was crowded for the verdict, with the merits still being
heavily debated by the spectators. No one doubted that Barnes was
guilty. But they doubted that the jury would convict. The foreman read
the verdict: Guilty, as to all counts, Guilty.

At the sentencing there was no crowd. The victims were there. They
had asked to be.

The defense attorney and I made impassioned statements—a lot was at stake. As far as I knew, Barnes was the first defendant in the state eligible to be sentenced to the new maximums. He was a young man, in his early twenties. Even with the new maximum, he would see the parole board when he was in his forties. Anything less than the maximum was unthinkable. I'd submitted a brief to the judge on the new law and on consecutive sentences. This was a tough sentencing judge. I wanted to make sure he knew he had the ammunition.

After the attorneys had their say, the judge spoke. He was eloquent. He spoke slowly and deliberately and with great dignity. He quoted from another legal proceeding where these words had a very different context, but what he said to the defendant was, "I cannot find it in my heart to forgive you." The judge imposed a sentence of thirty to ninety years imprisonment. I knew it still translated to twenty-five to fifty, but it sounded awfully good when the judge said it.

While the judge was handing down his sentence, one of the roommates, the "strong one," started to cry. At first it was just sniffles, but then it turned into sobs. Once she started, all the tears she'd held in since the rape poured out of her. It was finally over.

I probably should have taken a break after the Barnes trial. I probably got too taken with myself. It was overly ambitious to start a trial on the other pattern rapist, in front of a weak judge, with only the weekend intervening between the two. But I'd flown the victim in from Israel on a promise to both her and the judge that we'd finish the hearing (where her testimony was necessary) and then go to trial immediately afterward. It wasn't just a "firm trial date" (which is only as firm as the judge). It was a commitment. I kept my word.

Trials vary in the degree of animosity between the lawyers. Prosecutors have to learn how to be effective no matter where in that spectrum a particular trial might fall. I learned that lesson the hard way.

The judge did not control the attorneys in his courtroom. That's fine when both sides fight fair, but it is a serious handicap when one side resorts to dirty tactics. This defense attorney was from the school of Legal Aid attorneys who demanded that the rape kit be produced in court on every sexual assault trial because of an apocryphal story about a Legal Aid attorney who had found a pair of suggestive underwear in the kit and waved it in front of the jury, supposedly inspiring an acquittal.

I had to watch the lawyer every second. Too much my anger at defense-attorney sleaze was fueled into ignition by frustration with the judge for not curbing him. Even in jury selection we spent a lot of time in flare-ups.

It didn't take me long to realize that I was spending too much energy reacting to the defense attorney, getting diverted from the prosecution itself. He made me angry, but reacting to him was a luxury I couldn't afford. I told myself it was *my* courtroom. I had to take control of what was happening. I had a tough one-witness-identification case to try. I needed to concentrate on the issues.

The victim's testimony was wonderfully powerful. I was afraid at first that she was going to be too unemotional. She was trying so hard to be tough, especially in front of the defendant, that she wasn't letting her feelings show through. Juries hate that. They want to see rape victims cry, and don't trust them if they don't. I don't manipulate victims into crying, but I do talk to them about showing emotion and tell them that it takes real strength to let a jury see what's inside, what the rapist brutalized by his crime. I thought this victim did that. After the verdict, some court officer said her testimony was "too good." What do people want from rape victims?

The defense attorney treated the trial like a chess game. During his summation, he read from my summation in the Barnes trial. He predicted to the jury that that was what I was going to tell them in this case. What a fool.

During my own summation I embarrassed myself. I was telling the jury that the defendant had had his turn, up on the roof, to be in power, to be in control, but that it was not his turn anymore. When I said that last part, I started to cry. Maybe I really shouldn't have been doing so many back-to-back trials. The only thing that made me feel better was that the defense attorney accused me of having staged the tears.

Jury deliberations went late. The jurors were sent to a hotel overnight.

When I woke up the next morning, my eyes wouldn't open. My husband rushed me to an emergency room. It turned out to be a combination of exhaustion and an allergic reaction. Even after the medical treatments, my eyes were all runny for days. I worried that I looked too vulnerable to the jury, not confident enough during testimony readbacks.

I brought the victim in the second afternoon of deliberations, to remind the jury silently how they'd felt during her testimony. It's not something I usually do, but I didn't like the questions the jury was asking. It was worth a shot.

None of that mattered. After what was now becoming the usual three days of deliberation on my cases, the jury acquitted. I knew that it was a one-witness-identification case to them (they never got to hear about the other parts of the pattern). The five alibi witnesses hadn't helped. But I worried that the animosity between me and the defense attorney had affected the verdict.

I asked the jurors. They said no, that they knew that no matter how much we fought, outside the courtroom we shook hands and were friends afterward. I told them, "No, we didn't." They didn't believe me. They were so wrong that it took me years to accept that they told me the truth about why they acquitted. They were genuinely unsure we had the right man.

Acquittals were always haunting. Even on convictions sometimes I woke up in the middle of the night cursing myself for mistakes I had made. Acquittals bred even more self-doubt. My husband told me I had to stop reporting verdicts to him as either "The jury convicted" or "I lost." I knew he was right. Trial lawyers who believe they're only as good as their last verdict have very short careers—unless they pick and choose real carefully what they're willing to take to trial.

Given the kinds of cases I was trying, I had to face plenty of acquittals. Mostly they amounted to the jury doing the wrong thing for lousy reasons. It was disheartening to watch a jury let a rapist go free because the victim was Hispanic, or because who could blame a teenage boy for whatever he did if a teenage girl visited him in his bedroom. But feeling disheartened can't mean the same as losing heart. Sex-crimes prosecution may be a war where we lose a lot of the battles, but it's one where we can never afford to surrender.

With all that was to happen, the one truth that remained more important to me than all the rest is that what the public is entitled to from prosecutors is not any particular verdict but the willingness to step into the ring again and again.

4

F or once I didn't follow the acquittal with another, immediate trial.
I needed to restore my energies and to take stock. I was growing increasingly frustrated with the Queens DA's office. In January I would be
completing my three-year commitment, and it didn't seem like my
career was going anywhere.

Whatever illusions I had when I started working in John Santucci's
office—and I admit there weren't many of them—had died in the face
of the everyday realities of big-city prosecution.

Appearances were everything. Santucci claimed that raises and promotions were dependent on "productivity," and left to his executives to
translate for the troops, that word meant "conviction rates." Within the
legal community, criticism of Santucci was common. Yet every year
Santucci's chief of trials announced that Queens had the city's leading
statistics.

Some of looking good by numbers is just plain hustle. Add pleas (no
matter how generous) to verdicts for an overall rate of conviction, and
any prosecutor can sound like a killer trial attorney.

Confusing sentencing laws and lazy reporters combine to mislead the
public even further. Actual sentences are far shorter than they seem.
"Life" is not the same as "life without possibility of parole," and most
lifers in fact serve less than fifteen years. Five terms of ten years each
sounds like fifty years, but if a judge imposes the terms concurrently, the

real sentence is only ten years. And even where a judge imposes consecutive rather than concurrent terms, there may very well be an obscure law on the books that limits the actual maximum aggregate to far less than fifty years. In New York sentences are even more confusing, since the judge names a minimum and a maximum term of incarceration—so that a sentence will be something like six to eighteen years or ten to twenty years imprisonment. Even these numbers are not what they seem, since "jail time" (credit for preconviction incarceration) comes off the minimum and "good time" (the prison's reward system for good behavior while incarcerated) comes off the maximum. The net effect is that the public is deceived into believing that criminals serve far longer sentences than they do.

District attorneys use these illusions to enhance their public images.

The worst danger is that beyond the hustle, deifying statistics sets prosecution policy—rewarding prosecutors with high conviction rates but no moral convictions, no agenda beyond personal ambition. No district attorney is required to prosecute every time a citizen complains to the police—otherwise there couldn't even be the pretense of investigation. But no one except the victims sees which cases are declined, and victims are rarely in a position to complain. Headlines come from botched cases . . . not aborted ones.

For example, it was not in the Queens DA's statistical self-interest to prosecute William Porter. Anyone looking solely at likelihood of conviction would have sent Laurie packing the first time she contacted law enforcement. And that action—which certainly would have exempted a rapist from consequences, and might well have resulted in Laurie's death—would never have appeared as a negative statistic.

If prosecutors decline all cases without incontrovertible proof, they can ensure that conviction percentages will be in the high nineties. (Given the jury system, absent corruption no verdict is guaranteed, so district attorneys don't aim for 100 percent.) The trade-off is that if cases are evaluated solely on the basis of likelihood of conviction, then the dangerousness of the offender or the predatory nature of the crime becomes secondary.

Even this amoral framework for case selection requires some competence—the ability to recognize probable convictions. The most common criticism of the then-chief of Special Victims was that she didn't know how to evaluate a crime. Her bureau indicted cases that were unprovable. Other cases that should have been indicted were dismissed. Years later I prosecuted a defendant, George Chavis, for beating a three-year-old to death. It wasn't the first time. Chavis had beaten another three-year-old into hospitalization, carved an X in his forehead, and left him for dead. The old Special Victims Bureau agreed that the case should be dismissed "in the interests of justice."

Scandals about Special Victims kept hitting the papers.

From the day I was hired I'd heard rumors that the chief of Special Victims was about to get "her" judgeship (presumably meaning that she was sufficiently politically connected to get appointed as a criminal-court judge by the mayor). Santucci seemed to grow increasingly dissatisfied with her, to the point that he was considering demoting her if she didn't leave the office. Still, nothing happened.

When I was hired, I'd asked Santucci if he would ever consider me for chief of Special Victims. He said I had to earn it. That was fine with me, but so far nothing I did seemed to be getting me any closer to that goal.

There were interim promotions I could have received. Plenty of other people had been promoted to the supposedly elite "Major Offense Bureau," with a healthy salary increase to go along with the transfer. I was still in the same general trial bureau where I'd started. I was the only woman in the bureau. They treated me like a mascot.

I tried speaking to Santucci but he wouldn't see me. He had his executive assistant in charge of trials find out what I wanted. The executive told me that Major Offenses was not a promotion.

Things got worse instead of better.

I was reassigned to a new judge who was notoriously unjudicious and inept. She had a habit of putting everything she did on the record, including when she took court breaks so that she could go shopping or to her hairdresser. She once interrupted an extremely serious plea negotiation to tell me that I had very green eyes. Her conduct was so bizarre that I took it into account when I decided on plea offers. With a judge this outlandish, I wasn't about to risk any rape trials. I left most of my caseload in Kew Gardens. I pleaded out what I could of the rest. My offers were so generous on the nonviolent crimes that at one point the judge told me (as always, right in the middle of a plea conference), "You're not so tough. Everybody said you were so tough, but you're not so tough. You're a sweetie-pie." A lot of people think soft-spoken means soft.

I complained about my Long Island City assignment to the chief of trials, often. He told me that he was on my side, that he kept telling the DA to promote me, to Major Offenses or even to chief of the Special Victims Bureau, but that the DA didn't think I was "ready" yet.

I tried the second trial of the second pattern in front of a different judge. Opposing me was the same sleazy defense attorney from the first trial. The victim had seen the rapist's face only in the flare of a match when he lit a cigarette after he raped her. Still, she was sure the defendant was him. The jury convicted despite both the defense attorney and the judge.

I had a long talk with the victim afterward. She was convinced that the path to safety was to avoid all black people, since that was the race of her rapist. I tried to explain that she couldn't afford that kind of prejudice. It put her at risk to all rapists of any other race. I went through the arrest photos in my case files with her. Look at these defendants: all types, all colors, all ages, all races, all economic status. You can't tell by looking. You have to find other ways to make yourself safe. I don't know if talking to her did any good—other than that she appreciated me going to the trouble.

There *was* one (at least initially) encouraging sign from Santucci. He asked me to be the first person in the state to videotape a child's grand jury testimony.

In the fall of 1984 there were a number of changes in New York State's laws that made it easier to prosecute sex crimes against children. As a general rule, New York requires grand jury testimony by the victim as a prerequisite to indictment. One of the new laws permitted prosecutors to videotape a child's testimony rather than requiring children to testify live before the grand jury. Children still had to testify live at trial, but this was a start.

There was a delay between passage of the videotape legislation and the date it became effective. A month before the law went into effect, a four-year-old girl was abducted and raped. The crime was all over the papers. Witnesses came forward. It turned out that the perpetrator had tried to abduct a thirty-one-year-old woman, who'd escaped. He had also tried a teenager, but she had managed to jump out of the car at a red light. Then he'd found the four-year-old, playing in a yard, out of her mother's sight for only seconds. The little girl was too small to run away from him. When he was through with her, she needed reconstructive surgery.

Afterward, he called his girlfriend, who was in the hospital. He bragged to her, laughing, "I just had a piece of ass and it was really tight."

Once they caught this subhuman, it turned out he was wanted by all sorts of law-enforcement agencies, so bail and the normal time constraints on quickly indicting defendants were not an issue. He wasn't going anywhere. Santucci decided to be the first district attorney's office in the state to use the new videotape statute. This would be the case.

I researched the statute, virtually memorizing it. Then I told the technical department what equipment we needed, and they promised to get it. Sure, no problem. The district attorney himself wanted this videotape.

I contacted one of the city's leading experts on sexually abused children. She gave me step-by-step instructions on what to do and say with this child, how to act, how to structure my interviews with her, what toys to use. It wasn't that this would be the first child victim I'd worked with. But it would be the first time I worked with a child from the beginning, before mistakes were made. I wanted to do it right.

I followed the instructions to the letter. The first time I met the little girl was just to get acquainted. I showed her the toys I had with me. We played a little and talked. I explained ahead of time what each of our meetings would be about. Each time she knew in advance whether she would have to talk about the crimes, exactly what the meeting would consist of. I always kept my promises. After each meeting I called my expert and double-checked what I'd done.

The little girl made it a lot easier on me. She was very smart—and patient with me when I wasn't. She interrupted my incompetent simplification of videotape technology by explaining that she'd already been on TV. I asked her when and she told me about being a flower girl at her uncle's wedding. She was indulgent. She understood that grown-ups still thought videos were high-tech.

The morning of November 1, 1984, the law went into effect and we were ready for it. The little girl was saddened to be talking about the crimes, but not afraid, and not surrounded by strangers. Having made sure ahead of time that she liked this, I gave her a big hug when it was all over. I told her she was great. She beamed proudly for a moment and then turned serious to ask me, "Why did the bad man do this to me?"

I didn't have an answer. For a moment I cursed myself for not having thought to ask my expert how to answer *this* question, but I still had an expectant little face looking up at me. I simply told her, "Because he was a bad man." I told her we could talk about that more if she wanted to, but she didn't. Maybe she understood I didn't have any better answer.

As proud as I was of the videotape, I knew it hadn't advanced my career. In the process of taping I'd gotten into a head-on confrontation with the executive assistant for investigations. Sure, doing the job right was more important than making friends in high places. Still, I was frustrated that the Queens DA's office always seemed to confront me with that choice.

I waited. I visited the chief of trials again. Nothing.

Finally, a few months shy of the end of my third year at the Queens DA's office, a transfer list came out with my name on it. I was assigned to Major Offenses.

While that transfer was pending, one of the golden boys in the office, David Finkel, came to me. He was leaving for greener pastures and had two pattern cases he was prosecuting. Would I take them over? Yes.

The first one was Robert Mitchell, the Flushing Meadow Park Rapist, the one who was getting all that press when Eric Barnes was stalking Briarwood. The defendant had been arrested with much fanfare and a lot of proof, but the case had fallen apart by the time I inherited it. Most of the lineups had been suppressed—I couldn't use that testimony at trial. The file offered no clues about where to find several of the victims. Two of the cases had already been tried (one of them twice). The results had been two hung juries and a mistrial. I'd inherited a mess.

The other pattern rapist was Emanuel Santana, the Astoria Rapist. Prosecuting Santana was an opportunity: Maybe someday I'd be able to explain bad men to a four-year-old child.

Studying rapists wasn't a pastime for me. It was a way to compensate for inadequate investigations. Sometimes it was the only way to understand the truth about a crime.

Representative of the way the old Special Victims Bureau investigated was their response to a teenager who reported that she'd been fondled by one of her regular baby-sitting customers. The surrounding circumstances sounded improbable, but the baby-sitter's mother, by the force of her own personality, convinced Special Victims to indict.

The baby-sitter did give a lot of detail, including where in the house the defendant kept the gun she said he'd used. If there had only been a search warrant, there might have been one verifiable aspect to the crime. Instead, all I had was a disturbing sense of doubt.

The teenager had reasons to lie initially and a background that made it possible she might invent such a story. Sustaining such a lie was different, but there were reasons why she might do that as well. Until she reported the sexual abuse, she'd had a rocky relationship with her mother—normal adolescence. Since the report, the mother had been everything the teenager wanted: loving, supportive, demonstrably and loudly on her daughter's side. Her mother's support was well-intended, but it left no room for recantation if that's what her daughter wanted to do.

Interviewing the baby-sitter, checking the facts and details, all that I came up with was that I couldn't tell.

I reinterviewed the teenager, this time for background on the defendant. She said he wasn't the respectable businessman he seemed. She gave me the name of the bar he hung out at and the places where she said he dealt drugs. I sent out a detective—no one at the bar seemed to know the defendant. Queens Narcotics didn't recognize the locations I gave them either. They agreed to send out undercover narcotics officers to try to make a drug purchase, and they set up surveillance at those locations. Nothing. These seemed to be some of the most drug-free locations in New York.

I complained to a detective I knew about my lack of investigative skills. He didn't have any new ideas, but he gave me a new insight. He said when you've done a thorough search, sometimes finding nothing means finding something. Maybe there was no information to be uncovered.

I went back to the baby-sitter with the results of my investigation. She said the cops didn't know who to ask. Like everything else she told me, it could have been true.

Even now, I don't know what was the right thing for me to do with that case. What I did was go to trial. The jury at least treated the case with dignity, but they acquitted. The teenager's mother told me it was because I stopped believing in the case. Actually, the jury acquitted because the defendant gave a much more persuasive explanation of why the teenager would lie than she herself gave of why what she said was the truth. But the mother's words haunted me into elevating investigation even higher on the scale of what I thought was important for a prosecutor to do.

For all the TV shows that feature cops, and all the pious proclamations from trial attorneys about doing their homework, investigation is always the stepchild of the criminal justice system. Everybody wants the action.

I didn't find that sex-crimes investigators were substantially different from other detectives. Some were stupid; a few had a genius for the work. Some meant well; others were collaborators. Most of them worked hard; those who didn't were shockingly lazy and proud of it. The only difference with sex-crimes investigation was that more harm occurred when the job was done badly.

Much of the work was robotic. Take the complaint. Have the victim look through mug shots. Go to the last known address of anyone she picks out. Put that person in a lineup, make the arrest, and close the case.

I'd learned over the years how to clean up after such arrests: Find out who had seen the victim a few days *after* the crime and saw the bruises that didn't show up in the emergency room records; check the 911 tape and track down the neighbor who had called in complaining of screams in the playground. Some evidence was inevitably sacrificed by playing catch-up, but often I had no other choice. The detectives I respected most usually did this work prearrest on their own initiative, and were always willing to do the extra, unglamorous legwork it took to track down more proof.

But there was a more fundamental form of investigation that didn't presume a goal of making an arrest or adding to the witness list at trial. Sometimes to solve a case, or to win a trial, the investigation has to start with looking for the truth.

The criminal justice system is so time-pressured that this form of investigation is rare. Often there's a limit to how much truth you can find, or need to find. Like with Eric Barnes. I knew what he was—I never found out how he got that way. It disturbed me that the few pieces of the puzzle I had made it look as if one day Barnes was a citizen and the next day he was a rapist. I knew that couldn't be true, but I couldn't find enough of the pieces to controvert it. I sent to the army for records—nothing. No one could tell me anything about where he grew up or how or give me any insight beyond what he did the summer he invaded Briarwood. Talking to the rookie showed me enough of Barnes's evolution to resolve any doubts about him being the right person, but not enough to understand it.

I had a new opportunity with Emanuel Santana. His life was spread over stacks of institutional records. His soul was smeared across years of crimes, stained in the lives of his victims. If I could look at it all, maybe I could understand it.

I started with the detective, George Greene. He hated Santana. I wanted to know why.

Greene and I went back a ways. There were detectives I'd worked with enough so that there was an easy friendship between us. With Greene, it was more like an uneasy friendship. Something about his personality made him hard to read—I could never even tell when he was joking. Still, I had real respect for Greene. I had prosecuted enough of the cases he arrested to know the sincerity of his sympathy for sex-crimes victims and his enmity for rapists. And over the years he'd done some genuinely creative detective work.

One of our cases together involved a predatory pedophile who had accosted a small boy in the rest room of a burger joint, orally sodomized him, and then thrown a dollar bill at him, ordering him not to tell anyone. The boy had immediately reported the crime to his family, who followed the molester out of the restaurant and flagged down a passing patrol car. The cops made the arrest and brought him to Queens Sex Crimes Squad.

Greene read the prisoner his rights, and the freak answered: Yes, I want to make a statement; I didn't do anything; you got the wrong man. The detective made no comment, just continued with printing the suspect and filling out the police paperwork to process the arrest.

After writing for several minutes, Greene put down his pen and extracted a dollar bill from his pocket. He ceremoniously opened a plastic bag, put the dollar bill inside, took out some baby powder and tapped it into the plastic bag. Greene sealed the bag, shook it up a few times, then reopened it. He pulled out the bill and put it on the desk next to the freak's fingerprint card. Greene retrieved a magnifying glass from his desk, then looked in turn at the two items on his desk. Then he turned to his detective partner and said, "It looks like we've got a match here."

The freak piped up, "O.K., O.K., O.K.! I did it, I did it, I did it! I'm sorry! I need help!"

We won the pretrial hearings on that confession (although the judge got distracted with whether it was the dollar bill thrown at the child or not) and the case was eventually sustained on appeal. The higher courts understood that the detective made the whole thing up. They just decided that even though it was not permissible to trick a defendant into waiving his right to remain silent, once he'd agreed to make a statement, it was all right to trick him into revealing the truth. The jury didn't care about any of the technicalities. When they heard the confession, they convicted.

George Greene and I didn't always win. There'd been one case that had been dismissed in the middle of the trial by Judge Soleil, the Long Island City judge I liked so much. That was back when the law in New York required corroboration whenever the victim of a sex crime was a child. The judge had let me put on the entire People's case. She'd warned me before I called the (then) five-year-old that it didn't sound like I had enough legally sufficient proof. The parents and Greene and I wanted to take the chance. The little girl did fine with telling the jury what had happened to her. But she got confused on cross-examination by questions like "Did he have a mustache?" (because she didn't know what the word meant). The testimony convinced the judge that there wasn't enough corroboration in the case. She dismissed. I know it was a hard decision, and Soleil made it based on what she thought the law was . . . I still think she was wrong.

I always thought Greene blamed me for that dismissal. Maybe it was just that I blamed myself. Now we put all that aside. I wanted Greene's investigative report on Emanuel Santana. He told me what he knew.

There were two pattern rapists preying on Astoria in the fall of 1983. The police believed (and it later turned out to be accurate) that one of them was Hispanic and the other a Greek national. The rapists' descriptions were similar, although their crimes were not—one of them beat up his victims before he raped them. The other one had his knife, and didn't choose to use his fists.

Greene had been assigned both patterns. No one could know for sure that there were two perpetrators until one or both of them were caught. One victim was particularly certain of the nationality of the rapist. The detectives credited her accuracy because she was Hispanic herself. When she identified someone in a lineup, the Sex Crimes Squad checked him against both sets of crimes. He didn't fit. Officially, they took that case out of the patterns. Greene never believed it.

The rapes continued over the course of the fall of 1983. With so many violent crimes concentrated in one neighborhood, the police presence there intensified. In early December there was a 911 call moments after a rape. Half the precinct responded. A sergeant and his driver cruised the area. They found a man fitting the description. He gave an alibi that didn't check out. They brought him back to the scene, where the victim identified him. It was Santana.

After the prisoner was transported to the precinct, the sergeant notified the Sex Crimes Squad. Greene was off duty. The first responding detective was someone who specialized in serial rapists. Nobody thought the rape that night was an isolated incident. But they weren't sure at first how much they had.

The detective checked the prisoner's record. Santana had a prior conviction for first-degree rape and assault in Manhattan. He'd served about six years and had been released just weeks before the pattern in Astoria started.

Santana gave a statement. Coupled with his record, it was what made the detective notify Greene.

Santana said he worked two jobs: a nine-to-five job in a Queens recycling plant and an evening job as a security guard in a Manhattan grammar school. (That fact always horrified me. It was true that as the night guard Santana had no access to students, but even a minimal background check would have told the school system they were hiring a paroled rapist. And the board of ed in New York City has certainly seen enough security guards wind up in front-page headlines to know that rapists seem to love that job.) On the previous day he'd worked at the plant and then visited his wife in the hospital between jobs. He returned to Astoria at around ten-thirty at night, stopping for only a few minutes in his apartment before going out to a local bar. He was supposed to meet a date there, but she never showed. He waited for a while, went home, then returned to the bar. As he was leaving the second time, the police stopped him.

By the time Santana wrote out and signed this statement, Greene had arrived at the squad and been briefed. He requestioned Santana and got essentially the same information. This time Santana refused to sign off on what he'd said. The hostilities between Santana and Greene had already begun.

Santana had intended his statement to be neutral, uninformative, but he made one mistake. Bragging about how hard he worked, he'd told them about the job in Manhattan. That detail could unlock the whole set of crimes.

The pattern had been distinctive, with each rape occurring about a month after the last. November was the exception, with no sexual assault that sounded like it fit. But a few blocks away from where the other crimes had been committed a woman was found near death in her car. The interior of the car was covered in her blood—her throat had been slit. She was rushed to the hospital, and somehow she survived.

Later she told the detectives what she could. She'd gone to her car in a parking lot in Manhattan. She was alone. She had started to put her key in the lock. Someone grabbed her from behind. She struggled, but he had a knife to her throat. He forced her into the car. She fought him, knowing what must be coming. That's when he slit her throat.

She wasn't sure of everything after that. She remembered him shoving her over to the passenger seat. He drove. At some point they went over a bridge. She thought she must have lost consciousness for a while. When he finally stopped the car, she knew she was too weak to fight him. But he didn't do anything. He just left her there . . . to die.

When Santana said he worked nights in Manhattan, the detectives checked it out. The details fit like handcuffs. The school was near the parking lot. He got off work just in time. He would even have wanted a ride to Astoria at just about that hour. Her car had been found just blocks from his apartment. If you forgot decency and morality, it was almost a "logical" crime.

It didn't make sense that he hadn't raped her. If they could ever get him talking, they'd ask him why.

The Sex Crimes Squad arranged lineups. Greene knew it was unorthodox to include the woman who had already identified someone else in the viewing, but being unorthodox was one of his strengths. His victims identified Santana. Greene told Santana the results.

Santana wanted to make a deal.

He offered to plead guilty to felony assault charges if they'd drop the rapes. He was told "no promises." Santana wanted to know exactly what charges there were. He upped the offer: He'd plea to robbery one, but no sex crimes.

Greene wanted a confession, not negotiations. First Santana had to admit to what he'd done. All right, yes, he was the guy. There'd been others besides the one last night—a "tall white woman" and a "short Hispanic one." The woman from Manhattan? Yes, that was him. He had meant to rape her. But she got so bloody he lost his desire.

Greene tried not to react. He tried not to show how nauseated he felt that Santana's reaction to someone's bleeding from a mortal wound was that it was a "turnoff." Greene wanted Santana talking. Later there would be time for judgments—legal as well as moral. Making Santana pay was a goal worth keeping him talking now.

By then Santana was being his most cooperative. The way everyone told it, Santana was the nicest guy in the world when he wanted to be. Actually, what the defense attorney later told me was that except when he was raping, Manny was one of the most likable people he'd ever met.

While Santana was in the mood to negotiate, Greene asked him what had happened to the jewelry he'd stolen from his victims. At first, Santana gave him a long story about a "fence" in Brooklyn named "Edgar," address and last name unknown. He offered to give information on homicides and gunpoint burglaries in which large amounts of cash had been taken. Greene listened. Nothing checked out.

Greene asked again what Santana had done with the jewelry and the other things he stole. Santana said he'd thrown last night's purse into a dumpster. Which one? He described the location. Greene tried to have the dumpster searched, but it had already been emptied.

Santana admitted that some of the jewelry was still in his apartment and described the locations where it was stashed. Greene got a search warrant. It turned up jewelry and other stolen property from each of the rape/robberies, plus a few items the detective could never match up to a known crime. He asked his prisoner about it, but Santana was getting tired of being a nice guy by then.

Greene had what he wanted—enough to wrap up the cases. He started the booking process, letting Santana know it was over. Santana had an answer. When the detective dropped his prisoner off at Central Booking, Santana bragged to him, "I'll never do a day in jail."

Greene asked me to take care of Santana's victims, especially Maria. She was fragile. Once I met her, I understood why Greene was so concerned. Maria was easy to worry about.

Santana's victims were an unlikely mix. Beth was tall, slender, elegant, very matter-of-fact. She had a lot of questions and was the one silently delegated by the group to be their spokesperson. In some ways it was Beth I always worried about the most. She was so methodical, so sensible about it all that I worried that someday she was going to start to scream and never stop.

Kerri was the opposite of Beth, everything on the surface, raw. Pain and heartache didn't have any place in her life, and she didn't know what to do with them when they came to her. She wanted to be back in her own world, a rock-music video technician, full of fun, with cropped hair, blue jeans, and whatever outrageous look struck her fancy at the moment—not sitting in my office talking about being raped.

Maria was small-boned, soft-spoken with delicate, exotic features and a shy, sweet bearing. She wasn't sure she had the strength to prosecute.

There is something about working with a group of victims of a pattern-rapist. It's like they've all seen the same face of evil. Listening to them, I started seeing it too. Later on, the defense team spent a lot of energy trying to convince me I just didn't understand Emanuel Santana. I thought I knew him better than anyone.

The first time I met Beth, Kerri, and Maria, they were feeling abandoned. I tried to talk it through with them. I explained my own background, how I'd specialized in rape prosecutions for several years, how their old assistant district attorney had come to me and asked me personally to take over this case because it meant a lot to him. Eventually they relented a little, but not before extracting a promise from me that there wouldn't be any other change in prosecutors. At the time I made that promise, I thought the trial was imminent. I was wrong.

Santana was too clever for that. He'd had years to practice, to prepare to beat the system. It was right there in his institution records, starting with his first conviction for rape.

The prison records contained only sketchy information on that crime. The victim was a woman Santana knew through her boyfriend. He tricked his way into her apartment with a story about the boyfriend being in trouble. She trusted him up until the moment he hit her over the head with an iron; before he raped her and robbed her. At trial he used an alibi defense and invented a convoluted story to explain why she would lie about him.

The crime must have been even uglier than what was in the files. Santana was sentenced to close to the maximum, and denied parole the first time around. (Manhattan sentences tend to be lower than those of other counties in the city, particularly for first offenders. And there is all that prejudice against treating it like a "real" rape when the victim is acquainted with the defendant.)

Santana used his time in prison. He took courses in law and psychiatry. He made the obligatory visits to the prison therapeutic staff. He knew the parole board would want some expression of remorse from him. He admitted the robbery, denied the rape.

Despite his show of cooperation, Santana was a problem inmate, with frequent infractions of prison rules. The records noted that he was manipulative, had trouble with authority. Later, psychiatric institutions would say the same things about Santana. He was always up to something, always playing one person off against another; he always had an undisclosed agenda. The psychiatrists complained, even in official reports, that he was manipulative.

Santana had a bad habit, once the game was clearly up, of flashing his defiance. Once, when he'd given up on getting what he wanted from one particular psychiatrist, he told him, "You do what you have to do, and I'll do what I have to do." The psychiatrist noted that statement in his report. It was vintage Santana.

Juries let too many things get in the way of conviction on sex crimes for me to believe that there are easy rape prosecutions. But if any pattern-rape prosecution looked strong, it was Santana's case when he was first arrested. None of the standard defenses would work. The victims were all respectable and articulate, middle-class and presentable, strangers to the rapist and willing to testify—everything a prosecutor would look for from a victim. There was plenty of medical evidence to prove it was rape. The rape kits had all come up positive for sperm. He'd used a weapon. The woman with her throat slit had come close to dying. He'd robbed all of his victims. Consent certainly wasn't going to be an issue. Between the lineup identifications and the recovered stolen property, the false alibi he'd originally given, the conflicting statements, and his ultimate confession, there wasn't much of an identification defense, either.

Maria *had* identified someone else in a lineup, who'd been indicted before Santana had been picked up. (That's something I kept reminding myself of later, whenever I was investigating a claim of misidentification.) But Santana had admitted to raping the "short Hispanic one." Her jewelry was in his apartment. When she saw him in the second lineup, she knew she'd been wrong the first time and this really was the one. Her original misidentification would create a little snag at trial, but nothing fatal to the prosecution. It could be explained.

Everything taken together, it looked at the outset like *People* v. *Santana* was a winner, one of those cases that would go to a golden boy in the office—it offered lots of good press, terrible crimes, and a good likelihood of conviction. The golden boy they gave it to was Finkel, the one who eventually asked me to take it over, but that wasn't until a whole lot of things had gone wrong.

The first break for Santana was a gift from the arraignment judge in supreme court: When plea negotiations broke down because the People demanded too much time, the judge dismissed the attempted murder case, claiming that only New York County (where the crime started) had jurisdiction over the case. I've never agreed with his interpretation of the jurisdiction law. (It was certainly not the only time I disagreed with that judge about a rape case. He was the judge who'd tried to undercut the plea on Shelvie Harris, and the trial judge on Johnny Washington.)

I hadn't been prosecuting Santana at the time, or I would have tried to appeal the dismissal. Finkel had just referred the case to Manhattan, and they indicted Santana there.

All along, Santana was looking for a way to minimize the consequences for himself, to play one end of the criminal justice system against another. When he wound up prosecuted by two different counties, he thought he might have found the edge he needed—somewhere in the middle. He was damn near right.

Santana waited until the pretrial hearings were over, when he knew just what he'd be facing at trial. Most of the proof against him was admissible: the physical evidence from the search warrant, at least as to Maria's case, the identifications, the confessions.

Santana tried plea bargaining again. He was a predicate felon (previously convicted within the past ten years), which meant he'd have to serve more of a sentence than otherwise, and he still owed parole time on his first rape conviction. But if Manhattan would give him low enough time, he'd see what he could squeeze out of Queens. He played the system back and forth for a while, but the numbers were just too high. He was facing too much time.

Since none of the three standard defenses for rape would work in his case, Santana took a drastic fourth option—one that might not get him entirely off the hook, but had its advantages. Santana decided he was crazy, "not guilty by reason of insanity." If a jury bought it, he would do "softer" time (in a psychiatric institution instead of a prison) and it would be up to psychiatrists, not the parole board, when to release him.

The defense retained a psychiatrist who came up with a diagnosis: Santana raped because he was compelled to rape. "Poor impulse control" was what made Santana a rapist. The only problem with that diagnosis was that it was not a defense to rape in New York State. It could be said about any rapist. This diagnosis, "rapism," is a favorite of some psychiatrists, and plays into popular perceptions that rapists are sick (implying that treatment will cure them). So far, it has not been recognized by either the psychiatric profession or the courts as a mental disease. ("Rapism" is not included in the *Diagnostic and Statistical Manual,* which is an official compilation of recognized psychiatric diagnoses. But the *DSM* is a political document, revised to reflect societal attitudes about such issues as homosexuality, so there is no assurance that "rapism" will not be included in future editions.) At the time, though, Santana might have been crazy by his retained psychiatrist's standards, but not enough to get him off.

Santana tried claiming he was too crazy even to go to trial, that he was not mentally fit to assist in his own defense. Even if he were successful in convincing the courts of this, it wouldn't get him off the hook, but at least it would buy him some time—and maybe save him a lot of it. His attorneys requested court-ordered mental examinations in the Manhattan and Queens courts. The psychiatrists disagreed with each other. The judges ordered hearings. Santana went on a hunger strike. The psychiatrists in Manhattan advised their court that Santana was unfit. Santana resumed eating.

When the psychiatrists sent word back to the Manhattan court that the hunger strike appeared to have been a ploy, and Queens notified Manhattan it had found Santana fit, the Manhattan court reopened its hearing.

The trials were approaching, and Santana was running out of options. He swallowed a razor blade. It was a standard jailhouse ploy: File the edges down to dull them, coat the blade with Vaseline, swallow it, then have it show up on an X ray. It worked.

The Manhattan court abided by its original position. Queens ordered a new hearing and did an about-face. According to the Queens judge, Santana was so depressed over the prospect of spending so many years behind bars that he was too despondent to assist in his defense. Santana had what he wanted—findings in both courts that he was unfit.

I took over the prosecution of the case a little before Santana swallowed that razor blade. The setup in the Queens DA's office was that the Forensics Bureau handled all the hearings on defendants' mental status. They kept telling me everything was going fine, that no judge was going to find anyone unfit based on depression. I kept asking them to get me a trial date—waiting was hard on the victims.

Forensics needed reminding. What happened in court was always all about Santana. Somehow his crimes and the people whose lives he traumatized were getting lost in the shuffle.

I was the one who had to tell Beth, Kerri, and Maria that Santana had been found unfit to proceed. It was hard to explain. There's no good way to tell someone their court case is in limbo, that it all depends on some psychiatric institution upstate, that if and when Santana was ever found fit, I would still need their testimony to convict him. I did the best I could. They didn't like it. Who would? But they agreed to prosecute if there ever was a trial.

So it ended with a gesture of courage, and I boxed up the file.

Afterward, I worried about having made a promise that I might not be able to keep. My own future at the Queens DA's office wasn't all that secure. If I left, I would somehow explain it to Beth, Kerri, and Maria. For now, they had enough uncertainties without me adding another.

Major Offenses *had* been a promotion, but it had also been a step back. Very few of my cases were sex crimes, and the majority of those, like the Flushing Meadow Park Rapist and Santana, were ones I'd taken with me when I was transferred. For most of the Major Offense caseload, it didn't make a difference who the prosecutor was. Either there was so much proof a moron could have gotten a conviction or else the case was indicted (despite a gross lack of proof) because the defendant's record was so bad.

Major Offenses was divided into teams of two ADAs who were supposed to share responsibility for their caseload. My new "partner" creamed all the winnable cases and called in sick any time a problem case was on the calendar. He bragged about a 100 percent conviction rate. Mistrials and give-the-courthouse-away pleas didn't show up on his statistics as acquittals. But he had a more important skill: He spoke fluent Italian. Rumor had it Santucci had him translate all the letters he got from the old country. The only time I got to speak to Santucci was to take messages to have my partner come up and see him.

I did a gun-possession trial. The defendants had long sheets for violence. The cop claimed he'd seen one of them give or sell the gun to the other. My new partner, or one of his cronies, had done the hearing. The transcript had the cop seeing things he couldn't have seen. The defense capitalized on that during the trial. The jury didn't much care, but as far as they could tell, there wasn't much to concern themselves about in the whole case. They weren't allowed to know the defendants' records. What's one more gun possession in New York City? I worried I would get a "who cares?" acquittal.

The day I was to sum up, I had the court officers watch me while I checked the gun and made sure it wasn't loaded. Then, when I started my summation, I told the jury that the case was very simple. "The People claim that this gun [I picked up the gun] was possessed by [I walked over to the defense table] these defendants. [I put the gun down on the defense table.] That's the crime."

I walked away, and all hell broke loose. The judge dove for cover behind the bench, screaming, "Take that away, take that away, take that away!" The defense attorneys ducked under the defense table. All the court officers rushed the defendants—who actually just sat there, paralyzed by surprise. The jury got the point that these defendants possessing a gun was not a "who cares?" proposition. They convicted.

The judge on that trial was notorious for believing that it wasn't rape if the perpetrator and the victim knew each other. He made a point of communicating his opinions to juries (who, inexplicably, liked him). I'd seen that once for myself, the hard way (with two little street-tough victims I'd convinced to trust the system this one time). So I felt some satisfaction when the judge yelled at me that I'd "compromised the security in his courtroom." I told him I'd made sure, in front of the court officers, that the gun wasn't loaded. The officers confirmed that. The judge had to settle for admonishing me never to do that again.

The defendants *were* bad guys, dangerous, so I felt some satisfaction in the conviction too. But not enough. I had stopped being a defense attorney after I stopped believing in what I was doing. I didn't want to feel the same way about being a prosecutor.

When my three-year commitment to the DA's office was over at the beginning of the new year, I made the decision to test the system. I'd always heard that only politically connected people got judgeships, especially in Queens County. There were a number of people in the DA's office then, such as the chief of Special Victims, who talked about "their" judgeships, waiting for appointment by the mayor as though it was a birthright. I decided to request the judgeship application papers from the mayor's office.

I had put in my ten years as a practicing attorney, which was the only fixed requirement for a judicial appointment. I'd been a public defender, I'd been in private practice, and I'd been a prosecutor. I'd tried something like a hundred felony cases. On paper I was as qualified as anyone else, a lot more qualified than the people in the DA's office waiting for what they considered their due. Maybe I could at a minimum make it more difficult for unqualified people to be appointed over me. Maybe I even had some kind of chance of getting a judgeship. And maybe, just maybe, I could force Santucci's hand and become chief of Special Victims.

An hour after I submitted my request to the mayor's office, I got a phone call telling me Santucci wanted to see me.

Because it was hard to match my trial recesses with Santucci's availability it took a couple of days before we had our meeting. I apologized for the delay. I was in the middle of trying the Flushing Meadow Park Rapist (the other pattern Finkel had given me—the one that had been tried three times so far without a conviction).

Santucci offered me the position of chief of the Special Victims Bureau. He said he would have done it sooner, but the chief of trials kept telling him I wasn't ready. Santucci told me he wanted the bureau to be a model for the country. I don't know how serious he was when he said that. I know I meant every word of it when I promised him it would be.

Between being offered a job I'd only dreamed of, convicting the Flushing Meadow Park Rapist, and my husband selling his first novel, the last week in January 1985 was one hell of a week.

Part Three

SPECIAL VICTIMS

© 1989 *New York Newsday*/Richard Lee

Photo accompanying a November 12, 1989, *New York Newsday* article entitled
"A Prosecutor's Best Friend"

1

The first time I walked into the Special Victims Bureau as its chief, I thought I was prepared for how much work it was going to be. In fact, I had no clue. Up until then, all I'd seen was the end result: the prosecutions I'd had to rescue from botched indictments; having to investigate months after a crime (and after the witnesses were already committed to their grand jury testimony) because no one had done their homework up front.

I wasn't prepared for the fact that, given its organizational structure, it was amazing that Special Victims functioned at all. There were no work assignments. Postarrest case files piled up on any semiavailable desk. ADAs took the files they felt like taking. A woman who'd flunked the bar several times and was supposedly only a clerk handled the rest. There was one pending investigation going nowhere. There was one half-time investigator. There was no training, no skills, and no accountability.

I called a bureau meeting and told the staff we were going to change everything about SVB (the Special Victims Bureau) except the name, and even that was open to suggestions. No one responded. Much later, one of them told me they were all terrified of me. At the time I thought they were just comatose.

I started with the basics. I created systems, forms, I taught the staff fundamental skills. All of that was just a predicate. Professionalizing the Special Victims Bureau was only the first step.

Santucci and I both wanted a radically different SVB. Santucci changed chiefs because he wanted a Special Victims Bureau that would try sex crimes, not just indict them. I wanted the position because I thought I could do better.

It wasn't just sex crimes, either. I started with the premise that traditional prosecution methods didn't work with any of the crimes the bureau handled. Initially, the bureau prosecuted six types of crimes: sexual assault, domestic violence, offenses against children and the elderly, and those involving schools and religious institutions. Later this was cut back to only the first four categories, but the challenge ahead was still huge. If I wanted to do the job right, it was time to innovate.

I made myself a promise that I was going to make at least one major change every day until the bureau was what I wanted. It was over half a year before I could ease up on that promise and cut back to one major improvement a week.

Some of what I did I knew was against office policy. I told the ADAs to forget conviction rates. There were two rules in the new SVB. Investigate—find out first what you had. Then, once you knew you had a bad guy—go after him with all your guns blazing.

The only way to teach the ADAs what that meant was with specifics, like trial strategy. One ADA had problems communicating with a jury because she tended to overintellectualize. Her heart was in the right place, but she wasn't effective. I told her to get up at the beginning of her summation and picture to herself that the jury had just returned a Not-Guilty verdict . . . and then to tell the jury exactly what she thought of what they'd done.

Another of the ADAs didn't need that lesson. Her first trial, the jury acquitted a therapist of having fondled one of his special education students. The boy had difficultly communicating; the adult was glib. When the ADA told me the verdict, I asked her if she'd stood up. She answered: Oh God, I was supposed to stand up when the foreman said "Not Guilty"? I told her: No, no, just tell me what you did afterward, and she said: I walked over to the defendant and I pointed a finger at him and I told him, "I'll see you again." So I told the ADA not to worry about it, she had stood up.

I couldn't count on all the ADAs being like that one. SVB becoming a vertical bureau meant that it was a place for ambitious people who wanted to bypass the normal route to becoming a supreme court trial attorney. That didn't bother me. I never objected to anyone doing the right thing for the wrong reason. But I needed to make sure nothing else got sacrificed to ambition. Supervision seemed like a delicate compromise between encouraging creativity and assuring competence. It was difficult to know when to trust the staff to know the right thing to do—and to do it.

I got so attuned to an uphill struggle that it took a hurricane to make me realize I was making progress.

It was storming badly that morning even before I left home early, caught a bus instead of walking, and trudged the two blocks from the bus stop to the courthouse. I figured I'd spend a few hours working alone— who else would be stupid enough to be there? The city never officially closed court that day. The courthouse was open but empty. No warrants were issued; even defendants were excused because of the weather. The hurricane was in full force by normal working hours, one by one almost every Special Victims ADA showed up.

One of the ADAs brought cookies, and we made the hot chocolate that we normally saved for child witnesses. We listened to the wind and radio reports of the hurricane. Somehow, everyone at SVB wound up staying in my office, or coming back to it after working an hour or two in their own cubicles. We talked mostly about work and cases, a little bit about ourselves. I told them about the most fun I'd ever had in court.

It was my last trial as a Legal Aid attorney. The prosecutor was arrogant and pompous and looking to make a name for himself in the Manhattan DA's office. During jury selection he literally told prospective jurors, "I may be an assistant district attorney, but I still put my pants on each morning one leg at a time."

The case itself was a run-of-the-mill robbery with an abundance of proof. The only reason the ADA turned down all plea offers and insisted on a trial was that it would be perfect for his conviction rate. The crime was a mugging on Wall Street, during a blizzard, with plenty of upstanding citizen eyewitnesses all willing to testify for the prosecution. They had chased down the perpetrator and caught him with the goods, and he had confessed and offered to return the proceeds. Even the judge knew why this case was going to trial and just whose ego it was massaging.

The trial was endless. By the time summations came (four weeks later, for what should have been a one-week trial), I had lost my battles with the Legal Aid Union and my client was buried, but at least we were both going down with a lot of flash.

By this time *everyone* in the courtroom, including the judge, hated the prosecutor.

The jury was out deliberating. Given the evidence, that should have taken about six minutes, but the jurors shared the general animosity for the ADA so much that they wound up spending over six hours before finally figuring out there was no way to convict the prosecutor.

While they were deliberating, the ADA came running into the courtroom, purple-faced, demanding the presence of a judge and a court reporter so he could "go on the record." When everyone was assembled, he announced, "I was in the hallway, and I overheard two court officers talking, and I heard the phrase 'that fucking ADA' and they were talking about me! I want to object. I want to object! There were no jurors around [in fact they were deliberating on a different floor], but there could have been. And, Judge, I want you to reprimand these court officers, and I want this to go on their permanent record because this was an outrage!"

While he was ranting, the court officers were standing behind him, fondling their weapons. He showed his usual sensitivity by not noticing his impending danger.

I got up and requested permission to respond, which the judge granted. "Your Honor, I have been here all along. I overheard everything said that could be overheard by anybody. And I did not hear a single soul utter the words 'that fucking ADA.' I didn't hear anyone say, 'that fucking asshole' or 'that fucking prick.' I didn't hear anyone say, 'that whining shithead' or any similar phrase. I didn't hear anyone say . . ."

I went on like that, on the record, until I'd exhausted every single curse word and insult I'd heard in my life. By this time the judge was laughing so hard he had to excuse himself from the bench. While I'd been talking, the court officers had collected all their brother officers to hear this (they used walkie-talkies because no one was willing to miss a word), so I got a round of applause before the judge returned to the bench to say, with as straight a face as he could manage: "Well, you've both made your records, and I think that's a sufficient remedy."

The ADA paid me back by saying something vile to me after the jury reluctantly convicted. I don't even remember anymore what it was, but I do remember my husband, who'd kept me company waiting for the after-hours verdict, holding me off the floor by my elbows, my feet still going, while I begged him to let me hit the ADA just one time. Years later I asked my husband why he'd stopped me, and he said simply, "Because he would have pressed charges."

The ADAs at Special Victims weren't used to a defense perspective or a bureau chief telling trial stories. I was still feeling my way around this new job. This time it felt right.

The hurricane taught me something about us all working together. I started trusting the staff more. To show it I started a tradition of throwing an annual party to announce and celebrate awards that the bureau staff voted each other for their accomplishments. The award itself varied from year to year, but it was always some form of star. Whether it was a silver necklace or a gold stickpin, it was a badge of honor . . . shared pride.

By then there was a sense of excitement in Special Victims about the work, about the future. The bureau even *looked* different.

We had new quarters on the ground floor of the Kew Gardens DA's office. They were rat- and roach-infested and periodically plagued by flooding from the ceiling. Compared to our old quarters, we were stepping up in class.

I convinced the office to hire exterminators. The rats moved to more welcome areas of the courthouse. The mice moved in, and stayed. The city wanted to put down glue traps. I said no. I wasn't going to have screaming glued mice in the place. The mice agreed to keep a low profile. The roaches thrived on the city's low-bidder insecticide sprays. We all bought commercial roach bombs and did the job ourselves.

I took on the city over the leaks. There were four floors above us. This stuff pouring in couldn't be rainwater. The Department of General Services told us (unofficially) that it was the Department of Corrections's fault. The DA's office was sandwiched between the Queens House of Detention for Men on one side and the criminal courthouse on the other. Just above our ground floor was a transport corridor for prisoners, with pens that included bathroom facilities. The inmates would stuff the toilets, they would overflow, and liquid waste would flood into Special Victims.

The Department of Corrections said (unofficially) there was nothing they could do. Inmates would be inmates.

I called the Department of Health. They found no health hazard, no "cause for action."

The flooding got worse. People had to use umbrellas to negotiate the corridors. There were pails of standing water everywhere. It was nauseating to know what this stuff was.

We knew that the ground floor had flooded like this for years. But still, we couldn't just accept defeat, even by the city's bureaucracy.

The detective/investigators documented the leaks with photographs and reports. The Civil Forfeiture Bureau researched whether we could institute suit, and Santucci agreed to sue Corrections if they didn't fix the problem. One of the executives wrote a letter of complaint to one of the directors for the Department of General Services. I wrote a formal letter of complaint to the Department of Health, threatening to go to the media or to institute suit, sending copies to the mayor, the warden, and various commissioners.

The Department of Health issued violations against the Queens House of Detention for Men. General Services budgeted and scheduled repairs. The captain at Queens House called me. Why hadn't I just asked him? He'd be happy to do anything he could to help. The policy on inmate transport was altered.

The leaks stopped. First every couple of months and then about once a year they would recur. Then they stopped for several years at a time.

We picked the nicest space, and the only one isolated from flooding, and designated it a playroom. There were a lot of children at the bureau for one reason or another. Some of them were there because they were victims of sexual or physical abuse or neglect. Some were there as witnesses to domestic violence within their families. A lot of them were there simply because, given SVB's crime categories, the majority of victims were women, and children just came with that territory.

The physical setup of the old Special Victims had sent a message to children that they were unwelcome. We had the playroom carpeted and shelves installed. Then we took the entire budget from a small grant the bureau had from the state and bought a year's worth of new toys.

We left the room open. At first we were worried that someone might steal the toys. But instead of toys disappearing, we routinely found sweet surprises in the morning: a box of brand new children's books; a baby doll with homemade clothes; hand-designed coloring books—all left there by different secret allies. I caught one once. It was one of the mail-room clerks, trying to sneak in a huge teddy bear. The teddy ratted him out.

The playroom looked beautiful for about the first week. Then two very abused and disturbed little boys visited with the adult temporarily responsible for them. The story that initially hit the newspapers was that the boys had jumped out the window because they were trying to fly, like Superman. It made a better story than the truth: They had jumped out the window to escape abuse. When we first saw them, they were still broken and angry. It took them less than an hour to total the room. They painted their names on everything. They Play-dohed all the working parts of all the toys. They ground all the crayons and chalk they could find into the rug. And *then* they started being destructive.

Later on it seemed like justice when their abuser, who had eluded police custody, jumped out a window to escape recapture. He wound up very broken too—and in prison.

We learned our lesson: Having an unattended playroom wasn't going to work. Abused children aren't all passive wounded sheep. Despite "Movie-of-the-Week" expectations, some of these children were very angry, and they found ways to express it.

Santucci agreed to hire an attendant for the playroom. One of the paralegals found someone whose own children were old enough not to need so much of her daily attention. Her first day on the job, the two of us cleaned the room top to bottom. We threw away anything damaged, replacing it from the store of toys and games too nice to be left out unsupervised.

After that, she kept the playroom spotless and well stocked. She started Scotch-taping to the windows drawings that children made while they were there. Initially she meant it simply as a privacy screen, but it didn't take long for all the walls to be covered. She grandmothered the place into a haven for little ones. We started to have a new problem: Children didn't want to leave the playroom when it was time to go home.

While SVB had still been relying on volunteers to staff the playroom, one of our sources was an agency for the handicapped. They had sent us a blind volunteer. Her handicap was not a problem, but she was afraid of children. When she left for new volunteer work, everyone missed her Seeing Eye dog. That got me thinking.

The SVB secretaries had talked me out of gerbils or goldfish for the playroom: too much work, too dirty and smelly, who would take care of them? I had read an article that said that the Seeing Eye Institute put up dogs for adoption: rejects (hand-raised puppies who turned out not to have the right temperament for guide-dog work) and retirees (guide dogs who had reached their tenth birthday and been replaced by younger, healthier dogs). I contacted the Seeing Eye Institute and registered. I wanted a retiree.

The Institute warned me that they didn't get retirees too often. They encouraged the blind people whose dogs they were to find them adoptive homes. It was only when they couldn't that the Institute took the dogs back. I said I would wait. A couple of months passed.

It was the week before Christmas when the Institute called. They had a retiree, a shepherd mix; did I want her? Yes. I drove out to New Jersey on Christmas Eve.

When I first saw Sheba, she was a sorry-looking mutt. They brought her into the kennel from some cages in the back. She ambled over, an old, tired wolf, her coat slack and limp instead of shaggy, peering up at me through white eyelashes and listless, cataract-dimmed eyes. Another dog barked at her. She glanced at him with disdain and backed under a table. They handed me her leash and I took her for a walk. She waited to see what I wanted from her.

We got stuck in gridlock traffic on the way back. The dog didn't react. She slept so motionlessly in the backseat that I kept checking on her to make sure she was all right.

I thought Sheba would perk up when I got her home, but she didn't. My living room was under reconstruction at the time, and she found some drop cloths in a corner and lay down on them. She looked so unhappy, so defeated, that I got some roast-beef scraps from the refrigerator. Sheba showed her first signs of life. She gobbled what I gave her faster than I thought possible, then gave me a tentative sigh of approval, as if maybe things weren't going to be so bad here after all.

I took her out to the yard and threw a ball for her to chase. She ran over to it, sniffed it to see what kind of food it was, then gave me a look of betrayal. It wasn't edible.

I was off for Christmas week and I spent it bringing Sheba back to life. All she wanted was food, sleep, and affection. I obliged her. I checked the medical records the institute had given me on her. She'd been kennelled for the past six months. They wouldn't tell me why or give me any other nonmedical information about her. It seemed like she'd gotten a lousy reward for a whole life as a guide dog. It was time for a second career.

After New Year's, I took Sheba to Special Victims. Walking to work the first day, there were icy puddles along the way. Sheba shoved me out of the way; I wasn't allowed to step in puddles.

Sheba had already adopted me as her person, so instead of leaving her in the playroom, I kept her in my office. She found a corner and went to sleep, a peaceful, silent presence. A clerk stopped by and accidentally stepped on her. (That turned out to be the only hazard of having Sheba around: She was so quiet she got stepped on a lot.) SVB's social worker ran across the Boulevard and bought dog treats. Sheba could live with that. Being stepped on was a small price to pay for a good snack.

The first day all Sheba did was meet staff and get used to the place. It was a lot of adjustment for an old dog. She was happy when we got home. What's for dinner?

By the next morning she was used to the routine. She'd memorized the way to work already. If this was where I insisted on going, she was prepared to guide me there. She was just disgusted with me for waiting for red lights instead of charging out when there was a break in traffic. The way she walked, it was like she was saying to the world, "Out of my way—there's an important person coming."

By the second day, I told the ADAs it was O.K. for them to bring children into my office to meet Sheba. The children who had dogs at home were comfortable with Sheba sooner than the rest, but just about all of them came around pretty quickly. They would toddle up to her, and when she just lay still, they would give her head a tentative little pat. She'd look back solemnly. Soon they would be telling her their problems. She was a good listener.

Sheba was also an excellent diagnostician. Most of the abused children she met were upset but not disturbed. Occasionally a child would visit whom the dog didn't trust. Sheba would patter over and sit near my chair, watching. Every time Sheba reacted to a child by being protective of me, it would turn out that the child needed serious therapy.

The first time I saw Sheba actually aggressive toward someone, I found out that her diagnostic abilities weren't limited to children. A stranger had stopped me in the street to ask about Sheba. It happened often—I was used to explaining that she was a retired Seeing Eye dog. This time the stranger leered at me. He said, "They train those dogs really *hard,* don't they?" It was obvious he enjoyed the thought of it. It was equally obvious that Sheba enjoyed the thought of tearing him apart limb from limb. I reluctantly talked her out of it.

At first (before Sheba had too many fans for this to be practical) I left my office door open all the time. Sheba wasn't going anywhere. People would walk by and see the dog sleeping and do a double-take. It wasn't what they expected to see in a DA's office. Many of them asked me if she was a stuffed dog. Sheba never got insulted. She just slept through that sort of stuff.

Originally, adopting a retired Seeing Eye dog had been strictly for the benefit of the children who had to be at Special Victims. It never occurred to me that adults needed her too.

With so many upset people around, it didn't take long for those who needed her to find out that Sheba was wonderfully comforting. There was something so calm and sweet about her that it made everyone feel better. Sheba didn't even extort treats from a lot of them, although she did try to communicate that she appreciated tribute. Her treat supply grew almost faster than she could consume it.

Sheba even got videotaped. The little girl testifying insisted on it. She would only talk if Sheba was with her. The video team set up in the video/interview room, with all the formalities that the law required for this taped grand jury testimony. Then we opened the door between the video room and my office, and Sheba sat at the door so the little girl could see her. With Sheba there to make her feel safe enough, the little girl was able to tell what had been done to her. Other children came up with the same idea. Sheba became a new kind of guide dog, through a darkness that was sometimes more frightening than blindness.

Sheba wasn't the only innovation we brought to videotaping. Because the process was brand new, it had a lot to teach us about creativity, and about finding unexpected allies.

There was a video team under contract to the DA's office—technicians with customized equipment mobile enough to set up wherever they were needed, who would respond regardless of the hour of day. The team taped defendants' confessions at the precincts. Once we discovered how kind they were to little ones, we "borrowed" them for SVB to videotape children's grand jury testimony.

There was a lot of resistance from unexpected sources to SVB using videotape so much. The Grand Jury Bureau hated it. Their court reporters complained that it was too much work to transcribe the tapes. The bureau chief complained that it was too time-consuming and he couldn't spare precious grand jury time on hectic days. Some of the Special Victims ADAs wanted live testimony from children, claiming it was easier to convince the grand jurors to vote an indictment if they saw a live little victim.

I met with what was referred to as "the counterparts," the women running bureaus similar to SVB in the other NYC counties. (Given city politics, being female was a prerequisite for the job.) I asked them when they videotaped. One of them said she only used video if the parents had heard of the law and demanded it. No one else had any more useful suggestion. Queens continued using videotape whenever it could.

A few months before I took over Special Victims, New York State had made another change in the law that drastically affected child sexual-abuse prosecutions. The old rule, that all such crimes had to be corroborated before a case could even be brought to court, was thrown out. The corroboration rule, by eliminating even the possibility of prosecution from the majority of child sexual-abuse allegations, had made it easy on DAs. They couldn't be blamed for not prosecuting—it was the law. I thought the new law meant that now prosecutors had to learn how to do the job.

There were new opportunities to do that. By 1985 the family courts in New York had begun to accept testimony on something called "validation." It was my husband who broke the ground with the leading case: done right, experts could corroborate whether abuse had occurred. When an expert "validated" intrafamilial child sexual abuse, s/he compared the symptoms that a child displayed to those that have been recognized as common among children suffering such abuse, to see if there was a match. It was like a psychological fingerprint of a crime. It wasn't a magic formula or a substitute for investigation, but like a competent medical examination, validation could give much-needed information.

Queens became the first county with a policy requiring validation interviews as part of the police investigation. It was a dramatic change but only one of many. SVB started to gain credibility for its investigations. Judges and defense attorneys began to understand that when we prosecuted child abuse, we meant it.

We found out something else about child sexual-abuse cases. I had believed for a long time that for many sex-crimes victims, regardless of the outcome of a trial, the act of walking into court was empowering. It was like saying 'I'm not a victim anymore.' What I didn't expect is that that would be true for children too. But many of them wanted to fight back, and a courtroom was a place where their size and age wasn't supposed to stop them from trying.

Elderly rape victims were the one exception. My experience was that regardless of crime, many elderly people are intensely frightened by going to court. With crimes as traumatic as rape, most elderly victims simply could not overcome their fears. As a result, the court system sees very few such cases and therefore mistakenly assumes that very few occur.

Sometimes I feel that teenagers are the population most often raped and least likely to get justice. Often they don't report because they don't see it as rape. And when they do report, they aren't believed. People don't trust adolescents about sex, and adolescents often don't trust themselves.

Adolescents are also the most likely age group to put themselves at risk for rape. I had learned early on with jurors that if the victim was a teenager, one of my questions in jury selection had to be "Did you ever do something really stupid when you were young? Did you ever put yourself in a dangerous situation?"

It's hard enough to overcome the "she deserved it" mentality, but many teenagers compound that problem by initially lying about how they got themselves into the situation in the first place. The rape allegation itself might be completely legitimate, but instead of admitting that she'd gone to the defendant's house voluntarily, the victim says, "He snatched me off the street in broad daylight and dragged me six blocks, up five flights of stairs, past his family and into his bedroom, and I was kicking and screaming the whole time." It's damn near impossible to get a jury past that story, to look at the actual sexual assault.

No matter what the fact pattern is, teenagers have a tougher time in court. In one case I tried, the victim was a newspaper-delivery girl. A customer had tried to molest her. By the time she testified, she was at that stage that some young women enjoy of being softly, breathtakingly beautiful. Although the jurors believed her, her appearance made them uncomfortable. They convicted the defendant of lesser charges, not the attempted rape.

There was even a study that said that, contrary to public opinion, people did not think children are generally untrustworthy when they made allegations of sexual abuse—but that teenagers are.

SVB tried to develop an expert who would specialize in teenage sexual-assault victims, to evaluate them for rape trauma syndrome and do a general investigative interview. Eventually we used the same experts we used for adult rape victims. Teenage sexual assault didn't seem ready to become a special area of expertise.

We had to be careful how we used experts and what experts we chose. For investigations, and to explain a victim's behavior to a jury, expert evaluations could be enormously persuasive. But even then there were developing classes, one of incompetents and the other of professional apologists, who were endangering the field. One so-called validator told children what to say. Child-abuse experts seem to divide themselves into two religious camps, one believing that children never lie and the other believing that children never tell the truth about sexual abuse—to the point where it was difficult to find an impartial expert. Even experts who work solely with adults, when they try to dispel myths about victim behavior, make it seem as if there is no reason ever to disbelieve a claim of victimization. Some of SVB's best investigations resulted in us deciding not to prosecute. A good expert could give us additional data to make those decisions.

Besides having rape victims evaluated for rape trauma syndrome, we had mentally incompetent people evaluated for their ability to "consent" to sex. We found doctors who could do adequate medical examinations of sexually abused children. We found experts in domestic violence and what was just then starting to be recognized as "elder abuse."

We hired the elder-abuse expert as SVB's new social worker. Santucci had created the slot shortly after I became bureau chief. The previous social worker's expertise was in child abuse. SVB was a nontraditional worksite for a social worker, and it took someone rare to be comfortable as part of a prosecutorial team. Before I found the elder-abuse expert, I interviewed forty-three social work candidates. All those interviews taught me a lesson: to make it clear that my job was to put rapists in prison. Anyone uncomfortable with that didn't belong in SVB.

SVB's new social worker didn't think there was a conflict between being sympathetic to victims and wanting predators incarcerated. She also had a lot to teach the bureau about elder abuse. The city was just beginning to notice the chronically mistreated elderly. For law enforcement, it was an easily overlooked problem. Old people can get injured in so many ways that unless investigators kept the possibility of elder abuse in the back of their minds, they didn't see it. SVB started seeing a lot of it. Queens was definitely the county in which to start looking. Although the borough has only about 20 percent of the city's population, 30 percent of New York's elderly live in Queens.

The first professionals to look at elder abuse made a terrible mistake. They equated it with child abuse, even implying that abused children grow up to abuse their parents. That theory may have a certain symmetry, but it isn't born out by reality. Elder abuse seems to be a form of domestic violence that occurs often between spouses more often by children, grandchildren, or caretakers who have a history of mental illness. Like all domestic violence, it is potentially deadly, and the victims tend to hide the abuse in shame.

There is a long list of SVB's innovations. SVB even turned out to be the first in the state—and I think the second in the country—to try a case in which the rapist was identified by his DNA. The police commissioner and two pattern rapists combined to make that not only possible, but necessary.

The old SVB had so botched the use of forensic evidence in identifying rapists that more often than not the fact that such tests existed was used as a *defense* tool. Defense attorneys kept asking juries why the state had neglected to perform things like electrophoresis (the technology then available to test semen deposits for identity). This wasn't an oversight that could be fixed by the trial attorney. Electrophoresis had to be done very early on.

The availability of sophisticated investigative tools is a tremendous advance *if* police and prosecutors have access to them, use them appropriately, and are prepared to explain to the public (and juries) why in most cases such techniques probably bear little fruit. When such techniques are used faddishly and ineptly, they cause more harm than good.

In the one case I got from the old SVB in which they'd used electrophoresis, identity wasn't even an issue. The victim had met the rapist at a bar, and it was true that there was some question as to whether she could identify him. But half the people at the bar had known the defendant for years and (when I asked them) were willing to testify that on the night she was raped the victim left the bar with him. The victim knew that the man she had left the bar with was the one who'd raped her. Special Victims spent almost six months delaying the case and obscuring the issues by testing blood, saliva, and a rape kit on a nonissue. After I told the defense attorney about the bar witnesses—and before he decided to plead guilty—the defense was transformed from identification into consent.

SVB's handling of forensic testing was one of the areas I was determined to turn around when I took over the bureau. We did improve the procedures for electrophoresis, but electrophoresis was still cumbersome and often impractical. It was DNA analysis that pushed the bureau to the head of the field.

DNA testing (to unravel the mysteries of the human gene) had already been around long enough to revolutionize medical research. Once the technology started outgrowing its infancy, scientists began looking into ever-expanding fields of application. Most recently scientists had been perfecting a means to identify individuals through chemical testing of the chromosomes within their body fluids.

Lifecodes, the leading private lab—which stood to make its reputation and a lot of money if the procedure was adopted generally by law enforcement—was pushing for ways to bring what they called DNA fingerprinting into the limelight. When the Forest Hills Rapist started makings headlines, they thought they'd found the way.

What the newspapers were headlining was a series of sexual assaults in an exclusive section of Queens, called Forest Hills. Sexual assaults in Forest Hills got a lot more ink than an average pattern. Then the politicians jumped on the story, holding rallies against a rapist . . . as if that would keep him quiet.

In fact, the crime methods and descriptions of suspects actually formed two entirely separate patterns. The perpetrators' races were not even the same—let alone the method of access to the victim, the weapon used, or the words said by the rapist.

So many sexual assaults happening in so short a time the two patterns going on at once—especially in an area that was generally considered one of the safest—made the entire city feel at risk. One rapist was burglarizing sometimes and other times preying on street pedestrians—doing both at night. The other rapist was hitting in the parking lots of shopping malls during daylight hours. It was right there in the headlines: Rape could happen anytime to anybody.

I don't know if the police commissioner thought he was calming the city by the press conference he held. I do know that several detectives told me he refused to be briefed on the patterns before he announced to the entire city that there was only one Forest Hills rapist.

It was the next day that Lifecodes contacted the Queens DA's office, volunteering to test the rape kits in the Forest Hills sexual assaults. If the tests were successful, they could prove whether there was more than one rapist. The lab's calls worked their way down the chain of command. We sent all the rape kits to them.

Eventually, both Forest Hills rapists were caught. The trial of one of them, Victor Lopez, marked the first time in New York that a jury heard testimony that the rapist had been identified by his DNA. The testimony by Lifecodes caught the public's attention. Santucci gave press conferences, relying on his high school science and a fictionalized account of the discovery of DNA fingerprinting in England.

The media became so fascinated by DNA that many of the issues surrounding its use got obscured along the way. My own impression didn't change much. DNA testing is a highly effective investigative tool, but it's only one tool. It is highly persuasive evidence, but it's only one piece of evidence. It's not what everyone seems to want: "the rape test"—the scientific one-size-fits-all substitute for sex-crimes investigation or juries having to make hard decisions.

There were no shortcuts. With the Special Victims Bureau's case load and my dreams, I needed an extraordinary staff. Since I didn't get to select the lawyers assigned to the bureau, what I wound up doing was convincing the people I had that they were extraordinary.

And to some extent, they were.

2

I knew Jim Jeffers was going to work out as a Special Victims ADA the first time I assigned him a case involving a child. It was a parental abduction. The father had snatched his little girl, a two-year-old who needed her asthma medicine, from a mother who now needed to know that her child was safe. The father refused to disclose the two-year-old's whereabouts. SVB got the call initially from the precinct detective unit.

I walked into Jim's office a few minutes after he'd succeeded in reuniting the mother and the little girl. They were outside hugging each other and crying. Jim was pretending he was busy with paperwork, giving them a few minutes alone. I asked him how he was doing, and he answered before he had a chance to think about it: "I'm on cloud nine." Afterward, Jim denied having ever said that. I guess it didn't fit his self-image.

Jim was a big, handsome man who easily qualified as SVB's most eligible bachelor. There were times that his penchant for dating women who worked within the court system (several of them simultaneously) caused a few less-than-comfortable moments on the unit. But it was always women furious with each other, not at Jim. Jim was so charming, and so candid about not wanting to limit himself to one woman, that they seemed never to direct their anger toward him.

It was important to me to have someone like Jim in the bureau. Sex-crimes prosecutors are so often typecast that units like SVB are traditionally staffed predominantly by women, preferably of diverse ethnicity, with a few "sensitive" token white men. Jim was black, self-confident of his manhood, and embarrassed whenever his heart showed too openly. He was exactly what I'd been asking for.

Jim's first big case involved the same cult that had picketed the Wendell Nance trial. By the time Jim's case broke, the Yahwehs had firmly entrenched themselves in Queens County. They had two temples. They were highly visible. And, as it turned out, they were dedicated to the ritual torture of children.

Fridays at Special Victims were rarely uneventful. No one ever relaxed and looked forward to the weekend until the four-thirty Friday-afternoon crisis was over. It didn't surprise me that the first call I got about the Yahwehs came on a Friday. But it did offend me that the emergency had actually occurred two and a half weeks earlier.

The call came from a casework supervisor at the local field office of what was then called Special Services for Children. (Whenever a scandal about the quality of New York City's child-protective agency reached crisis level, they changed the name. It's now called the Child Welfare Administration. Most people still call it BCW—the Bureau of Child Welfare.)

The caseworker had consulted with BCW's attorneys and finally decided they should tell law enforcement about a complaint they'd received: Two little boys had run away from a cult in Queens to their father's home in Brooklyn. They told their father about having been beaten and half-starved at the temples. The father rushed his sons to a Brooklyn hospital, where doctors found them malnourished, with whip marks and scars all over them. The hospital reported the case immediately to the Child Abuse Hotline.

A BCW caseworker visited the temple and found nobody there. She stopped by a few more times, same result. After a few weeks, she happened on a day when there were obvious signs of life at the temple, but still no one would let her in. She went to her supervisors, who eventually contacted the agency's lawyers for a court order to allow her access to the premises. It was the lawyers who thought someone should inform law enforcement. The casework supervisor was told to call me.

Child Abuse Hotline complaints in New York City are supposed to be referred by the local child-protective agency to the local district attorney, so that they can be investigated by the police as well as caseworkers. The initial screening is done by BCW. They have a list of the types of cases that qualify for referral. When this cult/torture complaint reached the hotline, the list included sexual abuse and various types of injuries. Mayor Koch later defended BCW's inaction on the basis that pouring hot sauce into fresh whip wounds wasn't on the list of qualifying injuries. The mayor wasn't even embarrassed to raise this as a defense to charges of incompetence.

I asked enough questions of my caller to know this was serious.

I assigned the case to Jim, with another one of SVB's more meticulous ADAs as backup. I called Queens Sex Crimes Squad. The two runaways, their father, the caseworker, and her supervisors were all brought to the DA's office and work got under way for the search and arrest warrants. Somebody notified Santucci. He called, suggesting I alert the night-court judge that the warrants were coming. It was an overly optimistic estimate of how long it would take to get the necessary information and to put the case together.

The warrants were signed around midnight. It had taken that long to process what these witnesses had to say. The two little boys reported an entire lifestyle of child torture. It was their mother who was a cult member. All of what was done to them and the other children was done with the blessing of the mothers in the church.

The children were sent out onto the streets to beg money for the cult. If they were caught keeping a few cents in their little pockets to buy themselves food, there were various forms of "punishment." The mildest was to be forced to stand for hours on a chair with arms raised. Crying didn't help. Appeals for help went unheard. Nothing stopped the "disciplinarian" once he had decided on a course of action.

Repeated infractions were grounds for "stoning," where all the cult members would get together and throw shoes or other objects at the offending children. This would be done as part of the religious services. For serious food stealers there were whippings, sometimes with ritual staves, more often with tree branches. To imprint the memory of the punishment on the child, whip marks were treated with hot sauce to make sure they hurt as much as possible. The entire temple joined in these activities, watching and approving if not actually participating.

The children were allowed only extremely limited food, generally one small meal in the late-evening hours. They were constantly hungry. There were numerous food infractions, and whippings were frequent.

These abuses were apparently unique to the two local temples. The nationwide organization of the Yahwehs did not insist upon such treatment of children. The church as a whole was silent as to how children should be raised. Before the current leaders had joined the local temples, the children had better lives.

What the runaways were saying sounded incredible. But it was all verified by their medical records and by their father, who had some tangential knowledge of the temple from his experiences trying to free his children from their mother. He had received death threats warning him not to interfere with the cult's operations. The caseworker verified everything that could be observed from the outside about the temples.

Even with all the criminal justice system's built-in prejudice against believing children, this information was enough to get the search and arrest warrants we needed. (Later on, the warrants were appealed as far as the state's highest court, which officially approved the work we did that night.)

Santucci called me for updates until two in the morning. Around seven A.M. he called to tell me he'd decided that I should appear at the press conference on the case.

Santucci's reputation was that he allowed no stars in the office. He was notoriously unhappy about any media coverage of the DA's office that contained a name other than John J. Santucci. Either this was a rare moment of generosity or Santucci was unwilling to be inconvenienced on a Saturday—or else he underestimated how big a story the case would be.

Santucci had no advice for me about the press conference, but he did direct me to announce that we were going to be investigating BCW for their delay in reporting the case to law enforcement. (That investigation was subsequently assigned to a different bureau in the DA's office—and went nowhere.)

The warrants were executed in a predawn raid on the two temples. The news stations had footage of stone-faced detectives leading white-robed and turbaned cult members into waiting police vans. The cameras also captured the recovery of the staves and other torture objects described by the runaways. It was good footage for a slow-news Saturday.

The press conference was slated as a joint one between NYPD and the Queens DA's office and was heavily attended.

This being my first press conference, I was completely unprepared for its intensity and chaos. Only two things helped me through it. One was that I had gotten so little sleep that I was too tired to be nervous. The other was a piece of advice from my husband, who has the skill to look completely comfortable being televised. While he was driving me to the precinct, he told me to just pretend the cameras weren't there.

When I got to the station house, the press conference was still being put together.

Another war about the Yahwehs was being waged within the precinct that was a more urgent emergency. (Special Victims taught people the need to rank emergencies.)

When the detectives had executed the warrants, they had rounded up all the white-robed people at the temple, scooping up as well any children they found there. Once they got to the precinct, they needed to sort out who were defendants and who were not, separate the children from the adults, get the children medically checked, and start all the various processing. To keep the peace pending these arrangements, the police placed the males in one holding cell and the females and children in another.

The detectives learned that one of the female cult members taken into the precinct was only a visitor, not involved in any known crimes. She had accompanied the temple members back from their recent trip to Florida. (Although everyone always suspected that this trip had been occasioned by the two runaways' successful escape, no cult member ever actually admitted this.) Two of the children were hers and another was an infant. All three of these children were in apparent good health. The detectives made the tentative decision to release the visitor with the three children.

The plan, after that was accomplished, was to separate the individual cult members and talk to them quietly, looking for statements that would support the runaways' account, detect additional abuse, focus on the primary actors, clarify the intermember dynamics within the cult. In the meantime, the detectives waited for an Emergency Services caseworker (the part of BCW that works nights and weekends) to approve the decision to discharge the children.

When he finally arrived, the caseworker thought he had a better plan. Maybe he was inspired by the power of speaking to "clients" who were behind bars (when presumably he could say whatever he wanted). Or maybe he just followed BCW protocol without adjusting to the circumstances. Whatever his reasons, he marched into the holding-cell area, and before anyone could stop him, he announced, "O.K. We're taking all your children away from you. These are your rights."

Child-abuse professionals often talk about an "interdisciplinary approach," in which law enforcement works with social work, medicine, and various other disciplines in a united effort to investigate and prosecute child abuse. Everyone agrees that's the way it should be, but it's taking a long time to get there. Cops have too many horror stories like this one. And caseworkers have comparable horror stories about police officers refusing to accompany them into dangerous situations to rescue a child.

Predictably, the cult's response to the caseworker's announcement was menacing fury. Single-handedly, he'd killed any opportunity to divide and conquer among cult members. All of the detectives' strategy had to be revised, the goals scaled down to bare minimums to avert disaster. Now the cult members were united against a common enemy sworn to take all their children away from them.

Tensions were so high that even fingerprinting and booking were going to be a problem. And now any police action would be time-pressured. The longer it took to bring these defendants to Central Booking and court, the more volatile the situation would get. No one wanted a physical confrontation with a bunch of incensed cultists, with children mixed in the middle, when the pen gates were unlocked.

Jim and the other ADA, the various detectives, the lieutenant, and I were forced to make decisions quickly. Who to charge with what was a matter of sorting through what the runaways had described and the people they described doing it. The observers needed to be distinguished from the participants. One of the worst of the abusers had stayed behind in Florida when the cult returned. Also left behind in that state were children whom the runaways had described as abused. Sorting it all out was additionally complicated by the fact that all the members of the cult used the last name Israel. Santucci's phoned-in advice was to charge everybody with everything.

By the time we made some progress with these decisions, the media was ready and waiting for us. I asked the lieutenant if he wanted to speak first. He looked at me like I was crazy and just shook his head no. Some official made a brief statement, I followed up with some details about the crimes, and the whole roomful of reporters started to ask me questions at once.

The crimes and the press conference got a lot of coverage. All of the major and local stations, and CNN (in a continuous loop replay), showed shots of the cult being arrested, the staves being carried out to police vans, me answering questions. It was an upsetting crime, and newsroom editors seemed to like me looking so upset about it.

As a result of the coverage we got an avalanche of information about the Yahwehs. When I'd tried Wendell Nance, I'd run a NEXIS report on the cult to get a computer printout of what had been reported in the print media about them. When the casework supervisor had first called me on the child-abuse case, I pulled this printout from my files. I updated it with a new NEXIS run the Monday following the press conference. I added in the data that was being phoned in from other jurisdictions.

The Yahwehs (also known as the "Black Jews") were a nationwide cult, claiming at times to be the lost tribe of Jews from the Bible. They'd tried locating in Israel but had been evicted for cult-related violence. Their central temple was in Miami, but there were news reports on them from several major cities across the country. There was one investigation for child abuse and neglect in Michigan, where sixty-six children were removed from the cult after a child had died from cult "discipline." The mother of that child was prosecuted for homicide. Everywhere and with increasing frequency there were rumors and reports of escalating violence by the sect. Other prosecutions involved various frauds. There was nothing directly bearing on the Queens case, but all of it was suggestive that these were powerful, networked, and highly dangerous people. Years later our impressions were confirmed when the cult's leader, Yahweh ben Yahweh, was convicted of homicide.

We'd taken all the precautions we could. Before the search warrants were even executed, we'd relocated our witnesses. Still, the threat of violence hung over the prosecution throughout the long months yet to come.

The case against the Yahwehs was probably over Jim Jeffers's head. SVB didn't have the depth of experience in ADAs that it needed, and I often had to choose the best of a very green lot. Despite my misgivings, Jim rose to the occasion.

The defendants varied widely in culpability. After the indictments and the hearings, the lesser defendants were permitted to plead guilty, according to how much they had actually participated. I fought Jim a lot on these dispositions. I didn't want to be lenient with any of these people. One by one he convinced me that he'd worked out the right plea for each of the lesser defendants.

There were two cultists who were the most responsible for the torture that had taken place in the temple. One was never apprehended. The other had to be tried. We wanted him in prison as long as the law would allow. Because these children survived, that wasn't nearly long enough.

In New York, child abuse is prosecuted according to the traditional assault statutes. That means that the degree of seriousness of the charge is almost entirely dependent on the degree of seriousness of the injury. Broken bones and soft-tissue injuries aren't worth much time in prison, no matter how chronic or repugnant the abuse. The New York State legislature has yet to enact legislation sufficiently geared to the crime of child abuse. We wanted to stretch the limits of how much punishment we could get for ritual torture.

The initial reaction to the Yahweh child-abuse case was what I had expected. What I hadn't expected was everyone's obvious disappointment that our major witnesses were two runaway little boys. Unless we could get more of the children talking, we were going to face an uphill battle at trial to get a jury past such disappointment.

The child who had the most information, who could give us the full picture of what had gone on at the temples, was the priest's grammar-school-aged son. Other children had come and gone, but he had been there for it all. The boy, Israel, was also the smartest and oldest of the children, but he didn't want to talk.

Jim did a remarkable job with Israel. The first time Israel's foster mother brought the boy to Special Victims, he was terrified. He was also hungry. Jim fed him cookies until he relaxed (and almost burst). Israel learned quickly to negotiate just how much he would open up based on how much food he would get. But he was very scared. Jim didn't push for information. He just wanted the little boy to start feeling safe.

Jim saw Israel regularly, trying to get to know him and to establish some trust between them. Israel would say something offhand every once in a while to let Jim know the runaways had told the truth. But it was always just a little bit. Israel had strict limits: He was ready to test, but not to trust.

The foster mother was wonderful. What upset her most was that Israel could never get full. (Her worry was exacerbated by the fact that BCW had told her none of Israel's history.) After the first few days of being afraid to eat anything, Israel ate like a starving person. Once he learned that he wouldn't be punished if he accepted offers of food, he wanted as much food as anyone would give him. He was skinny, but he wasn't in medical danger. The hunger was more in his heart than in his stomach.

The case dragged on. With fourteen lawyers for the fourteen defendants, the hearings took forever. Some pleas and dispositions had to wait until we proved we could convict the worst of the abusers, the one who called himself Yeshir Israel—the chief "disciplinarian" of the temple.

Jim walked into my office one day as upset as I'd ever seen him. He had a betrayed look in his eyes that was painful to see. The family court had decided to award foster-care custody to Israel's paternal relatives—the priest's family. The priest's liberty depended on the family convincing the little boy never to talk. Jim wanted to know if we could stop this, or do something about it. I told him to talk to the BCW attorneys, to Israel's law guardian (the attorney appointed by the court to represent the child in family court), to the family court judge if the judge would hear us. But I didn't hold out much hope. The law guardians in New York City are Legal Aid attorneys, prone to interpret representation of a child as trying to implement whatever wishes the child "expresses," even when those wishes are to return to an abusive family. BCW and family court had often shown a preference for placing foster children with their biological families. (Later this preference was codified into New York State law.) They didn't seem to view the practicalities of divided loyalties the same way we did.

Israel was placed with his paternal relatives and soon clammed up completely on the rare occasions when Jim managed to get him physically into the office. Before Israel was taken away from his foster mother, Jim hadn't understood that the so-called justice systems could throw children away. It was a hard lesson to learn.

In terms of the prosecution, losing Israel as a witness meant the trial would have to depend on the runaways. The other children were too young, or unfindable, or just too scared to speak. One of them had even apparently been spared of the abuse. All of the "discipline" had taken place at one of the temples. The other temple seemed to be mostly living quarters. A mother who wanted to protect her child could find a way to do so, if she was careful enough about it. Learning that made me blame the mothers who had acquiesced in the abuse even more.

It was a difficult trial. The audience was filled with white-robed supporters. The runaways were terrified. The truth was too big to have to depend on two little boys to tell it. Jim managed to get a conviction anyway.

After all the prosecutions were over, the remaining Yahwehs moved their temple just across the border into Brooklyn. Years later the Kings County DA's office called me about an investigation into more child neglect in the cult. You couldn't eliminate crime. But if you upped the stakes, sometimes you could move it—and make one limited place a little safer.

The Yahwehs moving out could have been coincidence, or could have been a sign that Special Victims was having a big-picture effect. Another "coincidence" was the pedophile who was on bail defending himself in two different jurisdictions. No problem—until his lawyer told the pedophile there were Sex Crimes detectives waiting in court to arrest him and take him to Queens. The pedophile jumped bail on the court break rather than appear in Queens. Maybe he'd heard about John German.

After the Yahweh case I had enough faith in Jim Jeffers's abilities so that when the John German case broke, and it was clear just how big it was going to be, I assigned the case to Jim.

3

Although I was unprepared for much of what would follow, I did
have advance warning of John German's arrest. There was a Pedophile
Task Force in New York City, a joint project between the FBI and
NYPD. The task force always notified me when they were investigating
something big, and John German qualified. He was the local Man of the
Year. As its director, he had taken the Flushing Boys Club and, according
to his press clippings, converted it from virtually nothing to a highly
functional and funded social and educational center for boys. German
was articulate and educated, with broad shoulders, an open, honest face,
and a "trust-me" demeanor. He seemed like the perfect "good cause"
for politicians to get photographed endorsing. (When his photographs
were seized by the FBI, the one on the top of the stack was of a grinning
Geraldine Ferraro and John German. German had his arm around two
of the boys later named as victims in his indictment.) His work for the
Boys Club was above reproach. It was his hidden agenda that was
criminal.

German was a pedophile. The Flushing Boys Club was the perfect
setup for him. He could spend as much time as he wanted in the
company of teenage boys, slowly drawing them out enough to cull the
vulnerable ones, the ones who were desperate enough for the trappings
of love to trade them for sex.

It was one of the Flushing Boys Club workers who broke the case.
This man was afraid of German—and afraid of the consequences of his

own actions. But it never stopped him. German tried to recruit another young staff worker to photograph sex acts between himself and some of the boys the club was supposedly helping. The younger staff member went to the one man at the boys club who seemed willing to stand up to German. That man went to the police. That's when the Pedophile Task Force got involved.

The arrest and search warrants were executed. Boxes of photographs (including pictures of several of the children from the Flushing Boys Club in sexual poses) were seized. German was arraigned in both the federal and Queens County courts (some of the boys had been taken on trips across state lines, but most of the sexual activity had occurred within Queens County). The case hit the papers.

I was in Borough Hall for a meeting the day the story broke. The local politicians, the borough president's staff, were white-faced. It had been less than a year since Borough Hall had been shaken to its roots. Donald Manes, the center of Queens politics and its borough president, had become the target of a corruption scandal. He first unsuccessfully attempted and then later died (in what was subsequently called) a suicide. His domain (the behind-the-scene dealings that had dominated city politics since he and Santucci had been ADAs together at the start of their careers) was jeopardized in ways that had seemed unthinkable. When German was arrested, Manes's death cast an even bigger shadow over Borough Hall. German was one of the local privileged—now behind bars for repugnant crimes.

While some of the shock waves of German's arrest were political, some were community-based. German was typical of the breed of pedophile who used trust and betrayal as weapons not only against the children he molested, but against their parents, teachers, and peers. Whether the molester was the basketball coach at a private school, a parish priest, or the neighborhood dentist, what SVB found over and over was that the arrest of a pedophile sparked shock and anger that bordered on disbelief. (If the case presented opportunities to blame or doubt the victims, it took very little to turn that shock into literal disbelief.)

The proof against John German was strong enough so that people couldn't doubt that the "Man of the Year" really was a monster. The disbelief turned into anger.

German retained a local Queens Boulevard defense attorney with a reputation for being effective in a courtroom. The lawyer came to me. He knew German had to do time, but may be we could cut a deal. German wanted to "spare" the victims of having to testify in the grand jury. How very generous of him. I named some numbers. They were too high for him. No deal. I assigned the case to Jim, to indict and then to prosecute in supreme court.

Jim came to me the day the case was scheduled for grand jury present-ment. He was unhappy with his victims. They weren't sweet little preteens. They were acting-out adolescents. Did I understand that?

I know I have a softer spot in my heart for teenagers than most people do, so I was patient with Jim, explaining that this is what he should expect from a pedophile as sophisticated as John German. Such people search out throwaways as easy targets.

I wanted to motivate Jim, so I alternated topics. I talked about what was heart-touching in boys so desperate for fatherly love that they would be receptive to the devil's bargain German had to offer. Then I reviewed the proof we had, the pictures, the legwork done by the Pedophile Task Force, the testimony of the worker German had tried to recruit.

Jim said he'd just wanted to make sure I understood about the victims. I did. He also wanted to make sure I knew the victims' ages. In New York, sex crimes against children are gradated in seriousness of punish-ment based on age ranges. The two most significant cutoff points for victims are eleven and fourteen. These boys were over the range for the two most serious levels of punishment. The crimes had taken place in an atmosphere that was more psychologically than physically coercive. It would be difficult to prove the "force" counts of sexual abuse. As a result, a judge who wanted to could give German probation.

Jim thought the numbers I was talking about for German were awfully high. It wasn't that German didn't deserve them, but was I being realis-tic?

I told Jim the Pedophile Task Force had done a good prearrest investi-gation, but they'd cut it short. German had been arrested, and the search warrants executed as soon as they had enough, since waiting any longer might have tipped him off. There was plenty left unlearned; Jim could take the case a lot further. There were probably more abused boys out there, and plenty more crimes. If we uncovered younger victims, a judge would have to impose mandatory imprisonment.

If not, I understood, we needed a strong judge who would be willing to impose consecutive sentences. All the press attention would help. What judge would be crazy enough to offer German short time or a walk with the whole city watching?

Jim indicted John German and the case was sent to the now-centralized arraignment part. There was a new judge in there, Stephen O'-Toole*. I didn't know him, but I'd heard he was good. In the meantime, Jim had a lot of background work to do. There was still an investigation to complete.

By then, about half of the Special Victims Bureau's ADAs carried vertical caseloads, meaning that they handled their cases from investigation through trial. Jim was one of them. Because SVB was always understaffed, all of the assistants, but especially the vertical ones, were impossibly overworked. I tried telling myself that that was why Jim was slow to investigate the rest of the John German case.

The defense attorney went to the arraignment judge with the same offers he'd made me. He understood the case was strong against his client. The feds were talking plea. If the numbers were right, the Queens case could be pleaded out too. Let's talk.

The case got stalled in the arraignment part in a "let's talk" mode. I'd been told by the DA's chief of trials that the guidelines for this new centralized part were that cases would only appear a maximum of three times before being sent to an individual part. This case wasn't being sent anywhere—John German wasn't following the guidelines. I guess that was his specialty.

I talked to the feds. So did Jim. They wanted to offer a plea I thought was way too low, especially since German fit every federal guideline I knew of for early release on parole. They were considering a plea of four years. They made it a firm offer. If I wanted more time, I'd have to get in on the Queens case.

I would have been happy to do that, but our case was still stuck before that arraignment judge, O'Toole. What *was* his problem?

I asked Jim. The judge was talking about concurrent time with the

---

*This is an alias. There is a great temptation to use the actual names of the parties in the John German case. I have kept to my original decision because it is not the personalities that matter here, but what they represent.

feds. He had the legal leeway to let German plead to the indictment over our objections and give him the sentence he wanted no matter what we said. I told Jim all we could do was fight—and look for other John German victims. Maybe with more cases O'Toole would feel that he had to impose more of a sentence.

Jim came back from the next court conference more disgusted than ever. O'Toole had come up with a new idea. There was no point in sending German to prison, he said. German was an articulate, contrite sex offender. Maybe with treatment he could do some good. The defense attorney should look into it. I told Jim that was insane. Jim already knew that.

Jim was convinced that O'Toole was sincere—misguided, but sincere. If that was the case, then maybe we could change his mind. We could suggest a prepleading hearing—have our victims evaluated and submit an expert report to the court on the damage that had been done them. Maybe, if they were willing, we could even have the victims come into court and tell O'Toole how they felt about German. If the judge was as disturbed about "pedophilia" as the flag he was waving about it proclaimed, then maybe he could be educated. Jim tried. Things just got worse.

O'Toole's idea was that German should go into treatment. Then, along with his therapists, he should lecture across the country, educating the public and potential victims about pedophilia. The judge could make this whole plan a condition of probation—as if German would have any reason not to comply.

Sending a pedophile on a public-speaking tour spit on everything I had tried to do to impose consequences on sex offenders. But it was legally permissible for the judge to do. The defendant would have to complete his federal sentence first, but that would just delay O'Toole, not stop him.

I told Jim about Shelvie Harris, about Judge Asserta barring me from his courtroom for life for fighting him on a plea. We might not be able to stop John German's judge, but we could make it hard for him to do what he wanted. At least we'd know we'd done everything we could. Jim looked dubious.

I tried going to one of the case conferences myself to see if it was Jim, but it was O'Toole. The conference was a standoff. I couldn't convince the judge his idea was god-awful. He couldn't convince me to go along. O'Toole even tried telling me that my husband would be in favor of his idea. As upset as I was by the conference, I was cheered momentarily by the mental image of the carnage that would have resulted if O'Toole had been stupid enough to say such a thing to my husband's face.

I finally got O'Toole to at least hold off his decision temporarily. Let's see how German's "treatment" team evaluated his progress. I could use the time to try to scratch up something that might convince the judge to change his mind.

Besides, I needed the time for more urgent responsibilities. The Forensics Bureau had notified me that Emanuel Santana was back in court. Three and a half years after his arrest, he had been returned by the upstate psychiatric institution, with a report that he was now psychiatrically fit to proceed. Santana was ready for trial.

4

When Santana was returned fit, I thought about not taking the case back. It wasn't only the promise I'd made to Beth and Kerri and Maria that decided me—it was Santana himself.

While he was psychiatrically hospitalized Santana had had the time to create a more viable defense. His new diagnosis was "Vietnam vet syndrome"; he'd found something else to blame for his crimes. Santana gave notice of an NGI (Not Guilty by reason of insanity) defense. Having an excuse, I guess that's what got him over his "depression."

I'd been telling people for years that rapists are not sick, they're evil. Now I had a chance to prove it.

The trial took place in the Jamaica courthouse. The building is surrounded by security provisions: a parking lot in back monitored by guards; a wrought-iron fence around the rest that must be twenty feet high; a bank of metal detectors and grim-faced court officers just inside the entrance. After dark the front entrances are sealed, and armed escorts accompany the few remaining brave souls out the back.

All these precautions are necessary. Jamaica is famous for its street crime, its drug- and gang-related violence. A policeman was killed sitting in his patrol car only a few blocks away from the courthouse, shot at point-blank range through the window. A lawyer was shot on the Jamaica courthouse steps. There was no safe place or uniform in Jamaica.

Inside, the courthouse is more imposing than frightening, with its marble staircases, dark paneling, and courtrooms spacious enough to dwarf anybody's sense of self-importance, at least visually. The setup makes everyone look small, insignificant. The judge and the defense attorney looked smaller than most. Santana loomed larger. It wasn't just his size . . . it was the force of his will.

Santana asked to be excused when the victims testified. He would find it just too upsetting. This attitude was marginally better than that of the rapists who enjoy watching their victims detail their crimes on the stand. It was also an encapsulization of Santana's sociopathy: Nobody's pain mattered except his own.

He was unhappy when the judge compromised, excusing him from all but the in-court victim identifications. The defendant didn't like that the victims were going to testify at all, let alone that they were going to point him out in front of the jury. His lawyer repeated Santana's offers to stipulate, not only to the identification, but to the entire proof of guilt. Santana wanted the judge to simply instruct the jury that he admitted to doing these acts. He was offended that I had the right to interfere.

At one point, he even asked to address the judge himself:

Your Honor, I have asked this question of my lawyer and he gave me an answer and I still really don't understand what's going on: this here. I am not contesting and I'm not denying anything, what any part of the court indictment that was charged against me. I'm not denying or contesting it. And I want to know why the complainants and also myself have to be put through this trauma again or ordeal again if I'm not contesting it, Your Honor?

Defendants don't often speak in court. When they do, it's rare for them to be so articulate and polite. The judge answered Santana, trying to reassure him that his attorney knew what he was doing. I interrupted. The judge was missing the point.

Now that we were in a courtroom, not in some shadowed alleyway, I wanted Santana to understand some things about power and control. The judge tried to soften the confrontation, so I repeated myself: "I just wanted the record clear that it was my decision and I refused [to go along with the defendant's request]."

Santana nodded, taking in new rules.

The ADAs at SVB already knew by heart the basic profile of the jurors that I wanted for sex-crimes trials: men in their forties to fifties who said they read *The New York Times* but really read the *Daily News*. I wanted people who had a veneer of sophistication about sexual assault, but who would still respond from the gut to ugly crimes. I wanted down-to-earth jurors, grounded in everyday realities of urban violence—not anyone who would ever consider falling asleep on the subway at night. Ideally, I wanted jurors whose jobs required interaction with the public so that their perceptions were tested every day—bus drivers instead of house-wives. And I wanted jurors who'd served on a jury before. Somehow they got better with practice. Mostly what I wanted to avoid was col-laborators—anyone who would take a tolerance for rapists into the jury room and express it in a verdict.

Trial lawyers can go on forever describing just what kind of jurors they want, but jury selection is actually a process of elimination. Because each side has a limited number of challenges, lawyers use them to eliminate the worst potential jurors from their perspective. What's left is the jury.

From the beginning, Santana played to the room. Sitting in court, he would hang his head practically to the table. Sometimes he would shake his leg for hours on end, so violently as to be audible.

I'd talked over the order of testimony with each of Santana's victims, and we had all agreed on Beth going first. Beth wanted to get it over with as soon as possible. I wanted to start with my most articulate victim. The other two women looked to Beth for leadership. Today, I don't know if their choice was right, which one was the strongest. I got to see three faces of courage—I can't say which one was more beautiful.

Santana was excused before I called my first witness.

Beth told the jury about putting the key in her lock and feeling a shadow over her shoulder. They were in the vestibule. She told the shadow that he'd frightened her. He grunted and pushed one of the buzzers. She unlocked the door. He shoved her inside, knocking her down.

While she was still sprawled on the floor, he grabbed her purse and rummaged through it. Then he hoisted her up by the back of her neck, squeezing for a better grip, leaving bruises. He pressed the knife to her throat violently enough to imprint a mark under her chin that showed up in her emergency room records. He forced her behind the building to an alleyway. When she tried to hold back, he shoved her along. He tried the door to the basement, seemed surprised when it was locked. He pushed her deeper into the darkness, where he forced her onto all fours. When he couldn't get an erection, he told her "white girls are no good." He turned her over to rape her. She saw his face in the reflected light from the church adjacent to the alleyway.

As she testified, you could see Beth's fear growing with her memories. She was precise, detailed, and accurate, but only by an effort of will. Visibly mastering the heartache and terror, Beth was vivid enough and injured enough for the jury to understand what rape was all about, its true ugliness. The jury saw Santana through Beth's eyes: angry, violent, cold, deliberate—sane.

Waiting for Beth to finish frayed Kerri's nerves. She had started the morning terrified. By the time she took the stand Kerri was so tightly wound that I thought it might interfere with her getting out what she wanted so badly to say. Instead, it made her testimony even more powerful.

There is a little-used rule in New York that victims can be asked about their state of mind at the time of the rape. Normally "state of mind" testimony—what a witness thought rather than observed—is not admissible. But because the prosecution must prove the element of "forcible compulsion" for a rape, that a victim's "will was overborne" by fear, she is allowed to tell the jury her feelings. Usually victims say, "I thought he would hurt me," or "I thought he would kill me." Kerri said,

At that point I had this strange picture in my head of dying there, stark naked on the floor in my building where I live. I had this vision [of] someone having to call my parents and tell them that that's where they found me, and I couldn't allow that, and I knew that if there was some kind of way that I was going to get through . . . I was going to find some way that that man could not get away [with raping me] . . . and I was hell-bent on getting through . . . and that's what I was focusing on during what happened next.

I was nearly finished with Kerri's direct when the judge called me up to the bench to remind me that it was getting late. Santana's insistence that he couldn't tolerate hearing the victims testify was about to backfire.

The day had been a hard one for the jury. From Beth they'd heard a tale of horror that they couldn't help but know was true. From Kerri they got to see raw pain—three and a half years later and still red and oozing. The man responsible had, up until then, been noticeably absent.

The judge sent the jury to the jury room. Kerri and Beth were brought to the judge's chambers, while the court officers escorted Santana from the pens. They sat Santana at the defense table, and the attorneys resumed their places. The jury was brought back down. Kerri was recalled to the witness stand. She stomped her way into the courtroom, not looking at Santana, using her anger to get her through being in his physical presence. When I asked her, she identified the defendant, stabbing a finger toward him. The judge excused Kerri until the next day and asked that Beth be brought out.

Beth too had to walk by the defense table. Even with a court officer escorting her, she flinched when she got near Santana. She was still trembling when she took the witness stand.

The judge reminded Beth she was still under oath. Then I asked her:

Q: [Beth] Earlier today you told us about the man who had robbed you and raped you on October 25, 1983?
A: Yes.
Q: I am going to ask you to step up and look around the courtroom and tell us if you see him here today.

She did, she stood up. She hesitated, as if she wasn't sure she had the strength, and then she said in a whisper, more to herself than to us:

A: O.K. Yes, I do.
Q: Can you point him out for us?
A: That man, sitting right there.

She pointed, her hand and her whole arm shaking, and when she said the last part, she turned her face away so she wouldn't have to see him a moment longer than necessary. But she'd done it. It was what the jury got to think about going home that night.

Santana had other things on his self-centered mind. After the jury was excused for the evening, he asked to address the judge. He took a little time leading up to it, then voiced his complaint:

One of the police officers that was just outside, when I came through there he made a smart remark, and I've showed everybody respect in the courtroom and outside the courtroom and I think he ought to show me a little bit also.

Even the judge had difficulty being attentive to Santana's concerns after this day's testimony. But he was, as always, polite:

All right, Mr. Santana. If it is true what you are saying, and I have no way of knowing whether it's accurate or what, however, I will make sure that that will not happen again because it's not the right thing under any circumstances.

By the time the jury came back the next morning, they were ready to convict. I'd seen that before. It always amazed me how easily a jury forgets that feeling later in a trial. I knew as well as Santana—excuses are powerful.

Kerri had buried within her land mines of unresolved trauma. I'd found out about and avoided one of them on direct. One of the things that Santana had stolen from Kerri was her Walkman. Normally I would have had her detail the theft, but Kerri felt guilty that she'd been wearing earphones, blasting rock music, when she'd walked in her lobby door—as if the rape was somehow her fault because she'd been inattentive.

It wasn't the Walkman, though, that exploded one of Kerri's land mines.

On cross the defense attorney asked Kerri to describe the jacket she'd been wearing—"a short, military-type jacket with epaulets at the shoulder." Given styles, it was unremarkable that one of the victims wore something that was in some way "military." I didn't think the jury would take this as proof that Santana was reenacting Vietnam when he raped.

But the lawyer was pleased enough to ask Kerri, item by item, about the removal of her clothing.

When he got to her shoes and socks, she was evasive. He persisted and let loose a torrent. Kerri tried to explain, spilling out the words with mounting urgency, that she had no choice, he had a knife, she had no choice, she had to do what he said, she had to live, he would have killed her.

The judge let me talk to Kerri in private. I didn't ask her about her shoes and socks. I just told her they didn't matter and that everyone in the room knew that none of what had happened to her was her fault.

I'd figured out by then that Santana must have made Kerri take off her own shoes and socks, and that somehow she felt guilty about having done it. To someone unfamiliar with what goes on for rape victims, it's hard to imagine that Kerri could feel guilty about removing her socks when she'd been ordered to at knifepoint. The defense attorney had no idea that was what was going on. But women like Kerri bear the cumulative weight of all our collective years of victim-blaming.

There was a briefly famous case in New York of a woman who was killed on a rooftop resisting a rapist. It made all the headlines because people from nearby buildings could hear her screams and the sounds of the struggle. By the time the police got to her, it was too late. When the ambulance attendants were loading her onto the stretcher, she was still alive, but barely. What she said about having resisted the rapist was, "It wasn't worth it." She died before she got a chance to change her mind.

Kerri blamed herself for not resisting Santana to the death. That other woman blamed herself for resisting. All I ever blame is the rapist.

By the time cross was over, the jury looked like they'd been beaten up. They needed a break before Maria's testimony.

My plan had been to call all three victims, one after another. It was deliberately overwhelming, intended to immerse the jury in Santana's crimes. But this was too kindhearted a jury for me to stick to the original order of witnesses. It would have been too much. I called a police chemist, and the arresting officer. Then it was time.

There was a moment during Maria's testimony that will stay with me for the rest of my life. Maria had said from the beginning that she didn't know if she had enough strength to prosecute. She had said the same thing the first time I talked to her after Santana had been returned fit. She'd married the boyfriend she'd quarreled with that night. She had a new baby. She wanted the rape to be over, to be a past she no longer had to think about.

Maria got as far as taking the stand, answering the first few questions about her name, a little bit about herself. Then she started to describe the setting: leaving her boyfriend's apartment in anger, the street, the night, the decision to call and apologize, the telephone booth, the seconds before being grabbed from behind, knife to her throat. She took in her breath. It pressed in on her: what had happened, what she was about to describe. It felt like suffocation.

The judge called a recess. I took Maria into the hallway. Sobs ripped through her. I tried to tell her the rape was over, she'd survived, it was three and a half years ago. For her, it wasn't.

I'd brought a rape crisis counselor with me for the day. It didn't help. We were both too outside and too far away. Maria was as alone as she'd ever been.

The door to the pens was twenty feet away from us. Santana sat in his cell, protected.

The jury was waiting.

Maria struggled for control, trying to climb out of her private hell. I didn't know if she could.

I gave her a choice: If it was too hard, don't do it. What I told her, urgently, trying to reach her, was, "You don't *have* to do this. Beth and Kerri already testified. We can still get him." I repeated it until she heard me.

She asked me what would happen to the case.

I told her we could go ahead with Beth and Kerri's charges.

She asked me what would happen to *her* charges.

I tried to soften it, to say it less harshly, but I told her the truth. Those charges would have to be dismissed.

She was motionless for a second. Then she shuddered. It went through her whole small frame. Then she straightened up and looked directly at me and said, "No, I can do this. I want to do this."

People who say women can't handle combat should watch a rape victim testify sometime.

We went back into the courtroom. I told the judge we were ready, and we brought the jury back in. Maria went back to the witness stand. The judge tried to help:

THE COURT: **All right, Miss [Rosaro], you were at the phone booth, you were calling your boyfriend and telling him you felt sorry, come and pick me up. At that point you felt a knife at your throat, is that what you said?**

A: **[whispered] Yes.**

THE COURT: **And then you screamed?**

A: **[another whisper] Yes.**

THE COURT: **All right, listen to the next question.**

Q: **When you screamed and you dropped the phone—just take this step by step—what happened next?**

A: **[halting, but louder] He threatened to kill me. He told me not to scream and he took my hand to put it around his waist and he took me across the street.**

Q: **I'm sorry to back you up a little bit, but what did he do with the phone?**

A: **[stronger] He took the phone and put it back on the receiver.**

Q: **He took you across the street?**

A: **Yes. . . .**

Then we were into it. Maria described what Santana did, she identified the jewelry he'd stolen that had been recovered from his apartment. She identified the pictures of the phone booth and the same church alleyway where Beth had been raped. Maria even marked X's where each crime against her had occurred, drawing a dotted red line along several photos to demonstrate the route they'd taken.

We broke for the weekend after Maria's testimony. The jury filed out with a haunted look in their eyes, like they'd seen too much pain to process it.

On Monday the jury walked in with a "let's get down to business" look. At least that's what I read in their faces. Santana was back in the courtroom, making a point of his emotions. I called the detectives, covered enough basics to let the jury know Santana had settled on an insanity defense because he had no other choice. As soon as I rested, it was his turn.

We'd gotten a preview of the defense case at the openings. The original defense theory, that Vietnam had made Santana a rapist, had been modified to add allegations of child sexual abuse. Supposedly these two different kinds of traumas combined to produce PTSD (Post-Traumatic Stress Disorder—one form of which was Vietnam vet syndrome). According to the defense, Santana suffered so strongly from the effects of PTSD that he didn't know what he was doing when he raped, and he couldn't stop himself. That was the excuse.

Some of Santana's defense troubled me as a prosecutor—the part about Vietnam vet syndrome didn't. It was one thing to use Vietnam vet syndrome to explain a shoot-out with the police, where there was at least some correlation between wartime behavior and the crimes. But to say that Santana raped because he had flashbacks of Vietnam was a fundamentally offensive idea. Implicit was the concept that he was raping Vietnamese women (and that that was O.K.) but when he got back over here he couldn't adjust to it being culturally unacceptable to rape Americans—like some rap video where the targets of sexual violence always seem to be Asian women.

There was no way the war made Santana a rapist.

But to say that Santana raped because he had been molested as a child was more disturbing. I knew that children are damaged by abuse, and that sexually abused children can grow up to be sexual predators imitating their oppressors, overcoming powerlessness by controlling others. Sometimes they don't even wait to grow up. Special Victims saw cases of eight- and nine-year-olds raping three- or four-year-old babies. SVB didn't prosecute eight-year-olds—but we did want to know how they got that way, and who was to blame.

This is what I believe: No one is born to rape—they are tortured into it. If we as a country want to interdict sex crimes, then we need to put our energies into child protection. But where it is too late for interdiction, incapacitation is the only answer.

Santana was a full-grown man. Whatever background he had, he had made some choices along the way. Unless he really was in an "altered state of consciousness" when he raped, his background was explanation, perhaps . . . but never justification.

The defense called Santana's mother, a sister, and his wife for biographical details. Santana settled down, with a posture respectful toward the testimony, submissive toward his mother, grateful to his sister, indifferent to his wife. Their testimony made Santana sound like a war hero, wounded in body and soul. They told the jury about his Purple Heart. We weren't looking at Santana the predator anymore, but at Santana the victim.

Two psychiatric social workers who had treated Santana testified for him. The first one repeated Santana's stories of war atrocities. On cross he admitted that Santana's war injury was self-inflicted. This wasn't in any of the records. No one besides my husband (who'd taken my "analysis" of Santana one step further) had even guessed that Santana had shot himself. I wish I could say the social worker's disclosure was due to the brilliance of my cross, but in fact the witness just popped out with it, to prove he truly was an expert on Emanuel Santana.

The other social worker told the jury Santana's accounts of his sexual abuse as a child and more of his war stories. She talked about how supportive she had been of Santana during therapy. Part of the so-called therapy for rapists inevitably includes working on their self-esteem, as if someone should feel better about himself for being a rapist.

For his part, Santana seemed pleased with the defense case. I couldn't tell whether he thought things were going well or he just liked the trial being all about him. Or perhaps, like the victims, he was reliving the rapes. For him, that meant feeling the pleasure-power rush again.

Santana's defense would live or die on the testimony of one expert.

When the defense psychiatrist walked into court, he carried with him a large, multicolored woven basket with a matching, hinged lid. He set down his basket, rearranging the defense table to display it to his satisfaction. One of the court officers mumbled a joke about there being a snake in the basket. The doctor answered that it was his videotapes. He sniffed when he talked.

The doctor was ordinary-looking, but with a prissy, self-important air. His professorial-casual clothes had been carefully preselected for their image value. He seemed aware that I was watching him, and pleased about it.

I introduced myself, stretching for neutral courtesy in my voice. The psychiatrist answered in a condescending whine, literally looking down his nose at me when he spoke.

The psychiatrist's testimony was a reinterpretation of Santana's biography to suit the defense theories. Some of the silliest parts of it came when the doctor talked about Santana's success with women. It sounded like Santana had bragged about his conquests, and the "expert" had bought these barroom stories as scientific truths. It confirmed my belief that psychiatrists are no good at fact-finding.

The most offensive part of the chronology occurred when the psychiatrist described Santana's earlier rape trial. It was his theory that Santana wasn't himself when he raped—he was in an "altered state of consciousness." Nevertheless, the doctor gratuitously adopted and repeated the convoluted excuse Santana had invented for why this first victim would lie. The doctor shouldn't have said it—it had nothing to do with Santana's "sanity." It was just an extra bit of victim-bashing that the psychiatrist exercised for its own sake, disclosing more about the witness than about his "patient."

According to the defense, Santana had first recalled the rapes under hypnosis. The judge permitted the doctor to quote what the defendant had said during these sessions:

We had been in hypnosis for a while and was [sic] at a point where we brought—focused Mr. Santana on the period just after his release from prison in July, late July of 1983, and began moving him forward with the calendar by time method. . . . [S]ometime in August he had an incident that began in a similar way to the incidents that happened here. He described it was a rainy day, that he was out, he was seeing people, he was seeing people happy, he was feeling angry toward them because he was thinking they were normal and he wasn't. He remembers crying, wanting to scream, feeling pressure in his chest, feeling his mind separate from his body and he remembers following a woman, then grabbing her, taking her to the park and then letting her go suddenly and says that he doesn't believe he did anything at all. This is not an incident, I believe, that has been reported anywhere before.

I'd always believed that Santana had committed more rapes than we knew about. This "disclosure" was more confirmation than I'd expected.

THE WITNESS: He then reports that it was three or four days later, which would be about the 27th of September—he describes that about three or four days later, again it was raining, he went out, was sitting on a bench watching people playing, they were happy, he was thinking again of his brother in Vietnam, he recalls seeing the faces of—
THE COURT: Thinking again of what?
THE WITNESS: Of his brother and Vietnam.
THE COURT: *And* Vietnam, not his brother *in* Vietnam. *And* his Vietnam experiences.

I didn't mind the judge clearing up what could have been confusing, but it amazed me that for nearly two days the judge had let the witness walk all over him, break every rule of evidence, and now he was going to be a stickler over prepositions. Like everyone else, the judge had a tolerance level. The witness continued:

He recalls again seeing the faces of the deceased Corporal Rand. At that point, for the first time in any of his reports, he recalled the name of the corporal, the squad leader who he had shot. . . . He felt angry at himself and he began feeling resentment toward the people in the park who were having fun and began doubting his manliness. . . . He described at that point seeing a girl come out of a store.

He described her with shoulder-length hair, black hair, with a package, an umbrella, and then proceeds to describe following her into her hallway, attacking her there. He describes that she had groceries and recalls wax paper in the groceries. He recalls taking her out of the hallway.

Beth had bought half a pound of turkey before returning home the night Santana raped her. Just before she took the witness stand, she told me it amazed her that she was still angry that he'd even stolen her supper.

He described that he has house keys in his hand. He says he took the girl to the alleyway thinking—and this is a quote—"what a bitch." He recalls thinking that it was her fault. He feels disgust for her and for himself.

He says in the hallway she's on her hands and knees. He feels like hurting her and at that point [in the hypnotic session he] stops and is unable to go further. This is where the interviewer—as I said before, one of the techniques was to shout a word at him, he began shouting the words "she's a bitch" to try to generate some feelings, and at the end of a series of these he reports "I raped her." . . .

He goes—he is then brought on in time and describes a second incident where he finds a girl. He is walking again, describes the same kind of anxiety. . . . There was a girl on the phone. He described that she was laughing and he thought she was laughing and joking with her boyfriend. He describes thinking that the girlfriend of the corporal he killed is home crying and not laughing, and that again [he] thinks of her as a bitch, this bitch doesn't have any concern, doesn't care about what that woman thinks.

It was possible Maria had been laughing while she was making up with her boyfriend. But it was hard to imagine.

He says he grabbed the phone, he remembers having a knife in his hand, threatening her. He remembers saying to the woman—the woman saying to him "don't hurt me" and that he is holding her around the neck. He says he is saying to himself that he should leave her alone, that she did nothing to him, but then he begins feeling hate, anger and blaming her for his trouble.

He describes the next thing he remembers is putting his pants back on and coming to his senses. He describes that night he went out and he bought a lot of heroin, that somebody told him it was too much, but that he wanted to overdose.

. . . He says December 7th stands out in his mind because his wife was in the hospital.

It was raining, he describes, he became nervous, upset. He had described that he had been working at two jobs . . . he had been to the hospital and he had come home after his second job and he was not home very long when he became nervous, he became upset and he felt a need to get out of the house. He went out. He said he walked very far. He remembers—he doesn't remember exactly where he was walking, but describes passing a police precinct and describes that he felt a need to go tell the police he had committed crimes and needed help and that he didn't do it.

Even in Santana's self-serving version of his criminality, he had a choice, and the choice he made was to rape.

He then described a feeling that he was hunting something again, like a predator, that a lot of wrong had been done to him and that he had to take it out on someone. He felt other people responsible for what had been done to him.

He began to follow a girl and he described having alternating feelings of wanting to hurt her and not wanting to hurt her. He remembers following her into the hallway or reports remembering following her into the hallway and telling her not to look at him, took her under a stairway and remembers cutting or ripping something from around her waist. He acknowledges having sex with her against her will.

He remembers not thinking clearly, telling her to lay down, feeling like an animal when he walked out of there, and he described at times having alternating perceptions of what am I doing here, I hate this woman, and alternating feelings of rage and kind of recognition with a sense of wonderment as to why he was there.

He describes stopping for a drink on the way home, being stopped by the police, who asked him some questions, that they left, that he went into his building, came back out and went back to the police, and he states he told them to bring

him to the scene of the crime because he thinks he did something wrong.

Like the experienced sociopath he was, Santana had interwoven at least some truth into the self-serving fabric of his lies. He raped because he saw women who were happy and he wanted to take that away from them. All those women who torture themselves with the question "Why me?" can't imagine how impersonal the choice was. And all those people who think rapists pick women because they dress too sexy—they just don't understand what rape is. Maybe they don't want to.

The defense psychiatrist wanted to reduce Santana to a clinical specimen. He wanted to test out his theories for the ego gratification of seeing if he could prove he had greater diagnostic abilities than other psychiatrists. And if he was wrong, if Santana was released and raped again, well, these things happen. . . .

Cross-examination wasn't an intellectual exercise. It was a fight with rules. And like boxing, there were plenty of times you couldn't depend on the referee to enforce those rules.

My style is not to be a dancer—I don't win my trials on points like some SEC attorney. I *expect* the other guy to be ahead on points. The way I fight I need to equalize the other guy's style by getting close enough to deliver the payload just one time.

I spent some of the cross on Santana's history. When I was specific, when it was right there in the record, I could force the concession. But as soon as I tried to challenge the defense theories with facts, the doctor evaded me. These should have been power punches. But every time I hooked instead of jabbed, the witness slid out of range.

I tried to show the jury where the *idea* of Santana's child sexual abuse had originated, using one of the prior psychiatric reports. The witness strained the syntax of the report to claim that it was unclear whether the psychiatrist or the defendant had first broached the topic. The witness did concede that the defendant had volunteered at some point that "there were some kind of deeper problems from his childhood" and that the psychiatrist writing the report had *then* asked him about child sexual abuse. Santana hadn't even been subtle. He'd said "deeper problems," and the psychiatrists had jumped in feet first.

But there was a diagnosis that *did* fit Santana:

Q: **Doctor, what is malingering?**
A: **Malingering means consciously falsifying in order to have a particular end.**

I thought I had him on the run, but he was ready with the rope-a-dope.

The doctor smothered my question with words. He danced away from the ropes, backpedaling for speed. I kept coming.

I had to get in close to hurt this guy. He could dance all night.

But this time I might be earning points for aggression, but I wasn't penetrating the doctor's defense. The punches I threw hit only air—hot air. The judge got into a debate with the witness. I had a few minutes—between rounds.

What I had to face was that I wasn't going to get a knockout. I'd have to go the distance and hope for the right decision. I switched to southpaw, so I could get in his face. I knew how I wanted to end the cross-examination. I took the risk.

Q: **Doctor, what is your prognosis for Mr. Santana?**
A: **I think the prognosis for Mr. Santana, with continued treatment, based upon what I think has happened so far in treatment, is fairly good . . . and I've given estimates that he [needs] probably another year or two and probably the best place for him would be in the Veteran's Administration facility where they are most skilled in treating Post-Traumatic Stress Disorder connected with Vietnam.**

Let the jury have time to think about the prospect of Santana being out on the street, in their neighborhoods, in a year or two.

I still had the title fight ahead of me. The big question now was whether Santana himself would step into the ring.

I walked into court Thursday morning not knowing what was coming next. The defense hadn't rested yet. If Santana was going to testify, it was going to be either this morning or after my expert. Either way, I had to be ready.

It was a big letdown when all the defense attorney chose to do was formalities. The defense rested. Like he had at the end of my case, the defense attorney moved to dismiss. It was protocol. Denied.

Santana, who'd been quiet and attentive during his psychiatrist's testimony, resumed his act—visible tension and stress.

The jury returned to the courtroom. I called my final witness.

My expert had been in Vietnam as a medic, and had been decorated for his service in the war. When he'd come home, he'd felt lost, but had managed to find himself; he went to college and then on to receive a Ph.D. in psychology. He took what he'd learned in the war and its aftermath with him. While most people in this country were still anxious to forget there had ever been a Vietnam, he found in his fellow vets a population most in need of him, closest to his heart and goals.

At my request, the psychologist had examined Santana. He found the defendant did in fact suffer from Vietnam vet syndrome—but that it wasn't what made him rape.

The psychologist explained the term "Post-Traumatic Stress Disorder" to the jury. This was familiar territory for me. PTSD was *the* diagnosis I had to work with, whether it was called rape trauma syndrome, or intrafamilial child sexual-abuse syndrome or battered wife syndrome. In other trials I needed it to explain why a victim's behavior didn't match the jury's myths about how victims are supposed to act. Now I was explaining why it didn't excuse a rapist.

The psychologist used numbered factors to define PTSD, giving brief explanations for each:

[1] There had to be a traumatic event ("an event that is sufficiently catastrophic that it exists outside the realms of normal human experience");

[2] There was a set of symptoms that involved re-experiencing the trauma (reliving, intrusive memories, nightmares, even unbidden thoughts);

[3] There was a set of symptoms involving numbing or denial (where the traumatized person's feelings in general are numbed, as a way of protecting oneself from the re-experiencing); and

[4] There was a set of miscellaneous symptoms that included a "startle" response to sudden events.

I knew about the "startle" response. When I first met my husband, he had only recently returned from trying to set up a food-distribution system in war-torn, famine-broken Biafra. Any sudden loud noise would make him react as if the bombs were still falling around him. It made me recognize where I'd seen it before—in a filth-strewn apartment in the South Bronx; working the floor at Andros II. Later, when I started prosecuting so many sex crimes, I saw that reaction in myself.

The psychologist clarified that Post-Traumatic Stress Disorder did not mean the defendant was legally insane. There had to be something more. Some people with PTSD also had "dissociative states." The psychologist explained what that meant and that Santana didn't have them.

During my expert's testimony, I thought about calling a second expert on child sexual abuse. I added it up: more loss than gain. It was time to rest. I said so for the record. The judge turned to the defense attorney.

I don't actually know when Santana decided not to take the stand, or why. I didn't know until that moment what his decision was. I did know Santana would have overridden any decision made by either his psychiatrist or his attorney, if he thought it would be in his best interest. Santana understood control—it was the god he worshiped.

Once the defense rested a second time, what witnesses might have been called didn't matter anymore. What mattered was that after a few routine legal arguments to the judge, we were going to break for the day; the testimony part of the trial was abruptly over. It was all over except for the shouting—what lawyers call summations.

I wouldn't get a shot at Santana in the ring—I'd have to do it all on summation.

When I started the trial, I knew what I wanted to tell the jury. Santana was a rapist. All the rest of this was a blind over the truth. But the blind had been built into a wailing wall.

I explained the problem to my husband. I told him about my frustrations with the doctor, how what he said, when I tried to pin him down, was incomprehensible. My husband answered, with his usual ability to contain a volume of meaning in a few words: Maybe if what the defense expert said made no sense, it was because it was nonsense. Perfect.

I was nervous when I walked into court Friday morning, trying not to show it. It was one thing to let a witness dance away. I couldn't let a rapist do it.

When I was a defense attorney, I wore all white for summations, so the jury would think of innocence. When I became a prosecutor, I switched to black and white. I wanted to tell the jury that that's what it was—black and white. No gray areas. No excuses. Make them feel it—and deal with it.

The jury filed into the courtroom. They looked solemn and formal for this occasion. It had been a typically hot and humid New York City summer. Throughout the trial the jurors had dressed accordingly—slacks and T-shirts, presentable but nothing fancy. Now they were all dressed up. I'd never seen a jury do that for deliberations. I didn't know what it might mean.

The defense attorney got up to speak. He reviewed Santana's life with the jury. For everything bad the defendant had ever done, he had an excuse.

You go a little crazy and you shoot your hand without thinking about it. On the other hand, after you've done it, you wake up in the hospital and you tell them what happened. Why do you tell them it was a shrapnel wound? Why don't you tell them 'I shot myself in the hand because I couldn't take it anymore'? Because he considers it shameful. He is not an immoral person. . . .

This was the theme. It was repeated about a variety of topics—none of them rape.

It was my turn. I had that moment of terror that I always have just before I sum up. By then I was standing in front of the jury with my last chance to convince them. Santana had watched, absorbed, while his lawyer spoke. If he was watching me, I didn't know. All that mattered to me right then was the jury. I would bring the defendant into this when I was ready.

First, I had to take this case away from the psychiatrists. I used my husband's words:

[I]f at times during this trial there was evidence that was confusing to you, it is the fault of the evidence, and not your own

faults. . . . There was a lot of debate about a lot of things that may or may not have made any sense to you. If they didn't make sense, you are entitled to assume that's because they were nonsense. . . .

[T]his is not up to the psychiatrists or the psychologist to decide. That's their testimony. It's given to you for whatever aid it may or may not be to you, and that's it. We know that there are plenty of psychiatrists who have interviewed Mr. Santana and we know that very few of them have ever agreed with each other on anything. Everybody agrees that he has some disorders.

It seemed like I'd been waiting a long time to say this next part—as if it were some piece of truth waiting out there for me to get to.

We know he has some disorders. He is a rapist. There is something wrong with anybody who rapes. There is certainly something wrong with anybody who rapes over and over again. That doesn't mean that he is insane. That doesn't mean that he didn't know reality at the time of the crime.

There is no dispute that there is something wrong with this man, but it is something criminally wrong with him. He commits crimes. He commits offensive, obscene crimes. We're here to try him not for his personality, not for his whole life. . . . We're here to try him for specific crimes.

I pulled out two pieces of evidence, two little gold charms. My hands shook as I held them up to the jury.

After this case is over—you have heard testimony that this is a cross and a painter's pallet that belonged to [Maria Rosaro]. After this case is over the state will, if she wants them, return these to her. He took other things from her that night that cannot be returned to her. He took other things that night from [Kerri Woods] and [Beth Tyler] that cannot be returned to them. He took their sense of safety. He took their sense of being secure from violation, from rape, from robbery, from a knifepoint attack. He took that away and they may never again have that in their life, and that's what he is on trial for.

He was a rapist. Didn't they get that? His excuse was "blame my life" instead of "blame the victim." But it still came down to "don't blame me." Santana was a sociopath. Now they call it "antisocial personality disorder." Whatever the words, it means the same thing:

Mr. Santana is somebody who never in his whole life felt anybody's pain but his own. He feels only his own pain, and his pain comes first. . . . The man is a liar and a manipulator and he is willing to go to great lengths to get himself out of consequences.

The crimes were the trial. It wasn't my words that could convince this jury. But Santana's could. I read the jury what Santana had said to Maria and Beth and Kerri while he raped them. I pointed to the defendant. Now was the time I wanted him in this, up front for the jury, not some spectator. This wasn't Roborapist. This was deliberate. Santana's malice was visible, audible.

When she tried to look at him, he would respond to that. "Look at the wall! Look at the wall!" and he shoved the knife in harder. He rips her clothes, he cuts off the sash. She makes eye contact with him and he is surprised by that and he gets angry. "Close your eyes. Lie down or I'll kill you." . . .
It has nothing to do with flashbacks or anything else. He is raping her because he wants to. This is a man who will go to any lengths for what he wants. That doesn't make him crazy. That makes him a lousy human being and that's all it makes him.

All the truth the jury would ever need to know was in those crimes. It was the jury's decision whether to give aid and comfort to the enemy. I brought it back to them.

You know as much as anybody can about what was going on in Mr. Santana's mind in 1983, when he was committing those rapes and robberies, and you know it the way we judge any man, and that's by his acts, what he says and what he does.

Mr. Santana's game is to manipulate the system . . . and it is going to be up to you to decide if that game is over or not.

At some point after the Judge's charge and when you are in the jury room, the only people of relevance here are going to be you and Mr. Santana. You have something to say to him. You can either say to him: Poor Manny, you've had such a tough life, I guess you weren't responsible for these crimes. Or you can say to him the truth . . . and that one truth is Guilty.

I tumbled out a few more words, afraid to stop. And then I was done and sitting down, shaking like I always do after it is all over. The judge was giving the jury a break before he said his own piece.

Like all instructions on the law, sitting through this judge's charge was an exercise in self-discipline. The defense attorney and I tried to look interested and concerned. Santana didn't even bother with the pretense. As soon it was over, his lawyer said the defendant wanted to be excused from jury deliberations. He was tired and wanted to be sent back to Kings County Hospital for the night. I didn't know if the law permitted him to leave. The judge said he didn't know either—nobody had ever asked before—but that he'd research it. In the meantime the defendant would remain in the courthouse until the judge found out.

The hardest part came next: the wait. All during the trial what had gotten me past the obstacles was the certainty that letting Santana go free was unthinkable. Now I *had* to think about it to make plans in case the jury voted NGI.

Now that I had time to look at the whole trial, I was scared. There was a lot more proof against Emanuel Santana than I was used to having—and a much more elaborate excuse. There was plenty there to convince a jury, *if* they didn't let anything get in the way. But that was incalculable.

Santana wanted his excuse to be true. He wanted to have a sickness that meant all the harm he'd caused was not his fault. But he went to trial because he believed, like every rapist, that a jury wouldn't condemn him. He understood collaborators. And like all rapists, he underestimated the Resistance.

No matter what the verdict, this battle wasn't the war. But if the verdict was NGI, the casualties were going to be very heavy.

After half an afternoon's deliberation, the light went on in the court-room, indicating a note from the jury.

The judge called for extra security. The clerk called the case into the record.

THE COURT: Bring the jury in.

COURT OFFICER: Jury entering.

THE COURT: The Court has received a written note signed by the foreperson which reads as follows: Your Honor, we the jury have reached a verdict. It's signed by the foreperson. . . . This will be marked Court's Exhibit 4.

THE CLERK: Jurors, please rise. Defendant, please rise. Madam Forelady, under the first count of the indictment, robbery in the first degree, how do you find the defendant?

THE FOREPERSON: Guilty.

Convicted all counts. Guilty as charged.

Thank God.

The judge needn't have bothered with extra security. Santana didn't react at all. Up until the moment when the foreperson started speaking, the jury had some power over Emanuel Santana. Now we were all irrelevant. Santana was in that dark, locked room. He didn't need to reach out to feel the walls. He had everything he needed inside him. If he ever gets out, he'll make a lot of people pay.

5

When I got back to Special Victims Monday morning, there was a tidal flood of problems and decisions waiting for me. It had been a long time to be away from someplace where anything could happen from moment to moment. It took me a few days just to reorganize. It took Jim even longer to get around to telling me that, while I'd been on trial, O'Toole had taken the plea on the John German case. Thanks a lot, Jim.

German had been promised probation and a speaking tour.

Jim was disgusted enough so that I didn't spend a lot of time asking him how he had let that happen, or what had prompted O'Toole into action. I told Jim to step up the investigation into other boys that German might have molested. He promised he would.

The plea showed up in the papers with only a minor splash. There was some talk in the courthouse—but people went on about their business.

I heard a story from the executive assistant who was my current supervisor. Apparently O'Toole wasn't satisfied with seeing to it that German got the deal of a lifetime from Queens—he wanted even *fewer* consequences for the defendant. Supposedly O'Toole had called the U.S. Eastern District Courthouse to speak to his counterpart on German's case. Wouldn't the federal judge reconsider German's four-year federal sentence? According to the story, the federal judge had refused to take the call and had ordered his clerks to refuse all other calls from this guy in Queens. The executive laughed at what a Nervous Nellie the federal judge was.

I asked Jim if he'd known what his judge was up to. Sort of. O'Toole had said he was going to make phone calls—Jim had stopped listening to the particulars by then.

Temporarily, we lost German to the federal system. They needed him for sentencing and then for classification. Months went by with no return of German in sight. Jim resigned, trading in Special Victims for private practice. This wasn't a "prosecution" that could be reassigned to another ADA, so I inherited the job of seeing it to its ugly end.

Every time I thought about German's "sentence," it made me angrier. It wasn't only that this was an unthinkable disposition for a predatory pedophile. Despite all the obstacles, SVB was by then well on its way to becoming a model for the country. If German got what he wanted, if the judge imposed this obscene sentence, we would be a national symbol of how pedophiles get rewarded for preying on children.

Now that the plea was a fact of life and it was closing in on a year since the arrest, I didn't know how practical it would be to indict German on additional crimes. It would look like bad faith; we would run the risk that a judge would dismiss the new indictments on that basis. Still, I wasn't ready to abandon the idea, if all else failed. What I really needed, though, was to change O'Toole's mind.

Educating O'Toole about the crimes or the victims hadn't worked. All the focus, during all the conferences, had been on German himself. Maybe if I joined in that perspective, I could have more impact. It wasn't much, but it was my best shot. I started the research for a presentence report.

Everything I read said that pedophiles weren't treatable—they never stopped being pedophiles no matter what was done for them . . . or to them. There'd been fads where they'd tried everything from brain surgery to chemical castration to "aversion" therapy (in which after he's been "cured," the pedophile is supposed to snap a rubber band against his wrist every time he wants to rape a child). Occasionally there have even been cases in which physical castration has been considered—as if removing a body part could change what someone is, as if they wouldn't just use Coke bottles or broomsticks instead. None of it has worked. The worst part is the way the experimenters have found out they failed: at the expense of children.

I found enough to be encouraged. I could put together a powerful report, tangible opposition. While I was researching, German was busy too. One Friday afternoon a week before his next scheduled sentencing date, I got a document in the mail. It was written by the defendant. The defense attorney later tried to claim that this "proposal" was part of a presentence report, but it wasn't—it was a cry of victory.

German set forth his "credentials." It was supposed to be remorse. It sounded more like bragging. Like all sociopaths, the only true pity he felt was for himself.

At my arrest in my office at the Flushing Boys Club in New York City, the FBI agent told me, "it's all over now!" For seventeen years I had been sexually involved with children aged 8–17, all boys whose families knew me very well and loved, trusted and respected me as a "big brother" father image to their fatherless sons. . . .

At the age of nine, as a fourth grader in Catholic schools in 1959 in Massachusetts, I was sexually abused on three different occasions by three men who forced my friend and I to perform fellatio, anal intercourse and masturbate each other. I didn't understand what was happening. I was confused, scared and curious. I was sexually molested several times again when I was 11 by a swim instructor at a city pool who fondled me while teaching me to float and stared at me nude in the shower and changing. He also ridiculed me in front of younger boys who were able to learn where I wasn't and I was scared, repulsed and afraid to tell anyone for fear that I would get in trouble and be punished for doing so. There wasn't anyone I felt I could really tell anyway. I was raised in a working class family of seven children in a strict, Catholic background. Sex was sinful and not discussed. At age 14, I was fondled by a woman who picked me up hitchhiking from school to work, and, that same year, by an old man who showed me some nude girl pictures in his truck in a park while fondling my ass. I finally related what happened to a couple of my friends who didn't believe me about the old man and laughed at me for not doing more with the woman. I couldn't relate to them how scared and confused I was.

I became more and more disassociated and alienated from peers and adults and unable to relate to them and trust. Dating girls was very platonic and felt inadequate and scared in intimate situations. At ages 14 through 17, I was routinely approached, fondled and caressed by three Catholic brothers in a private College Prep School I attended. Many other boys were similarly abused and other boys only laughed and joked about it and nothing was ever done to stop such behavior. During this time, at age 15, I became a counselor in an orphanage for disturbed boys ages 10–13 and was responsible for organizing thirteen boys each day in recreation, home-work, meals, bathing and chore activities and listening to their individual problems and concerns. I became very emotionally involved with the boys and assumed a role as father for them at the same time I became interested in a few of the boys in a more intense way. I did not understand the special attraction I had and continued to date girls. My sexual feelings were first acted upon four years later as a college freshman. I usually became involved with shy, fatherless boys who were having difficulty communicating and opening up. They lacked social and athletic skills and were getting into trouble in various ways. They were like myself as a youngster in many ways. We went on camping trips, shopping, doing chores, visiting my family and friends, going with me on dates, to PTA meetings, job interviews, sports events, concerts and medical appoint-ments—all the things a parent often does not have the time to do. Observers would remark how wonderful a job I was doing and, in my mind, that sort of justified the affection that led to sexual involvement with them. My work and volunteer life centered around children and clouded the problem I had and was not dealing with. I could not see the wrong in what I was doing. . . .

On two occasions, overwhelmed by guilt and fear of being "uncov-ered," I went to confession for what I was doing. One priest heard my sexual involvement with boys and gave me a few prayers to say as pen-ance—that's all. The other priest, after hearing my confession, proceeded to seek out the boy I was involved with and confessing about, and took him to a church camp alone for a weekend where he had sex with him. I have always had problems with trusting adults and relating to the Church and this only compounded my difficulties a lot more.

My experience as a victim started 28 years ago and as an abuser the past 17 years should make one stop and wonder how it could be that so many acts could have taken place with nine "little brothers" and contacts with about three dozen other boys could have happened and no one saw it. No one complained, no one got help.

There is a concept in the law called *res ipsa,* meaning "the thing speaks for itself." This proposal said everything there was to say about German. German *enjoyed* talking about his own victimization, reverting from more technical terms to the phrase "fondling my ass," reveling in being "hot stuff." He had no sympathy for the boy who was remolested by the priest, only for his own crisis in faith. He fulfilled "parental duties"—like taking the boys he abused along on dates[!] "No one complained": no harm, no foul, so "no one got help"—he didn't need to.

By now I expected this kind of justificatory drivel from sex offenders: the sleazy undercurrent to this "confession" that said that German shouldn't be blamed for his crimes—they weren't that bad; he'd done so much good; blame the victims—other victims, of course, not him.

What I wasn't used to, and what was so hard to stomach, was the context. This wasn't a defense, being argued to a jury. It was a "proposal" endorsed by a *judge*.

I read the whole thing through, all the carefully constructed details for this organization supposedly dedicated to eradicating a social ill, featuring Pedophile of the Year, John German.

There didn't seem to be any realistic possibility that I could convince O'Toole to change his mind. I went home, discouraged and sickened, to think about what I could do. Maybe if I hadn't been so upset by German's proposal, it wouldn't have taken me all weekend to realize he'd handed me a weapon.

I went back to the paragraphs about O'Toole. There were several of them. When German described his pedophile speaking tour, he said:

> This effort is being encouraged by New York Supreme Court Justice [O'Toole and the group of "therapists" who were treating him and planning this project]; and the many prominent organizations that constantly deal with this problem—seeking a better way to detect, prevent, understand, educate, and offer help to those involved.

Then, when German talked about "pedophilia" (from what he claimed was his unique perspective as both victim and victimizer):

> The painful and destructive isolation it causes leaves thousands—millions of children with no place to turn and that is exactly what one of my own victims related to [Judge O'Toole] who had the foresight and courage to see that there must be a solution—a better way. He has pioneered this effort to educate thousands of professionals who deal with this problem and work with and for children.

When the proposal described the setup for the organization itself, German bragged:

> In conjunction with sex offender treatment specialists . . . [evaluators and treatment specialists for Mr. German]; [the defense attorney] and myself [Judge O'Toole], has envisioned a large scale, national prevention/education program involving lectures and presentations to major organizations that deal with children and media coverage and publications in psychological, legal and educational journals and literature on this problem and its solutions. [O'Toole], along with the group above have contacted over 100 professionals to date and we have recruited sharp interest and support from over 16 organizations to date.

There was even an implicit promise that O'Toole would get in on the speech-making part of this:

> Additional speakers will be utilized as need exists for a particular purpose or focus (i.e.—a judge, an FBI agent, a victim or victim's mother, etc.).

When he'd taken the plea, O'Toole had acted within the bounds of what judges were permitted to do. That's why we couldn't stop him. But German's proposal said O'Toole had (enthusiastically) crossed beyond those bounds.

According to German, O'Toole was an active participant in something much larger than a sentencing plan. The judge (together with the defendant's therapists, his attorney, and the defendant) was in some stage of creating a legally questionable and morally repugnant organization, supposedly designed to provide "training," make speeches, publish. German himself wanted to "educate" children about sexual abuse (although the other participants later tried to disclaim this). Even if it didn't provide the defendant with further criminal opportunities, the organization would not only make German a specimen-hero, it would get him out of jail. There was an implied promise that it could do the same thing for other pedophiles. All taken together, there was plenty of money to be made here, and no one was even talking "nonprofit."

I knew there were judicial canons of ethics, guidelines for what a judge could or couldn't do. This plan had to violate *something* in there.

Monday I spent on legal research. I read about Judge Asserta saying "there had to be another nigger in the woodpile." Disciplinary proceedings against judges were secret unless the judge chose to appeal. Asserta had. It hadn't helped him any.

The case law suggested that the misconduct that had actually gotten judges in trouble tended to be more grossly felonious than what I had here. Still, there was enough in the canons themselves about "avoiding the appearance of impropriety" and "avoiding business dealings with litigants" to give me some ammunition. Now that I had firepower, I started a war.

I didn't tell anyone except my husband, what I was about to do. Technically I didn't need approval to file motions on a case assigned to me. If I won, the office wouldn't do anything to me. And if I lost, there were other jobs.

Tuesday and Wednesday I prepared a motion to recuse. In one of those anomalies of the law designed to protect judges, if a lawyer in New York wants to argue that a judge should be removed from a case, the motion must be made to the judge in question. I had to argue to John German's judge that he didn't belong on the case.

I knew what I was doing was going to have major consequences—I just didn't know for who.

After it was filed, the motion became "public record." The press got hold of it. All hell broke loose.

The first coverage was a column in the *Daily News* Thursday morning, February 25, 1988, by Bob Herbert*, headlined SWEETHEART DEAL FOR A CHILD CHASER. It was a declaration of hostilities:

> Big-time civic leader and major child molester John German is about to spit squarely in the face of the criminal justice system. And he is going to do it with the support, encouragement and collaboration of his own sentencing judge. . . .

*My source citations do include the real names of the reporters. The quoted passages delete the names of all but defendants and politicians. The newspaper coverage allowed no one involved in the case this anonymity.

By the time I got to work Thursday morning, SVB had plastered the whole unit with copies of the column. The phone was ringing off the hook. Mostly it was the press—the office didn't comment. The higher-ups were waiting to see what would happen.

I had to run to court for some emergency on an unrelated case, and when I got back, my secretary gave me a message: German's lawyer had called. He had refused to leave a number where he could be reached; he was in court in the Bronx and would phone again later. My secretary told me there was no way this was a pay-phone call. There was no background noise at all on the line—more like expensive private-line silence. I figured the defense attorney had called me from O'Toole's chambers. If I was right, German's lawyer spent a lot of time that morning cloistered with his judge. It was a couple of hours later before he called back, with the same lack of background noise on the line.

The defense attorney asked me if I'd leaked German's proposal and the victims' reports to Bob Herbert. He chose his words carefully—I was sure he wasn't alone. I felt like somebody should be giving me Miranda warnings. I refused to answer.

The attorney wanted to negotiate. This time it didn't sound like his client was John German. He asked me, if German got *some* time, would I withdraw my motion. I said no—I couldn't do that. Having done the legal research, I was convinced this was judicial misconduct. The defense attorney responded that in that case there was nothing else to say, then hung up.

I got off the phone shaken. Up until that conversation, I had believed O'Toole's conduct could have been only "the appearance of impropriety." What German said about the extent of O'Toole's involvement could have been solely a reflection of German's arrogance. But this conversation translated for me that this *was* impropriety. They were all in bed together.

In the newspaper coverage that followed, the attorney defended the judge, not his client.

Friday was the scheduled sentencing date. Late Thursday afternoon I got messages that O'Toole was postponing action "to consider my motion." There was no need to show up in court. The case would be put over without the parties present.

Friday morning I got a message that there were demonstrators in the courtroom. I decided I should be there. I did know O'Toole wasn't going to be happy to see me.

The tension in the courtroom was palpable, the proceedings rigidly formal. Neither the defendant nor the defense attorney were present, but some of the press was. I asked permission for the demonstrators to put their names on the record. O'Toole decided to give them the opportunity to speak. I was uncomfortable with this—I didn't like doing anything with only one side present—but O'Toole took the statements anyway. They weren't going to affect his decision.

The way Saturday's *Daily News* article (JUDGE FEELS THE HEAT IN QUEENS ABUSE CASE) described it, the proceedings were dramatic:

> [The worker who was] physical education director of the Flushing Boys Club, who initially contacted the FBI about German's behavior, told the judge he opposed the light sentence because "there is no justice for the young men involved."
>
> The mother of one [unrelated] abuse victim, who cried uncontrollably in the courtroom, told [O'Toole] the effects on her son lasted "for years and years."

When she couldn't stop crying, I'd taken that woman into the courtroom hallway. We were only a few feet away from where Maria had recaptured her soul from Santana. I tried to say something soothing to this stranger, to compliment her on her strength for having said her piece. At some point, when she continued to cry, I patted her back. It quieted her. Then she turned to me, looking at me full-face, and said, "Who *are* you?" So much for self-importance.

O'Toole said nothing about my motion—at least not to me. To one of the protestors he still insisted that his plan would help stamp out child sexual abuse.

Publicly, it was the defense attorney who was doing all the talking. He defended the proposed organization, talking about how many children it was going to save from victimization. The *New York Times* coverage on Saturday included a boldface break-out quote that would become a favorite line of the defense attorney: "Act of Prosecutorial Terrorism."

This was the way the defense attorney described my motion to recuse. In its typically "balanced" coverage, *The Times* included a quote from me as well. I said the sentence was a national invitation for pedophiles to come to Queens County.

The *Times* reporter (Mark Uhlig) brought Santucci into it, attributing my actions to him. I wondered how long it would take the DA—if I lost—to disclaim any knowledge of what I was doing—and of me.

The newspapers had become my only sources of information about what was happening with the case. The judge and the defense attorney weren't telling me anything. I suspected O'Toole hoped things would die down so he could deny my motion and proceed as planned. Nothing anybody was saying publicly sounded like I was having an effect on his "sentencing" decision.

On Tuesday Bob Herbert ran a follow-up column, headlined IN QUEENS, JUSTICE IS BEING MOLESTED. He called the proposed sentence grotesque, the plea bargain a sleazy deal. He quoted the part of my motion to recuse that talked about financial arrangements for the organization. The column ended with a comparison:

> Meanwhile, the March 1 edition of the American Bar Association's Law Journal mentions a remarkably similar case in Tucson. A defendant named Lawrence Taylor was convicted of 85 counts of child sex abuse. The sentencing judge was named G. Thomas Meehan.
> Meehan sentenced Taylor to 2,975 years in prison.

The pressure was still on. The opposition had to come up with something.

In Wednesday's *Newsday* (MOLESTER "OVERSTATED" JUDGE ROLE: LAWYER) I found my answer. Besides the headline, the article quoted the defense attorney twice with the same language about German's proposal:

> German's lawyer . . . would not confirm the document's assertions yesterday. "German may have mistakenly overstated what has happened. . . . It could simply have been an inaccuracy," [the attorney] said.

In a position never repeated by the opposition, and with no source ever given, *Newsday* added:

> According to a source in the court, [Judge O'Toole] has not advocated the unusual sentence, but spoke with some church groups about the idea of such a program without asking that German be the speaker.

Newsday ended by quoting a couple of law professors to the effect that the sentence was not improper, and that "creative sentencing" should be encouraged. More collaboration.

At least according to the defense attorney, O'Toole hadn't budged. They were not just defending the sentence, they were advocating for it. The judge hadn't acted improperly; German had just exaggerated. This news might have spelled defeat, except that by now things were happening too quickly. They'd underestimated the Resistance again.

As a result of all the press coverage, phone calls and information had been pouring in. Most of the agencies German had listed in his "proposal" simply denied involvement. But one of the callers was a national agency director who'd been contacted in writing by O'Toole urging his participation in German's speaking tour. So much for *Newsday*'s "source in court"—I had a smoking gun.

O'Toole started his letter to the agency director by thanking the recipient for writing (to *oppose* the sentence) and "welcom[ing] the opportunity to respond." After glorifying his own ideas, O'Toole wrote:

> I want your help in that effort. Yours could be the single most important voice in the prevention of more victims. Victims in [your national agency], victims anywhere. Let me remind you that Mr. German was himself the Executive Director of the Flushing Boys Club. . . .
>
> I ask you to meet with me at your convenience and join with me in this ambitious effort.
>
> Since I will be away from the office during parts of August, I am giving you my home phone number . . . in the sincere hope you will discuss this with me.

The agency director responded with dignity and an impassioned last plea for O'Toole to reconsider; copies of the letter had been sent to others within the agency, one of whom felt it was appropriate to forward the entire correspondence to the FBI. When my motion became public, the FBI forwarded it all to me.

Judges weren't allowed to go into business with defendants. I filed a supplemental motion to recuse, attaching this correspondence.

I wasn't the only one who'd come up with new information. Across the front page of Thursday's *Daily News* was a headline that trumpeted: A MOLESTER AND THE JUDGE. I had known some of the facts behind this copy. I just hadn't known they were this potent.

The report set out the basics ("Judge's Plea for Molester Bids Fed Court to Drop Jail Term"), directing the reader to Bob Herbert's column, and adding as a tag the facts about my new motion to recuse.

Herbert's column made the other headlines seem tame. Its own headline was straightforward: [O'TOOLE] NOT FIT TO RULE IN GERMAN CASE. He started off by calling the plea bargain squalid, then turned up the heat, exposing O'Toole's efforts to influence the federal judge.

The coverage was exciting, but it wasn't results.

And I was in over my political head—not knowing how "insiders" might affect the outcome. I knew rumor had it that O'Toole wanted to be the next DA. I also knew the rumors that he and German came from the same political background—but I didn't know what or who that was.

I wasn't so naïve that I didn't understand that there is a political agenda to prosecution—a political agenda that controls what cases and what kinds of cases get charged and the level of commitment by the DA's office to any one of them.

When nothing else interfered, Santucci was proprosecution on Special Victims cases. It sounds simplistic to say that he was offended by sex crimes, child abuse, domestic violence—but plenty of people (especially in law enforcement) aren't.

Santucci put me in charge because he wanted someone who knew how to evaluate and prosecute sex crimes. But he had no idea that I would indict and insist on prosecuting the class of cases I did. SVB's caseload was determined by the degree of criminality and the dangerousness of the offender, not the ease of prosecution. Conviction rates couldn't approach those of a DA's office that accepted only sex crimes with medical evidence, eyewitnesses, a confession, and Good Victims.

I got away with breaking the rules because no one within the office was looking that closely. When I first started as bureau chief, I would get into head-on confrontations with the Intake Bureau. If some derelict was trying to snatch children in a schoolyard, they wanted to charge it as disorderly conduct (a petty class of offense called a violation because it is one step lower than a misdemeanor) and I wanted to charge it as attempted kidnapping (a high-level felony.) When a woman wanted to press charges because her husband had raped her, they wanted to tell her the penal law exempted marital rape*—even though the courts had found the exemption unconstitutional. After I learned to bypass Intake, and bring such cases directly to the grand jury, the arguments stopped. When I could keep it quiet, SVB's attitudes didn't enter into prosecutorial politics.

A courageous DA could have used what we were doing, incorporated it into his own politics. There was a victim population out there, and an even larger population afraid of victimization, who were enormously responsive to what was happening at Special Victims. Win or lose in court, it meant something to people that the state had listened to them, treated them with dignity, backed them. Word spread.

But in New York City, district attorneys are elected officials—politicians. Courage didn't seem to be an overabundant commodity at the Queens DA's office. Santucci wasn't about to get involved in the pendulum swing of American sexual politics. One year we make it impossible to prosecute rape cases under the theory that "it is a charge easy to make and difficult to disprove." And by the next year rape prosecutions are so hot-topic that they invite a class of extortionists *threatening* to bring charges. Santucci settled for being satisfied that Special Victims wasn't making him look bad.

He was waiting to see how John German would make him look. He wasn't the only one.

A local Queens paper, which openly admitted its long-standing opposition to Santucci, front-paged the John German story and ran an editorial demanding: GIVE GERMAN THE MAX. It marked a turning point.

If O'Toole was not feeling enough pressure, a *Daily News* editorial resolved that. It headlined his actions as AN OBSCENITY OF JUDICIAL ABUSE. The editorial pulled no punches:

> John German has pleaded guilty to 82 crimes of sexual abuse of boys. God alone knows how many other secret, sordid acts of sick-mindedness

he has accomplished in 17 years of confessed sexual exploitation of boys from 8 to 17 years of age. He probably long ago lost count.

One thing is clear. [Judge O'Toole] doesn't give a damn. Not for the boys whose lives were scarred, many almost certainly forever. Not for the message the case is sending to other sexual psychopaths. Not for anything that is publicly known and makes any sense whatever. . . .

The appellate courts of New York must set that right. Publicly and immediately. And in the process put [Judge O'Toole] and others under oath to determine what he or others may have stood to gain from the circus—what conceivable motivation he may have been operating under.

The rest will be up to the New York State Commission on Judicial Conduct. Which can't move fast enough.

The *Daily News* is one of New York's most powerful newspapers. This wasn't the Queens section, or even a main-section major columnist. This was an editorial. It was powerful stuff, maybe too powerful for O'Toole to ignore.

The media attention had been unremitting, not only in the newspapers but on local TV news as well. According to motion papers later filed by the defense, John German even came up as a topic on the Phil Donahue show. The response to O'Toole was virtually universal: The city was outraged. It was effective.

Saturday's headlines said it all: [O'TOOLE] QUITS CASE: JUDGE REMOVES SELF IN MOLEST SENTENCE and QUEENS JUDGE LEAVES CHILD-MOLESTATION CASE; and, in the newspapers that had to catch up in subsequent days: JUDGE SHUNS CASE OF CHILD MOLESTATION and JUDGE QUITS GERMAN CASE.

O'Toole didn't bow to my motions—they were only the impetus to what really mattered. The judge bowed to what was overwhelming public sentiment and outcry. Even New York City had a limit to its tolerance levels.

There were various commissions responsible for investigating judicial misconduct. As the *Daily News* pointed out in a follow-up editorial, these proceedings were secret. I didn't hear any results from any investigation of O'Toole's role in the John German case. I still haven't.

Before a new judge was selected, Santucci held one of his periodic staffwide dinners. There was a new chief administrative judge for Queens—because the old one got convicted of perjuring himself to the grand jury—who made a pitch for the DA's office to work with him. I was seated in my assigned place among the bureau chiefs, near the podium. While the judge was speaking, we made eye contact—just as he was saying to the crowd, "If you have a problem with a judge, come to me—" Then he decided to add my name to the end of his sentence. It got me a standing ovation from the crowd. (I should have known I'd have to pay for that. Santucci never let anyone besides him get a standing ovation at these dinners without consequences.)

The chief administrative judge reassigned German's case to a substitute judge, one who was notorious for giving child molesters lengthy sentences. As it turned out, though, the new judge was more interested in the lesson he had to teach me than the one he had for John German. But that judicial conduct came later.

The defense attorney broke ranks with a former ally—making a motion to O'Toole to reconsider his decision to remove himself. In essence, he asked O'Toole to voluntarily resume the hot seat he'd just escaped. O'Toole declined.

Reluctantly, the defense attorney turned his attention to the new judge. He filed a lengthy brief, backed by stacks of "documentation." There were letters of support from politicians from German's days as Man of the Year; copies of all the newspaper coverage, the plea minutes, and even a few letters supporting German the defendant. In case his client's "merits" were unpersuasive, the defense insisted the law required the new judge to honor O'Toole's plea promise.

I invited the defendant to withdraw his plea altogether—let's have a trial. But the defense turned down that offer cold.

They accused me of misconduct, demanded that the case be dismissed because of my "acts of prosecutorial terrorism."

German's case had been so mired in "off-the-record" dealings that it was a relief to respond in writing. I argued the law: There was no prosecutorial misconduct. And the new judge wasn't bound by a prior judge's promise. He could instead give German his choice: Take back his plea or take whatever sentence *this* judge thought was appropriate.

These response papers were finally my chance to submit the research on how pedophiles were not treatable that I'd done so naïvely before I got German's proposal. As part of the presentence arguments I included copies of some of the photographs that had been seized during the search warrants. By then I'd seen enough child pornography to know what the worst part of it was. As disturbing as it is to see young ones in sexual postures, it is their eyes that haunt you. There is a look of such despair and betrayal in them that it is impossible not to understand the terrible nature of the crime. It was hard to be well-reasoned instead of simply viscerally mimicking the headline that demanded: GIVE GERMAN THE MAX.

The prosecution won the arguments on the law—the new judge found no prosecutorial misconduct, and no way that he was going to honor the old promise. (Later the appellate courts ratified both these decisions.)

The only decision left was the sentence. It was what this had all been about. The new judge had a full range of options. He could sentence German to probation. Or, if he imposed all the sentences consecutively (on top of the federal time), all together he could impose ten to twenty years incarceration. Or he could pick something in the middle.

It was here that the new judge decided to teach me a lesson: Who do you think you are, little girl, to be taking on the judiciary? He gave German a sentence of four to twelve years, concurrent with the federal sentence. At the defense request, German would serve his sentence in the federal prison system. At my request, it would be up to New York, not the feds, when he would be paroled on the New York case.

The original federal sentence was four years. Unless the parole board came through, German would not serve an extra day in jail for the Queens cases. It was a hell of a lot to have gone through for that result.

The day of the decisions and sentencing, the courtroom was filled with all manner of media. Afterward, one of the reporters asked me if I was disappointed that German would be doing "soft" time in a federal prison. I told her I didn't care where German did his time, so long as he was in prison. That quote didn't make the evening news.

I got over being disappointed. This hadn't been a fight for some magic numbers. It had been a fight for the imposition of consequences. German had thought that because he picked vulnerable victims, and because he had the right image, he had a license. It took some doing, but the state finally told him: license revoked.

As it turned out, German did serve additional time on his New York sentence. After he served the minimum, he saw the board and was denied parole.

6

Santucci's office got such strong public and press approval for fighting the judge on the John German case that there weren't any immediate consequences to me for breaking all the unwritten rules.

But I knew there would be. It was always clear who was in favor or disfavor with Santucci at any given time. The list varied, but the small-mindedness behind it didn't. People in that office specialized in courting approval—to the point where what they served at staff dinners was hard to swallow.

There was one staff dinner for which Santucci chose a different kind of tribute for himself. The head of a local bar association fancied himself a singer/songwriter. He was invited to perform a one-time rendition of an ode to John J. Santucci put to music normally reserved to honor the country. Most of the audience was very drunk by then—a lot of people found that the best way to survive one of these dinners. During the performance of this musical homage, a couple of drunken bureau chiefs started to laugh. Santucci didn't see the humor. Within the year, both of those bureau chiefs were out of jobs at the Queens district attorney's office. Afterward, whenever they criticized him publicly, Santucci dismissed their statements as coming from "disgruntled former employees."

Santucci wasn't openly treating me like a pariah—but I didn't see a whole lot of him either. I had more immediate problems.

Shaping Special Victims was harder than I thought. Putting the backup services into place was an ongoing project, but all it took was hard work. Increasingly, the bureau's overriding frustration was that there was simply too much work and too few people and resources. Law enforcement had always given sex crimes low priority. Queens Sex Crimes Squad didn't even have enough detectives to run a midnight-to-eight shift—as though sex crimes happened more frequently during normal working hours. Instead of adding detectives, the city added to the caseload by renaming the units "special victims squads" and making them responsible for investigating sex crimes *and* child abuse.

Like Queens Sex Crimes, Special Victims always seemed to have less with which to do more.

It was difficult to pinpoint the bureau's actual caseload, but between all the trial-level cases, the preindictment felonies, the misdemeanors, and the prearrest investigations, SVB carried between five hundred and a thousand cases at any given time. Gross numbers are always misleading. Some cases required less work than others. But many prosecutions required massive amounts of energy. And beyond even the work required to prosecute to an acceptable standard, new issues always cropped up.

One of them was about Santana. While the battle lines were being drawn with the John German case still in limbo pending sentencing, Santana's sentencing was pending too. I wanted Santana to serve as much time as the limits of New York's sentencing provisions allowed. That much wasn't at issue for me—it was why I'd done the trial. But there was a new consideration.

When I had talked to Kerri, Beth, and Maria about the sentencing, Beth told me she was afraid Santana had given her AIDS. It was a fear that had been echoed by many of the bureau's stranger-to-stranger rape victims.

The law in New York made no provision requiring rapists to be tested for the HIV virus. There had been a case upstate in which the appellate courts ruled that prearrest defendants could not be required to undergo HIV screening. That case, though, was about the rights of people who had been accused but not convicted.

Santana *had* been found guilty. He had a history of intravenous drug use. If his bragging to "his" doctor had any grain of truth, or even if you only took into account all his rape victims, he had had multiple sexual contacts.

I put in my time at the library researching, then made a motion. Test Santana for AIDS. Disclose the results to the prosecution or the victims.

I tried to back up the motion with documentation, but it wasn't easy. I had much more trouble with the medical research than with the legal precedents. The literature itself was hard to understand, with only the Gay Men's Health Crisis speaking in plain language, but I was used to wading through foreign terms and extra clauses. My real problem was the content. What was known about detecting AIDS seemed to change from day to day.

Every time I thought I knew what I was talking about, it slipped away. Originally I thought it would help my arguments that because of his mental hospitalization, four years had now passed since the rapes. If Santana tested negative after all this time, then wouldn't that be a definitive answer? Wouldn't it mean he couldn't possibly have exposed his victims to HIV? (Nobody wanted to think about it, but if he tested positive, it would at least alert all his victims to be tested. And it wouldn't necessarily mean that he'd had AIDS in 1983.)

The first articles on HIV screening seemed to confirm that testing Santana now would give enough of an answer. But later texts kept extending the time a subject could test negative and still be infected. Just how much did these tests mean? What answers did they really have for people who needed life-or-death information?

Ironically, the defendant was one of the few people who wasn't an opponent in this battle. Santana agreed to have his blood drawn, to have the results sent to his victims. Probably he was curious about the results for himself. And he got to look good at no personal cost.

I had more powerful opposition—the city and the state, the various correctional departments, and the health agencies—all lined up to say no. Besides insisting that I didn't understand the state of medical knowledge on the topic, they argued that HIV results must be kept confidential regardless of the circumstances of the testing. They said that the public would be less willing to be tested for AIDS if confidentiality could not be assured. My own suspicion was that underneath these arguments lurked an ulterior motive. No agency wanted to be responsible for the potentially massive amount of testing that setting a precedent in the Santana case might require.

The debate lasted so long that Beth took matters into her own hands.

She still wanted the results of Santana's tests. But she asked me for referrals for her to be AIDS tested. I got an even greater education.

There were so many agencies with titles and ad campaigns promising counseling and AIDS testing that it never occurred to me that anyone in New York City would have trouble getting screened. I gave Beth the number for the Queens agency set up by the city. No, they didn't do testing—but did she want counseling? I gave her other numbers. Nothing.

Beth found her own solution. She volunteered to donate blood at a private hospital that routinely screened all blood donors for HIV. If the tests came out positive, they informed the donors of the results.

The people opposed to my motion bombarded Santana's sentencing judge with so much paper that he ducked. He granted my motion, but limited the basis of his decision to Santana's consent.

If Santana had hoped that being cooperative would lessen his sentence, his strategy failed. The judge also imposed the maximum.

I got what I'd wanted—especially when Beth's and Santana's results came back negative. But I hadn't set a precedent.

While I'd been fighting this battle, I'd trained the bureau's ADAs on the work I was doing. I had set new policy: Include HIV screening in their sentencing requests for convicted rapists. I backed off after Santana's sentencing, dissatisfied with what I'd learned. The new position was: Make the motion if a victim requests it. But don't create the issue for victims who hadn't considered the possibility. The test results provided too little information to make it worthwhile.

SVB did seem to wind up in the midst of controversy. I guess I believed that's where we belonged.

The criminal justice system is so inherently conservative, so committed to doing things the way they've always been done, that even when we wanted to change things for the better, the change itself was viewed with hostility. When I was a trial attorney inheriting cases from the old Special Victims, one of my biggest frustrations was having no say in what crimes got charged. More often than not, although the crimes on the indictment would be difficult to prove at trial, there would be other uncharged crimes that a jury would have less trouble with. Marital rape was a classic example. Jurors are still uncomfortable with convicting a husband for having sex with his wife regardless of the circumstances. But if he had forced her to crawl around on the floor on all fours just before the sex, that was a separate crime of coercion, and if he had beaten her up the week before, that was assault. Those crimes might not be as high a level of crime as Rape 1, but they helped a jury appreciate the context of the crime. And at the very least, a conviction on a lesser charge was a lot better than nothing.

The new Special Victims had more counts in their indictments than the courts were used to seeing. Law secretaries—those highly paid lawyers who are purely political appointees and whose job is supposed to be assisting the judges—complained about our indictments because they were "too much work."

SVB's plea policies didn't make us many friends in the courts either. It wasn't only that we insisted on more prison time than the defense bar was used to, we also insisted that rapists plead to the sex crimes. We were shocked, when serial rapists were rearrested postparole on a second or third series of rapes, to find out how many sex crimes are allowed to go in disguise. Defendants who had committed a dozen house-invasion rapes had been allowed to plead to one robbery or burglary. Such pleas were defended on the grounds that since the offender received the same time he would have received for rape, justice had been served. The problem was that neither the prison classification system nor the parole board treated such convicts as sex offenders.

Judges and lawyers thought SVB's plea policies were unreasonable. One Special Victims ADA came back from one of her first plea conferences in shock. The judge had told her the plea offer was way out of line, much too high, and why did the defendant have to plead to rape? He demanded to speak to her bureau chief. When she told the judge who it was, he told her not to bother. The ADA wanted to know whether I was insulted that the judge had said, "She drinks blood for breakfast."

The parole board welcomed an ally. They agreed to send us lists of released sex offenders. They asked us to tell them which robbery and burglary inmates were actually rapists, and when a paroled rapist was a suspect or rearrested. Several serial rapists in Queens were caught because of joint investigations between Queens Sex Crimes Squad and parole officers.

By then, SVB's working relationship with the Sex Crimes Squad had changed dramatically. Although they are supposed to be on the same side, police and prosecutors have sufficiently different goals (arrest versus conviction) so that there is inherent tension between them. Where resources are limited on both sides, tensions increase. Add to that a setup where each side tries to blame the other when things go wrong, and the animosity between police and prosecutors interferes with getting the job done. SVB had a lot of damage to undo to build a working relationship with Queens Sex Crimes Squad.

When the bureau first provided a prearrest validation expert for child sexual-abuse cases, the police viewed it as just another way in which the DA's office was trying to tell them how to do their job. When validation turned out to be a resource rather than an encumbrance, it was a first step. Then the detectives found out they could rely on SVB for search warrants when they wanted them, and the ADAs learned they could depend on the detectives for postarrest investigation. There were still mistakes and sometimes incompetence on both sides, but the standards were higher and the work better.

Special Victims began to win tremendous recognition. Outside the office we were heros. Within it, we were villains.

SVB never had the personnel to keep all the cases it indicted. The cases we prosecuted in supreme court were the pattern rapists, any case involving a child victim, and any case with a particularly vulnerable victim or unique issues. We kept the most difficult cases, but not all of them.

Outside the bureau the trial lawyers who wanted to make their careers on a rape case were disappointed when what they got from Special Victims wasn't a quick ticket to stardom. They decided we were keeping all the Good Victim cases for ourselves.

SVB indicted unpopular cases. The other trial bureaus misunderstood, perhaps intentionally—or spurred by collaborators within the office who didn't like what SVB was doing. The perception among other bureaus was that SVB was creaming cases—that there was some class of automatic-win sex-crimes prosecution that we were hoarding for ourselves.

Defending the bureau didn't work. It was obvious that the criticism would never go away until SVB kept all its cases. For that I needed more ADAs. I made the request to the DA and whatever executive happened to be my supervisor at the moment.

Instead of giving me more ADAs, Santucci progressively cut back on the number and experience level of ADAs assigned to Special Victims.

The gradual erosion in the number of staff had far more devastating effects on SVB than Santucci understood. When he made the bureau vertical, what he had had in mind was some token, team approach, where various individuals still handled separate tasks. It is a truism of the American workplace that assembly lines require fewer workers. What I aimed for at SVB, although it was often hard to achieve, was one ADA handling a case from investigation through trial.

If a rapist was represented by a different lawyer at each stage—one when bail was set, another when the case went to the grand jury, another at arraignment, a fourth at the hearings, another for plea negotiations, and someone entirely different at trial—he would appeal on the basis of incompetency of counsel. But for victims, that happens all the time.

I tried to make up for the lack of staff by motivating everyone to work harder. But there was a limit to how much working hard could overcome the problem. There were times when a lot of arrests came in at once, when instead of doing their own work, everyone became a designated player. People were pushed ahead of their experience levels. People were handed case files at the last minute. Go investigate and indict this before the clock runs down (on the, on average, three-day time limit between arrest and indictment) and a judge releases the defendant. It wasn't the best way to do the job. But sometimes it was the only way.

It was in this setting, on a day of the worst chaos, that I had first met Laurie.

At the time, I had no idea that this was SVB at its best. But I did know we were beginning to have an impact. We couldn't guarantee results like Porter's sentence. But we could hold out the promise that people would be heard when they walked through the door, and that if we took a case, we would fight for it.

John German was just one example. The defense bar got the message that if they took on an SVB case, they were in for a lot of work. Legal Aid suddenly "remembered" that it was a conflict of interest for them to represent child molesters, since they represented the victims as law guardians in family court. They started getting excused from our cases.

We could see the difference when we shared pattern-rape cases with other counties. Each county had to come up with its own plea offer. In terms of negotiations, one or more counties would "go along" and one county would be dominant. SVB got to set multicounty plea demands.

By then I understood enough about collaboration to sense that SVB's success was a mixed blessing. One form of collaboration stemmed from an instinctive affinity and sympathy for rapists. But just as dangerous were collaborators motivated solely by self-interest who, for whatever reason, were threatened by what SVB was doing.

Part Four

SHOWDOWNS

He grabbed [the three-year-old] by the arm and he threw him against the wall. [The little boy] was crying . . . 'cause he told me that I didn't know how to chastise [the child] right . . . and I asked him, I said, "What you want me to do? You want me to kill him just like that?" And he said, "Whatever it takes."

—Codefendant testimony, trial transcript, *People* v. *George Chavis*, Kew Gardens, New York, February 25, 1991

1

After William Porter pleaded guilty, the *Parade* article about "tough" prosecutors ran—with predictable consequences. Santucci said nothing. Some of the other bureau chiefs put me on their enemies list—"Who does she think she is?" I got letters and phone calls of encouragement from people I didn't even know.

I got a phone call from a woman in her nineties who'd read the *Parade* article. She'd been abused as a child in upstate New York. What could I do about it? It was something like eighty-five years past the statute of limitations. I remembered a victim whose rapist had never been caught telling me that it had helped her to attend the sentencing of a different rapist who was a stranger to her. It had comforted her to see some justice, even if it wasn't her justice. I made some suggestions to the woman caller, but they weren't what she wanted to hear. Eventually she told me that she was done speaking to me, now she wanted "to speak to the real Alice Vachss, the one who fights for victims."

For all that it had accomplished, Laurie's case never resolved the statute-of-limitations issue.

Therapists had told me about adult clients who'd unblocked memories of childhood sexual abuse from years ago. Sometimes this abuse was ten, twenty, even thirty years old. Sometimes the child abuse so poisoned their adulthood that trying to recover had become a way of life.

Then there were the victims who'd remembered all along but didn't have the strength, or the support, or the situation that would permit them to prosecute. Being old enough to move away from home, wanting to marry but being afraid, finding that they couldn't escape feeling abused even after the crimes ended—many women were first starting to report child abuse when they reached their late teens and early twenties.

I issued an open invitation: Find me someone willing to prosecute. Find me the right test case, and we'll see what the courts do with the statute of limitations.

A few months after Porter pleaded guilty, I got a phone call from a man who said his daughter had been molested by her uncle when she was a child. The abuse had stopped when she was eleven—she was twenty-one now. He hadn't found out about it until about a year ago. At the time she'd said she wasn't ready to prosecute. Recently she'd come to her father to say she was. They'd gone to the police, who refused to even make out a complaint report. The crimes had happened too long ago— the statute of limitations had run out. Was that true? Technically, yes. Was there anything else he could do? Would I be willing to speak to him and his daughter?

Loretta was lovely, with huge, dark eyes and a face glowing with goodness. She was intelligent, able to speak about the crimes but still visibly upset by them. She was a college student, coming into her own and wanting to make things right in her life. For a test case, it would matter that she was a Good Victim. There would be enough insurmountable obstacles without adding another.

I'd told her over the phone that during our first meeting I wouldn't ask her about the details of the abuse; we would decide then if she ever wanted to talk about them. I did ask her what type of abuse it had been: fondling, not intercourse. This was a drawback for a test case. I knew cold-bloodedly that the less shocking the crime, the weaker our chance of defeating the law. Still, it wasn't a decisive factor.

Loretta and her father, Charlie, told me how these crimes had stayed buried so long. The abuse had started when she was five. At the time she had been too afraid to tell. Her uncle had done to her what molesters always try to do—scared and shamed her into keeping the secret. By the time Loretta was eleven, she was old enough to find ways to avoid being alone with her uncle. The abuse stopped.

Loretta's mother was an emotionally fragile woman. The abuser was her sister's husband. It took Loretta until she was eighteen before she was able to tell her mother. The results of her disclosures set Loretta back even farther.

The mother had been shocked, horrified—she couldn't live with this knowledge. She began a decline that ended three years later in a nervous breakdown. Just before she was hospitalized, Loretta's mother told her husband what Loretta had disclosed. The mother and father went to confront their daughter's molester. He apologized. That was supposed to make everything better.

Charlie had spoken to Loretta after the confrontation. This time Loretta found the response she needed—love, support, anger at the criminal. Charlie wanted to go to the police. It took Loretta months of recovery before she was ready. In the meantime, on Easter Sunday, Charlie had bumped into the molester in front of church. The molester asked for forgiveness—in light of the holy day.

Now they were here, could we do anything?

I told them what I knew. The law books said the statute of limitations had run out. I knew there was talk about testing the statute of limitations in civil cases, but I was no civil lawyer. If they wanted to sue, they'd have to talk to someone who knew that area of the law.

They didn't want money. They wanted to prosecute.

I told them we could try to test the law, but that it wouldn't be easy. Even if I could convince the DA's office to go ahead, getting this case to court was going to be a battle every step of the way. Probably it would be dismissed and there would be years of limbo while we waited for an appeal. Even if we won, which was unlikely, we'd still be facing a terribly tough trial, so many years after the crime.

I talked to Loretta alone. It was clear what her father wanted, but he wasn't the direct victim of these crimes. I understood about how devastating secondary victimization could be. Still, his daughter's considerations were more compelling.

This wasn't like the delayed reporting I'd seen before. We don't make sex-crimes prosecution such an attractive offer to victims that it encourages reporting. I'd seen women who'd only changed their mind about not prosecuting after they'd found out the hard way that the rape wouldn't go away, that they couldn't stand living with it and had no choice. (Despite conventional wisdom about immediate outcry, I found it difficult to discredit a woman who said she wanted to prosecute because she couldn't bear not to any longer.) But that wasn't Loretta. It was outside events, changes in circumstances, that had brought her to my office.

When Charlie had found out, he wanted and needed to find a way to make it right. He hadn't been there then—couldn't he be now? Although his impulse was born out of love and support for his daughter, it also put pressure on her. She needed to make this decision for herself.

I told Loretta I didn't want a final answer from her that day. Think it over, come back in a few weeks. In the meantime, I set up an appointment for her with SVB's social worker.

By the time I saw Loretta again, she was sure she wanted to prosecute. She told me about the crimes.

Every Sunday when she was little, the whole family would visit her grandparents. The grown-ups would stay downstairs talking. The children would go upstairs, to her aunt and uncle's apartment. Their uncle would accompany them. One Sunday her uncle cornered her when she was alone. He rubbed and touched her, put his finger inside her vagina. He told her he'd picked her because she was pretty and "mature" enough to keep a secret. When he was distracted, she ran and hid in the bathroom, locking herself in.

Loretta told me that into adulthood, she couldn't use a bathroom without being terrified, without checking and double-checking that she was safe from intruders.

The abuse had continued most Sundays until Loretta was eleven. When she started to develop breasts, her uncle fondled her there— another part of her body that wasn't hers to control anymore. Finally she refused to visit her grandparents on Sundays. On holidays, when she had to visit, she stayed downstairs with the adults. Still, having to see the molester at all marred her spirit. Now she was ready to start to undo that damage.

SVB's staff shortage had worsened since Laurie's case. I couldn't spare the time from the bureau it would take to handle a new prosecution. I assigned the case to one of the ADAs, and helped where I could. We did the interviews, the investigation. When we were ready, I went to my new executive with the prosecution memo.

Because the police refused to make an arrest, the only way that we could prosecute was to go before a grand jury. For that I needed official approval. I didn't know if I would get it.

The man I had to go to had recently run unsuccessfully for district attorney in Bronx County, losing in a campaign marred by ugly, hotly contested allegations among the various hopefuls. Santucci had hired him to be the executive ADA in charge of investigations. Officially, Special Victims was an investigative bureau.

I didn't know much about my new supervisor except that he claimed to be especially committed to children. I was about to find out if he meant it. My first executive and I had functioned under an unspoken deal that I could do what I wanted as long as I took the weight for it. Interim executives had pretty much followed that pattern. They never would have signed the prosecution memo—and I wouldn't have asked them. If any of them had still been in charge, I would have gone directly to Santucci. But Santucci was avoiding me, and this new guy was insisting on being involved in SVB's functioning; I couldn't pull an end-run on him.

There was one hopeful sign about the new executive. Over the years Santucci had promised me a deputy bureau chief to assist me—one I would have a say in selecting. When we couldn't agree on anyone, we reached an impasse that had lasted for years. Santucci had recently agreed to give me a deputy I'd requested, who'd come up through the ranks in Special Victims. The new executive told me that that was his doing. Maybe I had an ally.

I told him about Loretta, that the indictment was an attempt at a test case, what the issues were. He signed the prosecution memo. He told me, "Good for you."

When we went before the grand jury, we presented the whole case, including the fact that technically the statute of limitations precluded prosecution. It was up to Loretta, her father, and an expert to convince them to indict despite the law. During the grand jury vote, we all held our breath. They took an awfully long time before they gave us their answer. Yes. They'd voted an indictment. We'd done it. We'd jumped the first hurdle.

We rushed back to my office, where Loretta's father and brother were waiting. We all hugged each other with the news, with the excitement of what we'd accomplished.

During all the disappointments that followed in Loretta's case, I held on to the image of that moment of celebration. I thought I couldn't let that be taken from us.

When I told the executive the news, he paled before fumbling out some sort of congratulations. He hadn't expected an indictment. Signing the prosecution memo had been a gesture; now he was going to have to live with it. He thought about it and told me not to involve the police, to go to the lieutenant who ran the DA's private police squad to execute the warrant. I don't know what he told the lieutenant.

The executive wasn't the only one who had second thoughts once the indictment was a reality. Loretta was worried that her grandparents might find out; it would kill them. I told her we would do our best, but that there was a chance they would learn of the prosecution. Did she still want to go ahead with this? Yes.

When I dropped off the warrant, the lieutenant wanted the background. I sketched it in. He echoed the words of my supervisor: Good for you.

That was Friday afternoon. Monday morning I got a call from Santucci. He'd flown back from his vacation in Florida. He wanted to see me right away.

It wasn't a one-on-one meeting, it was a summit, attended by several executives, the lieutenant, some tame bureau chiefs, a representative from the Appeals Bureau, the ADA assigned the case, the DA, and me. The Special Victims ADA kept quiet. Everyone else told me that what I'd done was illegal, outrageous, unthinkable. Nobody once said they'd approved it. Nobody said, "Good for you." Santucci ordered me to dismiss the indictment.

I talked Santucci into holding off his decision for a few days. At least let me prepare the brief I would use in court to defend the indictment. Maybe I could convince the DA before testing this out on a judge. He looked dubious, but if I wanted to do all that extra work . . .

It didn't take Santucci an hour to call me after he got my papers. The decision was the same: Dismiss the indictment.

I'd been prepared for this moment. From the day I'd started in the Queens DA's office, I'd expected that sooner or later someone would order me to do something immoral. I had my answer ready.

Santucci told me it was an order. I told him I was a Jew, I'd learned all about "following orders."

Santucci reconvened a smaller summit, where we argued it out. Santucci said only *he* could approve a test case. Who did I think I was? It surprised and deflected him when out of anger I finally said that his executive had approved my prosecution memo. It surprised the executive that I hadn't said it sooner, but that didn't temper his enmity. Santucci didn't back off, even though he could no longer accuse me of violating "office policy," but he agreed to meet with Loretta and her father. I thought maybe they could convince him.

I was grasping at straws here. I thought that maybe Loretta being Italian, looking like she could be one of Santucci's daughters, might soften his decision.

Instead, he convinced them. He used their common background to charm them—he knew how to be a politician. Charlie told him the family had once used the services of Santucci's brother, the doctor. They small-talked for ten minutes before they even mentioned what had occasioned the meeting. Santucci talked them out of prosecution—think what it would do to the grandparents! He convinced them to settle for the DA's squad talking to the molester. The indictment would have to be dismissed. They agreed.

It wasn't what I'd expected—I'd been prepared to be fired fighting out this particular battle. I'd already changed my working relationship with the district attorney forever. The law was that all ADAs (including bureau chiefs) "served at the pleasure" of the district attorney. I knew there would be consequences for invoking his displeasure. But I couldn't put fight into people who used theirs up just getting past the first step. I agreed to comply with their decision. The ADA dismissed the indictment. The squad talked to Loretta's uncle. As far as everyone but me and Santucci was concerned, it was over.

It left a bad taste in my mouth. I took a week off, but it didn't help much.

I thought about a case I'd prosecuted years ago. The defendant's name was Terry Pittman. He didn't have in him what quality it is that makes the rest of us human. He'd lucked into a teenager who asked him if he knew where to buy marijuana. He took her to his apartment and raped her. She struggled so hard she kicked out a window. He twisted her neck so violently that he paralyzed her. She begged: "Help me, help me, I can't move." It aroused him, and he raped her again. When he was done with her, he flung her body over his shoulder and toted her downstairs— banging her head against the banister because it was too much trouble to balance his unwieldy load. He dumped her, naked, on the driveway. Neighbors called the police.

The victim's parents didn't think she had the strength to prosecute. I did. I believed her when she told me, "If I have to testify, I'll testify— whatever it is—just so long as he gets punished." Pittman pleaded guilty. The day she could walk on her own again, with crutches, she came to the courthouse to find me. She brought me a rose.

There were reasons to stay at Special Victims.

I tried meeting with Santucci to talk over our differences. He wouldn't see me. It wasn't the first time.

When Santucci finally agreed to a meeting, months later, it was because he had something else on his mind besides my defiance. Like the defense attorney on the John German case, he thought that the press on that case was my doing. He thought that if someone had enough media connections, they could tell the press what to say. That's the way connections were supposed to work in his world. His question was: Why wasn't I doing anything to help him?

By then Santucci was one of the media's favorite targets. Headlines about him were merciless, including one in the *Daily News* that read: WHAT THIS BORO NEEDS IS A DA.

There were serial scandals about Santucci. One of them was a fourteen-hour lunch he was reported to have attended with a mob figure. He had a long explanation. He said he didn't know the guy had mob ties. He said he was only there for seven or eight hours. It wasn't as bad as it seemed; he'd done nothing wrong. Santucci was offended when the press didn't reprint his explanations as gospel and apologize to him for ever doubting his integrity. For years he would repeat a twenty-minute version of his explanation during every conversation. He nursed his grievances.

The State Commission on Goverment Integrity investigated Santucci. His son had run for local office a few years back. There were allegations that ADAs in Santucci's office had been pressured to assist in the campaign. The fact that one of Santucci's staffers took the Fifth Amendment rather than testify increased suspicions. The commission made headlines, but nothing ever came of it, except that the ADAs who testified "correctly" got rewarded.

As with all the other allegations against him, Santucci denied any wrongdoing. *Manhattan Lawyer* later ran a profile of Santucci in June 1990 entitled: "Santucci: D.A. For Life, a Constant Campaign, a Lackluster Record." In it, Santucci defended his conduct regarding his son:

> "Does anyone think that I'm the only one who should be accused? Is there no one else who helped his son, or a relative, or gave a friend a job?" asks Santucci. "I think it's the height of hypocrisy to think that any father doesn't somehow take advantage of it when he somehow gets an opportunity to help his children. Lawfully, properly, but perhaps contrary to someone's own ethical ruling."

SVB wound up more understaffed than ever. And the ADAs it did have were a greener lot.

Amid all the headlines, Santucci ran for re-election in 1989. There wasn't much doubt about the outcome—he ran unopposed. *The New York Times* of August 7, 1989, expressed its regrets, in a "Campaign Matters" column entitled "No Opposition, No Explanations for Santucci":

> District Attorney John J. Santucci of Queens County who usually investigates others is hands down the most investigated prosecutor in the city. He is, as politicians say, accident-prone.
>
> He has been investigated by the special state prosecutor and also superseded by him. He has been investigated by a fellow district attorney and

the State Commission on Government Integrity. No indictments, no charges. A lot of smoke but no fire.

Nevertheless Mr. Santucci will get a free ride this year as he seeks his fourth term . . .

The Times followed up two weeks later on August 23, 1989, with an editorial entitled "The People's Non-Choice," which began:

> One of the discouraging aspects of the New York election campaign concerns a race that is failing to take place. John Santucci, District Attorney of Queens, is running unopposed for a fourth term, despite incidents that raise questions about his judgment and ethical standards.

I got a call from the pattern detectives at Queens Sex Crimes Squad. A student at St. John's said she had been raped by the lacrosse team. It had happened a month ago, but she had just come forward to the police. They were investigating, but they were going to need search warrants. Would I assign an ADA? I gave them the one they asked for. He was young but he seemed competent.

I told Santucci what I knew about the allegations. I didn't need to tell him the case was explosive. St. John's is sacred to Queens. Almost every politically powerful figure in Queens County, including John Santucci, Donald Manes, and Mario Cuomo, went to its law school. So far the press hadn't gotten hold of the story—but it was only a matter of time. Santucci didn't give me any orders about how to handle the case. He just told me to keep him informed.

I figured I was in a race against the politics of prosecution.

I got updates on St. John's during the next two weeks. The detectives executed the search warrants, corroborating some of the more unusual details the victim had given (such as that the offenders wore masks). The victim wasn't sure if she wanted to prosecute. The ADA scheduled an appointment with her, and in the meantime she was meeting almost daily with the detectives and with her counselors at St. John's.

The day the victim was supposed to come in for the interview with the ADA, I got a phone call from the local *Newsday* reporter. She'd gotten wind of the allegations; what could I tell her? Nothing.

I'd just lost the race.

I went to Santucci but couldn't get in to see him. I told his press secretary, a man who disliked me. It was an ominous way to start.

Santucci met with me, along with the press secretary and my supervisor, the "good-for-you" executive, who was furious that I hadn't told him first. The case was a career maker (or breaker). Everyone wanted either a piece of it or their backs covered, depending on the result.

For reasons I can't begin to guess, Santucci started the meeting saying this was the first he'd heard of the allegations. The press secretary was fielding phone calls from *Newsday*. What did I know? I filled the higher-ups in on the details. It was clear the woman had been treated like garbage. I'd know more than that once the ADA talked to her.

Santucci called every twenty minutes during the ADA's interview with the victim. What did I know? At one point the ADA told me he wasn't sure what we had. I forwarded the message. Santucci didn't like that much. He wanted a rape case.

Now that the brass was involved, dealing with them took up most of our time and energy. Whatever work got done on the case had to be squeezed in between conferences on the third floor.

Santucci, my supervisor, the new legal counsel, and I disagreed over how the case should be handled. No one was under arrest yet. The standard was supposed to be to do the job right up front. The press was screaming for action. Santucci wanted an immediate indictment.

The result was a compromise: I stole a couple of days to do it, and Santucci got his indictment as soon as Special Victims was convinced of the crimes.

My supervisor made noises that he wanted the case for himself. He'd had his fair share of bad press—I guess he figured this case could make up for it.

The new legal counsel was nervous, but that wasn't surprising. All I knew about him was that he often seemed to think the safest course was not to prosecute, make that double if it was a sex crime, and triple if it was a crime against a child. He nearly had heart failure when he found out we'd indicted a teacher for sexual abuse based on the word of two Down Syndrome children. It was like the very concept Blame the

Predator was foreign to him. At the time I didn't know that would become a trend.

Between the executive, the press secretary, and legal counsel, they convinced their boss.

Santucci took the case away from Special Victims and reassigned it to a man who had never tried a sex crime, supervised by the executive in charge of trials. I was out of it, and so, most definitely, was the bureau.

I got an intraoffice memo from Santucci. It was a list of cases. A huge chunk of SVB's trial caseload was to be reassigned. The whole bureau exploded in anger. Having the St. John's case taken away had been humiliating, but it was just one case. It had almost been a relief to get back to the daily caseload. This list was different, a direct blow to the bureau's work and to its self-concept.

The ADAs and I talked it over in a series of meetings. Many of them said they were willing to walk out. I found a city agency that might hire the block of us all together. More people said they were willing to quit. At least in words, some people stood up . . . and others didn't. It cut wounds between us that never healed. But that was internal. To the rest of the office we looked more cohesive than a unit in a DA's office was supposed to be.

I asked for a meeting with Santucci. I suspected he had heard what we were planning. Maybe he didn't want front-page headlines that read SEX CRIMES BUREAU QUITS OVER HANDLING OF ST. JOHN'S.

This time he agreed to see me. He was all apologies and conciliation: Of course he still believed in me and the bureau. What did I mean, I hadn't been consulted about that list? No, that was wrong. All he'd wanted was to cut down on our backlog. Rip up the list. See if it's possible to find some transferrable cases. He would make sure the people they were reassigned to would handle them right. He would personally tell them it was the most important case in their caseload; In the meantime, work on the backlog.

Santucci wouldn't budge on the reassignment of the St. John's case. He thought I should be satisfied that the "good-for-you" executive was off the case.

I took the results of the meeting back to Special Victims. Was this enough for them, or did they still want to quit in protest? They voted to stay.

But the damage had already been done.

Santucci settled for smaller but more effective methods. Day by day, the Third Floor chipped away at the cracks he had created in our unity and our belief in ourselves.

Even understaffed SVB was overcrowded. There was a law now requiring that rape victims be interviewed in private. That wasn't possible to ensure in our physical setup. In response, Santucci took some of our space and assigned it to another unit. There was talk, even blueprints, about SVB being moved to a brand new building. (Somehow I knew from the first time I saw the plans that I'd never see the new quarters.) In the meantime we'd just have to put up with the inconvenience . . . and the visible message to the rest of the office that SVB was out of favor.

The three detective-investigators assigned to the bureau were moved to another floor. Other bureaus were allowed to use them. Progressively they had less time to spend on Special Victims cases.

Santucci's moves started having spiraling effects. By that fall, shortly after he made the legal counsel SVB's new executive, three of the ADAs quit at once, followed within a few weeks by three of the paralegals. SVB had already been dangerously understaffed without losing over a quarter of its people.

It got worse. Even the flooding from the pens recurred.

It didn't help, either, that the first appellate decisions concerning closed-circuit TV came down around that time. SVB had broken new ground here, and the higher courts had to redefine the new statutes and the issues. Of the first two cases they reviewed, they reversed one and upheld the other. (The defendant in the reversal was a woman. I thought maybe the higher courts believed all pedophiles were male.)

On the basis of this one reversal, the legal counsel tried to convince Santucci that we shouldn't use closed-circuit TV for trial, or even videotaping for the grand jury. When I proved to Santucci that those were two different statutes, he stopped crediting the legal counsel and backed off. But it was clear all I'd done was temporarily stem the tide.

We gave Sheba a posthumous star at the awards dinner that year. We'd lost her a little while before to old age and illness. I was glad, later, that she didn't have to see what was to come.

I watched Santucci unravel all I'd worked to create. At some point I forced myself to relinquish my dreams. All along I'd told myself that someday we'd have enough staff, enough space, enough resources for the bureau to finally be what I envisioned. Instead, Santucci set out on a path of destruction. Worse, he was taking the one thing I'd counted on in the staff—their heart.

There was a boxing match I watched with my husband. A Golden Boy, promo'ed as a contender, against a guy who was supposed to only be an opponent—but nobody'd told him. The Golden Boy had lots of skill. All the other guy had was heart. Between rounds the Golden Boy's corner coached him on strategy; this was a fight to learn on, looking forward toward bigger things. At one point the camera showed the opponent's corner. All they said to their fighter was, "Get out there and fuck him up." He tried. He did some damage—and it showed. He stood up all the way, but getting knocked out was inevitable. It felt like that was me.

The one hope was that this time Santucci meant it when he threatened to retire.

The higher-ups began to act like these were their last days to play. With Santucci less and less in the picture, they ran the show. They did what they wanted.

For the first time, there were rumors that getting ahead depended on who you were willing to get in bed with—sometimes figuratively, sometimes literally. These rumors got so bad that when Santucci announced promotions, he prefaced them by denying that he was having an affair with any of the women he was promoting.

That particular speech was given when Santucci held a staffwide Christmas dinner. Most of the promotions he announced were of people who lacked the background or experience for their new positions. It was a raw exercise of power, simply to prove he was still DA and would do what he wanted.

Among the changes, the present deputy bureau chief of Special Victims was promoted to bureau chief of Major Offenses. In her place he named another female. She had no experience in sex-crimes prosecution. What experience she did have in homicide trials, had gained her only the reputation of being "a nice girl."

Nobody, especially not my new deputy, cared what I had to say.

Instead, she made a point of being obsequious to the Third Floor. And she made common cause with the legal counsel who was now SVB's executive. He was jockeying for position to be the next DA. In the meantime, he specialized in obstruction. He refused to approve most indictments on child sexual-abuse cases.

He specialized in refusing to approve most of the indictments on child sexual-abuse cases.

The rumors escalated about Santucci.

The county itself lost faith in the district attorney. Convictions became damn near impossible to come by. Morale was at an all-time low.

One of the problems was that there were so few staff that they started looking for shortcuts. I'd tried to teach them to reject conventional wisdom, to think for themselves. Now that meant not listening to anyone, just plowing ahead. I second-seated a trial where the ADA hadn't bothered to talk to the alibi witnesses. She told me she already knew they were lying and that the defendant was the right guy. It was hard not to worry all the time about what the ADAs were doing wrong.

The work itself started getting to me. One day there was a photograph in the news of a man holding a little baby in his arms. Behind him there was only rubble. The baby had miraculously survived a tornado completely untouched. The man was quoted as saying: God sent his angels to watch over her. I started to cry. Where were all the other angels?

I did what I knew how to do. I went to trial.

I'd taken over the prosecution of George Chavis and Geraldine Mitchell a year before when another bureau had refused to indict it. It was a homicide, originally without even a body, and according to the other bureau, without sufficient proof. It wasn't a sex crime—at least not technically. The victim was a three-year-old boy who'd been beaten to death by his mother's boyfriend (with her assistance). He had suffered months of torture under the blind eyes of the city's Social Services before he finally died. The mother, Geraldine Mitchell, had reported the child missing. The police knew he must be dead, but they held on to enough hope to mount a massive search. Cops worked triple shifts, came in on their days off. They braved rat-infested dumpsters, shrubbery, and undergrowth so dense they found an animal sacrifice from a voodoo ritual—all for a little boy who nobody cared about until it was too late.

By the time the body was found in an abandoned cemetery months later, the medical examiner could barely prove identity let alone find the kinds of forensic evidence a jury would want to hear about the cause of death.

When the police isolated Mitchell in order to question her without Chavis present, he became enraged. He went to her grandmother's house and beat the eighty-year-old crippled woman. Later the grandmother said that while he beat her, Chavis threatened that he was "going to do her like he did the baby."

Chavis had abused other children. He seemed to seek out girlfriends with ready little victims. The mothers of the other children told me Chavis could be nice but then he would become a different person; a pulsating rage would take over him until he satisfied himself with enough damage to a little body. Once, after he'd battered another three-year-old, he carved an X in the child's forehead. (That was the Chavis case that the old Special Victims Bureau had refused to prosecute.) It was power-rush violence—an ugly but familiar evil.

Mitchell said in one of her statements (although she refused to say it on the witness stand) that the final beating came on a night when the little boy tried to fight back. Chavis struck the child for having interrupted their intercourse. According to Mitchell, she tried to protest and Chavis hit her as well. The child reacted by making little fists in anger. It incensed Chavis. He beat the boy to death.

When it was done, they had an argument about whether the baby was still breathing. Chavis put the body in a garbage bag, and then into a pail underneath the bathroom sink. When Mitchell complained that the body upset her whenever she wanted to use the bathroom, he moved it. This time he put it inside their apartment-size refrigerator—where it stayed for a few days. On a moonless rainy night he told her he was going to "give the baby a good burial" and took the garbage bag out of the hotel room. Although these last details were hard to credit, human hair was found in the refrigerator, and the body was eventually discovered in an abandoned cemetery.

Mitchell's defense attorney postured for a long time about how I couldn't prove the case, and how the prosecution of his client was an outrage. Mitchell had an excuse—allegedly she'd been battered by the boyfriend too. He claimed that she was "the black Hedda Nussbaum." He claimed it was racism that had granted Nussbaum immunity in the headlined death of Lisa Steinberg, while his client was being prosecuted. (I don't know what race he thought the *victim* was.) The defense attorney demanded and received support from battered women's advocates against the prosecution.

Even the anthropologist who studied his bones had difficulty thinking about the kinds of pain that had been inflicted on this little boy. Geraldine Mitchell watched it, assisted. Night after night she smuggled Chavis into her room in a welfare hotel. During the day, medical attention was there for the asking, but she hid the boy's scars and bruises. She was the one person who could have stopped this slow, horrifying suffering, and she did nothing. She needed to pay for her crimes.

When the defense arguments failed to make the case go away, Geraldine Mitchell pleaded guilty for a prison sentence and a promise to testify against her boyfriend. George Chavis went to trial. It took almost a month. There were a lot of witnesses—maybe because none of them had a lot of proof.

During the trial, my husband wrote me notes of encouragement. Whenever our schedules conflicted, a note on the breakfast table would remind me he was on my side.

The day after I succeeded in getting out Mitchell's testimony against her boyfriend, I got a note that said:

> Keep the pressure on him, don't let him rest—he's already breathing bad—didn't train to go the distance—which is fine, because he's not going to.

When the judge precluded the proof that Chavis had been a security guard over the abandoned graveyard where the baby's body was found, and when it still looked like the judge wasn't going to permit testimony about Chavis's other victims, his note read:

> Today starts the middle rounds—keep banging.

On the defense case, in preparation for the defendant testifying, he wrote me:

It's the last round—and you've won them all, a couple 10–8—but go after the maggot like *he's* won them all *and* the judges are in his pocket *and* the ref is his cousin—he'll get a long count when he goes down too—so knock him *unconscious*—hell, knock him *dead!*

The morning I had to sum up, my husband shook me awake. "Alice, Alice." He had one final piece of advice: "Get out there and fuck him up."

I tried. It felt like it was my last day in the ring. I told the jury:

Andrew Mitchell's* life was short and painful. His death was slow and horrible. His burial, unsanctified, without mourners, without rites to mark his passage. His body was left for [rats] to gnaw on. If Andrew Mitchell's passage through this world is to be marked with any dignity and any justice, it is up to you to produce that for him.

It is not your job to deliver a particular verdict in this case. For that you must look to your own hearts and minds and to the evidence. It *is* your job to treat the death of Andrew Mitchell with the same solemnity that you would treat the death of a loved one. Andrew Mitchell learned more about the dark side of human nature in his few years on this planet than most of us . . . learn in a lifetime. He learned very little about decency or love or kindness. Maybe it is too late for him to learn that the human species can be good and just. I don't know enough about the ways of the Lord to know if Andrew Mitchell is watching down on this trial. . . . All I can do is ask you to treat your deliberations as if he is.

The defense attorney just spent a lot of time telling you about what the People allegedly failed to prove in this case. Some of what he says is true, although that does not change the truth. There's no decent, respectable, wonderful, credible witness who was there for the final moments of Andrew Mitchell's life who can tell us exactly what happened during that time. If

---

*I have used this victim's real name. It's his legacy.

there were, if Geraldine Mitchell were such a person, Andrew Mitchell would not be dead.

There's no pathologist who can tell you with precision as to the final moments of Andrew's life. The precise autopsy of his bruises, his injuries, and so forth. That is not this crime. There's not going to be that proof. There is no such proof. This is not a shooting of an adult with eyewitnesses. [That] is not this death. [That] is not this crime. All that we have left to find the truth is bones and pieces. Bones that are still screaming from the pain. . . . And pieces of the truth that we can glean from the testimony that you have heard before you. . . .

I took out two pieces of evidence and placed them on the ledge in front of the jury. Looking at them, it was hard not to cry. One was Chavis's sneaker. (It was just coincidental that it had been vouchered from him and that he had extraordinarily large feet.) The other was Andrew's little three-year-old's sneaker, with a picture of Alf on it.

I reviewed all the circumstantial evidence, all the carefully assembled details that might prove Chavis's guilt—the sole remains of Andrew Mitchell's short life.

It is not the final moments of this child's life that we are talking about. We are talking about a slow, long death. We may never know what those final moments were, and maybe that's a kindness. But we don't need to know. This is not a gunshot wound that causes death. This is months of torture . . . this was a crime of power. This was a crime that occurred because George Chavis was larger and stronger and capable of beating a three-and-a-half-year-old. And because Andrew Mitchell was small and weak and vulnerable and had nobody to protect him. . . .

All that is left to Andrew Mitchell is bones and pieces. He only had a little piece of life and that little piece was tortured. No POW was treated worse than Andrew Mitchell. . . . There was no army to come and rescue him. . . . Andrew Mitchell was about as alone on this earth as any child can be, and nobody should get away with that. Nobody. . . .

The defense attorney told you during openings that the death of Andrew Mitchell was a tragedy. When a child dies in a fire, that's a tragedy. When a child dies . . . in a car accident, or from illness, that's a tragedy. When a child is beaten and tortured to death, that's not a tragedy; that's evil. . . . The tragedy would be . . . for *him* to get away with that. . . .

You have an awesome responsibility, ladies and gentlemen. The truth in this case can only be spoken by your voice in your verdict. Andrew Mitchell is dead. Don't let the truth die with him.

The jury convicted Chavis of manslaughter in the first degree. The judge gave him the maximum. It felt like prosecuting Chavis was what had kept me at the DA's office, the final battle they were willing to let me fight.

There was nothing left for me. Special Victims had been my piece of desert. I bled for it. I grieved its losses. I sweated over it. Against the odds I made the crops grow. Now they were giving it away to the enemy in a peace accord. When I fought them, they salted the earth.

The media aired videotapes of police brutality in California. Santucci had a bunch of cops indicted in Queens County for police brutality and murder. The proof was questionable. The media was critical. Santucci announced that he was going to retire, and this time he meant it. He spent the remainder of his time in office openly criticizing the press. He said they didn't like him because he was Italian.

There really was going to be a change in district attorneys. It was a new chance.

2

There were months of speculation about who the governor was going to appoint as Santucci's replacement. Both the legal counsel and the "good for you" executive were acting as if Santucci had promised them they would get his endorsement. Either way, I knew I would be looking at unemployment. I'd come too far, though, not to play out this final string.

After the trial, my husband started to write me notes on a different topic—the deputy, who he'd started to call "the toad" (short for "toa-die"). One note said:

The toad can never break the code—or you.

To me the deputy came to symbolize everything Santucci had done to Special Victims. When she'd first arrived, I'd interviewed her about her background. Had she ever handled an investigation? No. Did she ever prosecute a sex crime? No. Had she ever interviewed a child victim or witness? No. Did she ever prosecute a crime against an elderly victim? No. Did she ever prosecute a case between family members? No. Well, any case where the victim and defendant at least knew each other? Yes. All right, I'd give her some materials to study and start her working on domestic violence. No. She refused and accused me of "decimating the position of deputy bureau chief." All along I had tried to motivate the staff by creating a unit where everyone *earned* their status. Now I had a deputy with no background in our work, insisting increasingly on her "right to supervise." I got another note:

> If your eye is on the sky
> you may crunch the toad in the road—
> which is how we measure progress.

If there really was going to be a new district attorney, if I had any shot at all of SVB rising from the dead under new leadership, then I wanted as clean a slate as I could manage. I took on the effort to try to get rid of the deputy.

I started small. I tried seeing Santucci. No. I tried a short-form memo. No answer.

I wrote Santucci a longer memo. I'd been told for years that it was impolitic in that office to put things in writing. I requested the toad's transfer, listing my reasons.

I waited again. Nothing. It was like punching a pillow.

I wrote the toad herself a memo. She didn't answer. Instead the executive handed me a sealed interoffice envelope with his response inside. He had already sent a copy to Santucci. The memo ended with a threat:

> I am quite upset by your inability to resolve this situation and I can only state that if you cannot accept the District Attorney's choice as your deputy and work with her effectively for the betterment of the bureau then you should consider resigning or asking for a transfer to other duties.

When my response was completed, my husband wrote me a note that said:

> Stomp them so flat even toads can't crawl under them.

I did the best I could, ending my memo:

> If the day ever comes when your criteria rule this office, you won't have to weasel around trying to manipulate me out of a job . . . I'll be gone.

I started going to work each day expecting to be fired. It seemed to be what everyone else expected for me as well.

Governor Cuomo played out his own string, waiting as long as he could before naming a replacement for Santucci. The new appointee was Richard A. Brown, a judge who'd previously been appointed by the governor to the appellate bench.

I was the only one from the office willing to be quoted by the media. I said this new guy better bring a new broom to sweep the place clean.

I was determined to force the issue with the new DA. Special Victims had succumbed to office politics. Brown could continue that tradition—choose politics over prosecution—or he could be willing to make a change.

On Santucci's last day, there was an officewide meeting to transfer the reins of power. Brown made a speech in which he said he wanted the office to be about justice. He told us all he carried with him no baggage, introducing his personal secretary and his law secretary as the only staff he'd be bringing along. He took the oath of office to be the new DA.

After Santucci left, I waited.

The memo exchange got more newspaper coverage as THE MOTHER OF ALL MEMO WARS. Several victims and victim agencies wrote to Brown supporting the work of Special Victims.

Within a few days of Brown's taking over, my deputy's executive and the "good-for-you" executive "resigned."

I'd put off training SVB's new crew of ADAs during all the chaos. It couldn't wait any longer. I ran a full-week's training course. We were so understaffed that most of them were too busy to attend most of the sessions. The toad had her own reasons not to attend.

SVB wasn't going to get any better unless Brown made some radical changes.

In a bureau chiefs' meeting early on, Brown looked around the room preparing us for an announcement: We all knew he was running for election in September; he wanted us to know that we were all out of it. He didn't want us doing anything. He had plenty of people working on his campaign. Our job was to do our jobs, not get involved in politics. I only hoped he meant it.

Brown created a new position: chief assistant. The DA was now to be one step removed from the running of his office. During his first hours on the job, the chief assistant and I wound up in a meeting together. He called me aside for a minute afterward, told me he just wanted to let me know: "Your ass is not hanging over a ledge." Like everyone else, he'd read the memo exchange between me and the executive. In case I didn't get it the first time, he repeated, "Your ass is not on the line." Somehow it reminded me of John German, who couldn't avoid the phrase "fondling my ass" even when he was supposedly being "professional."

I tried to make an appointment to see the chief assistant about SVB's future, but he was too busy to see me. As it turned out, he wasn't too busy to see the toad.

I wound up writing another memo to the deputy about her time sheets, detailing my reasons for refusing to sign off. I sent it only to her. The chief assistant called me into his office. He had a copy of what I'd written. He told me, "No more memos."

I brought up the bureau. The chief assistant was uncomfortable with phrases like "sharing a vision"; he kept looking at me like he was trying to figure out what I was up to. He told me to just be patient.

The chief assistant was going to be a roadblock, but that still left Brown.

I asked to see the district attorney. He was too busy. Somehow this didn't feel any different than things had under Santucci. It was getting harder to reserve judgment.

Brown hired a new executive for Special Victims. She told me to watch out for the chief assistant. She said she'd heard he would have been named to his position no matter who Cuomo had named to be DA. She wanted me to know that he was a powerful man: I shouldn't cross him.

Brown called a meeting on the St. John's case, which had gone to trial on the first three defendants. I wasn't invited.

The ADAs on the trial picked a terrible jury. The prosecution blamed all its problems on an unfriendly judge. (It was Judge Soleil.) The media couldn't understand it when the jury acquitted.

Brown brought in a new executive in charge of budget. One of the first policies he instituted was that ADAs shouldn't order hearing transcripts. They were too expensive; the defense having them to prepare for briefs and trial wasn't a good enough reason for us to spend the money.

Brown had said he was going to run the DA's office like a law office. I thought he meant professionally.

The new budget exec was horrified by SVB's expenditures. Why were we spending so much on consultant fees? Did we really need validation or experts on rape trauma syndrome? They cost too much—cut back. And what's this about a video team? Wait until he found out what DNA analysis cost.

SVB's state of mind showed. Even the anatomically correct dolls wound up in the corner of the video room, stacked any which way and often naked. I requisitioned a toy box to contain them. The new budget director denied the request: It wasn't an appropriate use of monies.

He asked my new executive whether she knew we had a baby-sitter on the payroll. His wanting to do away with the position of playroom attendant fit with my deputy's plans to convert the playroom into an extra office so she could keep her solo one. They only held off because Brown had praised the playroom when he saw it on his initial tour of the office.

I waited for Brown to start running the office and take these decisions away from the people he'd brought on board.

At one of Brown's weekly meetings he made an announcement. He knew he'd said that all of us were not to be involved in his campaign, he said. But so many of the bureau chiefs and executives had "begged" him to let them participate that he didn't want to abridge our civic rights. He'd asked his legal counsel to research the situation. At the next meeting, Brown reported the results of that research. It turned out that despite the general prohibition against ADAs engaging in political activity, we *were* legally permitted to work on his campaign—so long as it wasn't fund-raising or on office hours.

Brown finally talked to me toward the end of the summer. He wanted to talk about the media coverage he'd been getting. I wanted to talk about Special Victims. He mouthed the right words about his commitment to Special Victims, and repeated them at a bureau chiefs' meeting; they sounded like a politician's promise. I talked specifics:

I needed more staff.

There'd be a transfer list soon.

What about the deputy who didn't belong in Special Victims?

It would have to wait until after the primary; she had political connections.

I had specific ideas.

Put them in writing.

I did. It was my one shot, so I put on paper what I'd learned and stood for over the past ten years. We need to up the stakes for sex offenders. We as a public have the right to demand that our district attorneys wage an all-out war against predatory violence in all its variations. We can no longer afford to permit politics to take precedence over prosecution.

I got no response. Brown was busy with the election.

I did as much for Brown's campaign as I had for Santucci's: nothing. For a new DA, Brown made some very old choices.

Later* this item ran in the local gossip page of the *Daily News*:

> John Zacarro Jr. has put his 1988 drug felony conviction behind him and is following in the footsteps of his famous mother, Geraldine Ferraro. He's landed a summer job in the Queens district attorney's office where Ferraro began her career. . . .

The word-processed postconviction press-release copy that was always sent out was altered. Now it said, "District Attorney Richard A. Brown will demand the maximum sentence."

Brown promised the public that he was going to be the DA to finally go after organized crime in Queens. To prove it, he created an airport bureau.

A transfer list came out. There was one new ADA assigned to Special Victims. She was someone no one else wanted—and Special Victims wasn't where she wanted to be.

All I knew was to keep swinging. Lester Ford got himself arrested on three rapes and three murders. SVB disagreed with Homicide Investigations about how the cases should be handled. Afterward, they wanted to take the rape cases away from Special Victims. I said no. I got into another battle with the chief assistant.

It wasn't that I didn't know what I was doing. I wanted Brown's

*May 7, 1992

choice as clear-cut as possible. In that much, I think I succeeded. It was up to Brown.

Brown had so little opposition to his election that he consented to have an opponent on the ballot (withdrawing his original successful challenge to the opponent's candidacy). Still, Brown acted beforehand as if he could lose . . . he didn't.

Three days after the election, the chief assistant called me into his office. I was fired.

After years of training and preparation, they finally let me climb into the ring. But by the time I even broke a sweat, they started stripping the padding out of my opponent's gloves. They made sure I had no one working my corner. Then, when it looked like I still wasn't going down, their hometown referee declared a TKO and held the other guy's hand high in "victory."

That's O.K.—they don't own the only ring. I'll find someplace else to go out there and fuck 'em up.

Part Five

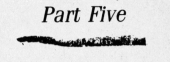

AFTERWORD

Writing *Sex Crimes* has been as difficult for me as any jury summation. I wanted so badly to put the words together right so that other people can see what I saw and feel what I felt. What has kept me struggling at this task is a belief that what happened in Queens is not limited to the petty politics of one borough of New York City.

I don't have a magic formula to fix things. All I have is some basic working principles.

When I decided to become a sex-crimes prosecutor, I had no idea what it would feel like to convict a rapist . . . to create a little piece of justice on this planet. All along, from the first sex crime I prosecuted to the last day I ran Special Victims, there were people "in the know" saying that what I wanted couldn't be done. For longer than I ever thought possible, and with greater success than I dreamed, SVB stood for the proposition that sex-crimes prosecution *could* be done differently than Queens County tradition dictated.

It still amazes me how readily we let district attorneys off the hook for crime. It may be that crime itself is inherent to the human spirit, but the degree of crime and its level of violence are always a function of societal tolerance more than of any other factor.

When there is a strike by the New York City Sanitation Department, the public outcry is immediate. No amount of press releases claiming that "Commissioner of Sanitation John J. Santucci demands the maximum trash pickups" would satisfy a public that looks out the window and sees garbage piling up and rotting on the street. We have lower standards for our criminal justice system, although the visibility—and the stench—of the refuse is no less apparent.

Although district attorneys run for office, we have somehow communally agreed that the garbage piling up on the street is not their fault. Instead we judge them, if at all, based on their response to whatever individual criminal incidents the media headlines.

"Tough on crime" is used by politicians to mean tough on anyone who comes to public attention. Newspapers never cover the shadow figures—the prosecutions "declined," the violence ignored, and the criminality thus condoned.

Of all violence, sex crime is the most vulnerable to the politics of prosecution. Few prosecutors are crusaders—and it takes an affirmative determination to raise the stakes for sex offenders to overcome the statistical liabilities of taking on difficult cases.

If we are going to evaluate prosecutors on performance, then we need to develop a template like the Olympics scoring system for diving—that is, according to degree of difficulty. Conviction rates cannot tell us what law enforcement is doing about the most dangerous criminals—they can only tell us what is being done about those defendants against whom there is the most proof.

The soft underbelly of collaboration in sex-crimes prosecution will never be seen on Court TV—it exposes itself in the cases that are *not* prosecuted.

When we find evil and violence coalescing within any individual, then the only sane self-protective goal is incarceration. To do that consistently rather than episodically we need to take the self-interest out of collaboration. And we need to look at what we are doing to spawn such sympathies.

We have allowed sex crimes to be the one area of criminality where we judge the offense not by the perpetrator but by the victim. There *is* an essential difference between sex crimes and other crimes, but it has nothing to do with victims. Most other crime is in response to a need that the offense itself seeks to meet. (Some) people kill because they are angry. (Some) people steal because they want money. But as each rape is committed, it creates a greater need. Rape is dose-related—it is chronic, repetitive . . . and always escalating.

Rapists cross a line—a clear, bright line. Absent specific, significant, *predictable* consequences, they are never going to cross back. Too often, instead of consequences what we give them is permission.

Collaboration is a hate crime. When a jury in Florida acquits because the victim was not wearing underpants, when a grand jury in Texas refuses to indict because an AIDS-fearing victim begged the rapist to use a condom, when a judge in Manhattan imposes a lenient sentence because the rape of a retarded, previously victimized teenager wasn't "violent," when an appellate defense attorney vilifies a young woman on national TV for the "crime" of having successfully prosecuted a rape complaint, when a judge in Wisconsin calls a five-year-old "seductive"—all that is collaboration, and it is antipathy toward victims so virulent that it subjects us all to risk.

When collaboration is judicially supported, it is a grave error to conclude that it is an individual aberration of a particular judge. Since judges are picked on a political basis, we have to expect their conduct to be reflective of the larger norm. Judges who get their positions by lifetimes of obeisance to the local clubhouse are going to go with what got them there. We should not expect leadership from such individuals—but we can certainly impose consequences for their performance.

A judge with a demonstrated record of being anti-Hispanic, or anti-Italian, or anti-Semitic—any bias against any particular class of defendant—would be subject to penalties up to and through removal. But if that same judge shows an overwhelming bias against victims, there is no remedy.

What "double jeopardy" has come to mean in American criminal justice is this: The victim only gets one chance.

There are always going to be rapists among us. We need to stop permitting it to be socially and politically acceptable to give them aid and comfort. We need to recognize rape for the antihuman crime that it is. Rape is neither sexual nor sexy; it is an ugly act of dominance and control. Just as rapists generally prefer knives, they use the sex act itself to make their abuse of power more personal. We need to start judging sex crime by the rape and by the rapist . . . not by the victim.

No political ideology "owns" the war against rape. Everybody uses rape for their own ends, and it is rare for the focus to ever be on blaming the rapist. Those who want to say that society is too permissive say that we have rape because of pornography. Those who want to say that society is too repressive say that legalizing prostitution would decrease rape. The truth is, society doesn't "cause" rape—but society's reaction to rape promotes it.

People can be collaborators even when that is not their intent. Legalizing prostitution doesn't reduce rape any more than pornography causes rape; sex offenses are not a function of excess hormones. But pornography that degrades women may very well cause collaboration. Any time we send the message that sexual violence is acceptable, we feed into the support system for sex offenders. Anti-female pornography may not motivate rape, but it does validate the rapist's self-perception as a member of a large, societally endorsed group.

We have a unified attitude toward all other types of crimes. We have recognized that an armed robber poses a potential risk to each of us. Whether he sticks up a bank or a bodega, whether the victim is running numbers or selling church supplies, we have a sense of universality. We understand that we could be robbed next. Until we have the same unified attitude toward sex crimes, we will continue losing this "war."

Sex offenders are experts in justificatory language and concepts. We have to stop believing their lies.

• Saying victims cause rape is like saying banks cause robberies. No one deserves to be raped.

• Kiddie porn is not a victimless crime.

• Fondling is not a nonviolent offense. No child's conduct invites molestation.

• Same-sex pedophiles are not homosexuals any more than different-sex pedophiles are heterosexual—they are *criminals*.

• Sexual violence is not part of the marriage contract.

• The rate of sex crimes cannot be reduced by dress codes.

The Supreme Court has struggled for years with a definition of obscenity. I'll give you one: letting a rapist go free . . . giggling behind his mask, confident of his endorsements . . . and committed to recidivism.

There is no greater stigma to poverty than the reality-based perception that violence is more tolerated within one's own community than it would be elsewhere. Racism is never more self-destructive than when it says that the color of a woman's skin determines whether she was "really" raped. There is nothing more damaging to the soul of an abused child than the belief that his or her molestation is sanctioned by the adult world.

We can't afford our prejudices against victims. Sex offenders exact too high a price for our tolerance.

If "rapism" were a disease, it would be an epidemic. When sex offenders are caught, and if they perceive serious consequences, they demand "treatment," even though no one is claiming to have found a "cure." The only viable "treatment" for rape is quarantine. There is a lot of talk about sex-offender therapy, but there is only one functional diagnostic criterion: dangerousness. We spend much too much time trying to "understand" rapists from a treatment point of view. If rapists are to be studied, we should study them from a combat point of view; we need to understand the enemy. Most fundamentally, what we need to know about rapists is how to interdict them, and how to put them down for the count once they are finally captured.

We are finally beginning to recognize the inadequacy of our current systems to protect us against a specific type of predator—one who is dangerous, but not crazy. Faced with the parole eligibility of Larry Singleton, a rapist who kidnapped a teenage hitchhiker, cut off her hands, and left her to die in the desert, California rallied against the danger his release represented. Granted parole, he could not find a community in the state willing to accept him as a parolee. More recently public outcry in Florida gained an extra five years incarceration for a rapist already granted parole after having served only a fraction of his thirty-four-year sentence. In New Jersey the town of Wycoff keeps twenty-four-hour surveillance of Donald Chapman, a rapist who completed his maximum sentence, thus requiring his release after twelve years incarceration despite universal diagnoses (and his own promise) that next time he will rape *and* kill. The state of Washington has enacted controversial legislation, now being debated by at least five other states, permitting postsentence incarceration in exactly such circumstances. While all of this represents a welcome growing intolerance for the rapists among us, each case represents a failure of law enforcement. Known, dangerous, convicted sex offenders have received such leniency from the criminal justice system that they are parole-eligible within a shockingly short amount of time.

We could use better weapons. New York is typical in that its sentencing structure is hopelessly inadequate. If sexual psychopaths (like predatory pedophiles and serial rapists) are going to commit themselves to a lifetime of sex offenses—we need to commit them to life sentences. We say that we grade theft offenses by the value of what is stolen and the force and violence used. If we judged sex crimes the same way, virtually *every* rapist would get a life sentence.

We need laws that recognize that child molestation can be an ongoing crime, not just an isolated incident. We must revise the statute of limitations to recognize that sex offenders can traumatize victims into years of silence. We enhance the penalties for robbery depending on the use of weapons and/or violence. We need to use the same formula for rapes that involve the abuse of a "power relationship," be it father-daughter, teacher-student, minister-congregant, or any other permutations of that dynamic. We need to enact laws against rape-by-extortion, whether it occurs in a sweatshop against an illegal alien or on a psychiatrist's couch against a patient.

Prosecutors now have statutorily created "discretion" with which to betray victims. The charge of "sexual misconduct" serves no function other than to give a district attorney the option to treat rape as a minor crime.★ Because incest is the lowest class of felony, prosecutors have the option of treating intrafamilial abuse as less of a crime than a stranger-to-stranger molestation. Either rape and incest should be the same high level of felony or we should take incest off the books and simply treat it as what it is: the rape of a child.

Some of these defects in the law may be unique to New York, but they are representative of the obstacles to sex-crimes prosecution throughout this country. It may be that anomalies occurred when the penal law failed to change at the same pace as societal values. But it is

★Krista Absalom, whose victimization was detailed in the foreword, is currently spearheading a statewide effort demanding the repeal of this statute in New York.

nonetheless intolerable that there is still a state in this union that requires a child victim of molestation to be "previously chaste."

Although individual states have made legislative advances in this area, they remain unsupported on a nationwide level.★ We do not even have a national registry of convicted sex offenders, which would allow us to check the records of rapists and molesters before giving them access to children in our schools, in our child-care and child-protective agencies, and as foster parents.†

The federal government declared a "war on drugs" when its citizenry finally recognized that even people who are not dope fiends are harmed by narcotics traffic. All the children caught in the cross fires of drug-dealer wars proved that the most innocent can still be victimized by dope. The federal government has never declared a war on rape.

I am not suggesting that "just say no" is effective—that transparent PR slogan is now a national joke. If there is a war on drugs, then we are all POWs to it. But unlike with heroin, whose poppies don't grow in this country, we do grow our own rapists. We could win at both ends, dealing with both the current and future crops of rapists. We could succeed even if we didn't rehabilitate a single rapist, by heading some off at the pass and dropping the rest for the count.

It is axiomatic that children are damaged by child abuse. Some overcome that damage. Some become lifelong victims. Some limit their destructiveness to collaboration. And some become full-blown predators. We could intervene in that assembly line if we devoted sufficient resources to properly trained, funded, supported, and scrutinized child-protective services.

As to the rapists who already walk among us, our only recourse is to fight. This is no politician's euphemism—a rapist is a single-minded, totally self-absorbed sociopathic beast . . . a beast that cannot be tamed with "understanding." We need to stop shifting the responsibilities, to stop demanding that victims show "earnest resistance," to stop whining

---

★The much vaunted and recently enacted Violence Against Women Act represented the federal government's best opportunity to date to do so. But instead the huge block grants to local law enforcement authorized by VAWA come unencumbered by obligations or incentives to genuine legislative reform.

†The National Child Protection Act was finally passed. See foreword.

and start winning. The battlefields are many—too many. The courthouse and the jury room, the back alley and the bedroom, the school curriculum and the voting booths. And one of our strongest weapons must be fervent intolerance for collaboration in any form.

We need to go to war. The enemy has already opened hostilities. The casualties are already far too high. And our ranks are already depleted by friendly fire.

Each time a trial of mine came to a close, when it was time for a case to be handed over to the jury, I felt the way I do now, as this book ends. Most of my summations began with some variation of one single theme. This is what I told the jury, and what I am telling you:

> You have heard all the evidence you are going to hear. After I finish speaking, the judge will instruct you on the law, and then it will be up to you to decide the truth in this case. *You* decide . . . not the judge . . . not the defense attorney . . . not the defendant . . . and not me.
>
> No one can control what you do in that jury room. You can choose to be narrow-minded and prejudiced. You can choose to ignore or misinterpret the evidence. You can choose to abdicate your own responsibility and defer your judgment to that of your fellow jurors. No one can stop you.
>
> All I can do now is ask you not to do that. I am asking that when you are in that jury room, you use your hearts and your minds and your lifetimes of accumulated knowledge to look at the evidence in this case. If you do that, there can be but one result. It is a profound responsibility that you take with you and a rare honor that this country bestows upon its citizens. You have the opportunity to create justice.
>
> Do it.

ABOUT THE AUTHOR

ALICE VACHSS served as a VISTA volunteer teaching literacy skills to prison inmates, worked as a floor counselor in a maximum-security institution for violent youth, and was a criminal defense attorney for indigents before joining the Queens County (New York) district attorney's office in 1982 as a prosecutor specializing in sex crimes. Later, she became chief of that office's Special Victims Bureau and served in that capacity until late 1991. She is married to attorney-author Andrew Vachss and lives in New York City.

ABOUT THE TYPE

This book was set in Bembo, a typeface based on an old-style Roman face that was used for Cardinal Bembo's tract *De Aetna* in 1495. Bembo was cut by Francisco Griffo in the early sixteenth century. The Lanston Monotype Machine Company of Philadelphia brought the well-proportioned letter forms of Bembo to the United States in the 1930's.